joining
the
tribe

Also by Linnea Due

Fiction

HIGH AND OUTSIDE
GIVE ME TIME
LIFE SAVINGS

Anthologies

DAGGER: ON BUTCH WOMEN

Growing up
Gay & Lesbian
in the '90s

anchor books
Doubleday
New York London Toronto Sydney Auckland

joining the tribe

Linnea Due

An Anchor Book
published by doubleday
a division of Bantam Doubleday Dell Publishing Group, Inc.
1540 Broadway, New York, New York 10036

Anchor Books, Doubleday, and the portrayal of an anchor are
trademarks of Doubleday, a division of Bantam Doubleday Dell
Publishing Group, Inc.

Book design by Jennifer Ann Daddio

Library of Congress Cataloging-in-Publication Data
Due, Linnea A.
    Joining the tribe : growing up gay and lesbian in the '90s /
Linnea Due.
        p.   cm.
    1. Gay teenagers—United States.   2. Lesbian teenagers—
United States.   3. Homosexuality—United States.   I. Title.
HQ76.3.U5D84   1995
305.23'5—dc20   95-7643
                                                         CIP

ISBN 0-385-47500-4
Copyright © 1995 by Linnea Due

All Rights Reserved
Printed in the United States of America
First Anchor Books Edition: September 1995
10 9 8 7 6 5 4 3

For everyone who believes telling the truth will make a difference.

acknowledgments

Any book of this nature depends on the goodwill of many people, most obviously the subjects. But there are dozens of others behind the scenes. The manuscript could never have been completed in the time allowed without the thorough and professional transcriptions done by Little Sun Heard and Hilary Mullins for far too little money. I can't thank them enough for their commitment to seeing this project through. E. Rikki Vassall, Tirza Latimer, and Marny Hall provided research material and ideas. In the Portland section, I want to thank Darlene and Barbara de Manincor for their help in contacting street youth workers E. Ann Hinds and Mark Stucker, who, in turn, introduced me to Tia Plympton. In the high school section, I'd love to acknowledge an author, but he must go nameless to protect someone who wishes her identity concealed; Al Chase and his *Speaking Out* newsletter were also invaluable. In the Missouri section, Elizabeth Howell, Jonalyn Siemers, and Martha Carroll gave of their time and knowledge with grace. In the New Orleans section, J. M. Redmann helped tremendously, as did Joan Ladnier and Brad Robbert. In New York, Sarah Lewis, as always, gave unstintingly of her enthusiasm for whatever crazy project I dream up next; Donna Farnum, Eric Bazaar, and David Nieves went far beyond the call of duty, and I thank Fred Goldhaber for participating in the worst of times. For the Introduction, I drew on the ideas of many people, among them Gayle Rubin's thoughts on the relationship between family and community, and Eric Rofes's work on suicide and sissy boys. I must, in fact, thank all the members of my study group: Gayle, Eric, Martha Baer, Larry Rinder, Will Seng, David Conner, Mimi McGurl, and Robin Stevens; and my writers' group: Ellen McGarrahan, Hilary Mullins, Jane Futcher, and Lucy Jane Bledsoe. Elisabeth Cornu, Martha Baer, and Sora Counts served as readers, a job fraught with the land mines of ego. While stepping gingerly, Elisabeth also had to make do with the mess, phone calls, travel, and tribulation that were offshoots of the writing. Another hero is my editor Charles Flowers, who has been unfailingly supportive and helpful. And, of course, I must thank Brent Calderwood, who started me off on this path and has provided contacts, ideas, and support ever since.

Contents

introduction

damaged goods or recruitable innocents?

In 1991, while writing a feature article, I tagged along with the East Bay chapter of Queer Nation on a couple of actions. Almost everyone in QN was under twenty-five; more than half were too young to get in the straight clubs they wanted to "liberate." After a debate, they decided on a mission of holiday visibility, and so a few weeks before Christmas, I met them in front of a crowded mall in Richmond, California. Cruising around with jackets bedecked with decals (DYKE, QUEER, FAG), flanked on all sides by grim-faced security men whispering urgently into walkie-talkies, the QN forces explored the mall, attracting stares, laughter, and a few startled thumbs-up.

After a couple hours, everyone was exhausted, so we headed for a sunken conversation pit to regroup before leaving. It was a bad choice. The pit was circled by balconies three stories high, and those balconies were soon mobbed by people, most of them also under twenty-five, many dangling over the railings to better pelt us with abuse, hard candy, and anything else they could grab from the nearest trash cans. There were just twenty of us, a couple hundred of them, and the hate and passion on their faces were all-consuming.

I don't remember driving home. In my dreams I saw those tiers of twisted faces looming over me, eyes bright with malice. For more than a week I wandered around in shock, feeling vulnerable and stripped. Then I went to the QN wrap-up meeting. "Terrific action," everyone said. "A real success."

"How can you call that a success?" I demanded.

"We got under their skin," they explained. "We made them see how they really feel."

How they really feel was exactly my problem. I had either never known, or not known with such immediacy, or blissfully forgotten *how they feel*. But the intensity of the revulsion with which we were greeted was no surprise to the Queer Nationals. After all, they said, they'd seen it every day in junior high and high school, and they were still close enough to the secondary school experience to remember how horrible it was. "But hasn't all that changed?" I asked. It wasn't like when I was a kid, when I believed I was the only lesbian on earth. Now we've had Stonewall and parades and a growing body of literature and film festivals and gay games . . .

"It's exactly the same," a couple kids asserted. "They don't televise the gay parade in Cincinnati, you know. And we could never get those books and records."

But a lanky guy in a leather jacket was shaking his head. "It's worse," he said.

"*Worse?*"

"Sure. Now they know we're here."

I am not a gay youth—nor even a lesbian youth. In fact, during the writing of this book, I strayed to the far side of forty-five. When I began this project, I worried about hubris, but I believed I could give my subjects a voice they would not otherwise have. And after my trial in the conversation pit, I was determined not to let my own experience intrude or provide a stretcher on which to mount the canvas of the '90s. I planned to approach people with an open mind, letting their lives burst fresh upon me, spurning simplistic links to the unsettled stories of gays and lesbians closer to my age.

This turned out to be a good strategy, though I was thankful for the perspective my years gave me. Because of that overview, I was able to put some flesh on a bone that is mostly of interest to those of us who are older: how different is it growing up in the '90s? At first I avoided this line of inquiry, fearing a natural tendency to use coming of age in the '60s as the "real" experience, as an unacknowledged measuring stick against which I might distort and misinterpret the experiences of those younger than myself. But soon I realized that wrong answers do not invalidate the question —and what I was discovering caused me such outrage and concern I no longer cared that the contrast between generations is not a burning issue to kids who presently have their hands held to a hotter flame.

My research for *Joining the Tribe* began with that revelatory excursion to the mall. There were other surprises during the writing of the Queer Nation article, as when I realized that many of the QNers were terrified of older gays—

or, more precisely, of their *image* of older gays; one girl said with horror, "What if I went into a bar and some forty-year-old woman asked me to dance?" This same girl could face down hysterical hets with aplomb, but older dykes were apparently the devil's work. Her contact with gays and lesbians had been limited to political groups organized in a university setting, with people her own age—very different from the '50s and '60s milieu of gay bars, sports teams, and small social groups that brought together those of different ages and experience.

In the spring of 1992, while working on another article, I attended several months' worth of Saturday afternoon gay youth meetings at the Pacific Center in Berkeley. At my first or second session, I met sixteen-year-old Brent Calderwood, at the group for his first time. Brent was anxious, articulate, and eager for someone to talk to. He was struggling with a seemingly insoluble problem: he hated himself for cowering in the closet ("I'm lying to myself every day I'm in school"), yet he knew he'd be subjected to unbearable harassment if he came out. His solution was to cut classes, so this formerly straight-A student had already been expelled from one school and was in trouble at the other.

Meanwhile I was hearing rumors that gay kids were three times more likely to attempt suicide than straight kids, and that thirty percent of completed youth suicides might be due to sexual orientation issues. The source of those rumors was a paper that psychiatric social worker Paul Gibson had written for the U.S. Department of Health and Human Services' *Report of the Secretary's Task Force on Youth Suicide*, a four-volume edition that, partially because of controversy over Gibson's contribution, was issued only in limited quantities. Gibson's clearly written report did a wonderful job of identifying problems specific to gay youth and galvanized right-wing saber-rattlers with statements like this: "The root of the problem of gay youth suicide is a society that discriminates and stigmatizes homosexuals while failing to recognize that a substantial number of its youth has a gay or lesbian orientation."

When I began work on *Joining the Tribe* late in 1993, I considered how to present the voices of the people I would interview. Telling their stories in the here and now, often in their own words and without analysis, seemed most respectful of their experience. This would entail both lengthy interviews and long narratives, but knowing Brent and what had happened to him in the eighteen months since I'd written my article persuaded me I could find others equally interesting. That turned out to be an understatement; I was amazed at how smart, thoughtful, and complex my subjects were, to a person. Nor was this due to a complicated selection process.

I wanted a good mix of kids: from urban areas and small towns, from poor families and privileged backgrounds, of different ethnicities and at different points in their schooling. I wanted gender parity, and I wanted specific experiences: a lesbian who was an athlete on a topflight college team and someone who had been institutionalized for being gay, for two examples. I pretty much got what I wanted except the specifics. Pursuing people for an experience I'd defined as illustrative didn't work; letting things happen organically was more successful and, I'm now convinced, fortuitous.

I found sixteen-year-old Renee George* (asterisks indicate a pseudonym) through a mutual acquaintance. Brandon Clark contacted me when I placed an ad on America Online

(AOL). When I journeyed to Portland to interview him, local street youth workers introduced me to Paul Johnson, and I ran into eighteen-year-old bartender Tom Winters* at the City, Portland's all-ages gay and lesbian club. Deerfield Academy's Allyson Mount was the friend of a woman who had been referred to me by an author. New Mexico's John Swensen*, the embodiment of isolation, responded to my AOL ad, as did Orange County's Lee Garrett*, whose situation could not be more diametrically opposed to Swensen's.

I called Missouri's Vic Edminster cold, referred through a friend of a friend, and discovered a tale that defied expectations. During my Missouri trip I met Lauren Dreyer*, whose experience is probably the closest to the "old days" of the '50s. Caroline Anchors* was enduring hell at Xavier University in New Orleans when I met her at a youth group, while Neely Boudier*, across the state in Lafayette, hemmed and hawed until she finally agreed to meet me. In New York City, I interviewed William at the Hetrick-Martin Institute's Harvey Milk High School, and also at HMI met Evann Hayes*, who belongs to a family that knows how to take care of its own. Brent Calderwood's story is here too, as well as that of Greg Fowler, a man with a very unique childhood who is just discovering who he might be.

Some turned me down, of course—almost always lesbians. And it was the lesbians who were certain I should interview someone with a better story, or who, even if they agreed, would stop in the middle of telling me something fascinating to apologize for being mundane. The few gay men who hesitated to be interviewed did so not because they doubted the worth of their stories but because they were concerned about future career repercussions. Clearly being lesbian does not exempt one from the lack of self-esteem that plagues women.

Another gender-linked difference that emerged is that women are more likely to continue engaging in heterosexual relationships long past the time they've come out to themselves. There are several reasons for this, one being the need to hide (Neely Boudier offers a cold-blooded demonstration). But even more important, the self-worth of junior high and high school girls hinges on their success at relationships, while boys have a broader range of success indicators (sports, academics, music, rebellion) and can take a break from relationships without losing too much face. In the past this has been interpreted as girls recognizing their homosexuality later than boys; while this may be true for some, I think the need not to be judged a failure at relationships—and relationships *means* boys—has more to do than a delayed self-awareness with prolonging heterosexual behavior by high school girls who have known they were lesbian "for ages."

These anomalies showed up very quickly. I filed them away and continued on my quest. But here I must admit to my assumptions, even though I didn't define them as such at the time. When I conceived the book, I made much of what I called donning the cloak of gay identity: I wanted to know what accommodations adolescents felt they had to make in joining the tribe, in becoming part of an established and often noisy gay community—a group which only twenty-five years earlier had been so circumspect and fragmented that it could hardly be deemed a community at all, at least not in most localities, and certainly not in the sense of contributing to public policy. Did today's teens feel that because of whom they bedded (or intended to bed) they must sign up for a lifetime term in the equivalent of the gay Marines? What aspects of the conflicting self-images we call gay identity have filtered down to high school students? By basing an identity on something so fluid as sexual orientation, so ephemeral as desire, had we stepped from a closet of impossibilities into a ghetto of certainties without ever pausing in the open air of self-definition? Had we, in response to straight misreadings, invented ourselves so thoroughly that now all of us must find a fit inside a smaller wheel?

But I soon discovered that the gay community—in any of its many guises—has remarkably little reach into the daily affairs of those who will soon join it. A number of my interviewees had tried for some expression of support from older gays and been greeted with hostility; others regarded the community as an incomprehensible, frightening world of adults they preferred not to think about. Yet those who were already members of the tribe barely remembered what it'd been like to live without it.

There are a number of reasons for this, and a variety of consequences. But first let's make clear that the existence of a visible gay community *has* had one very important effect: kids are realizing the truth about themselves sooner. To paraphrase my Queer Nation friend, now *we* know we're here. It is no longer feasible, as it once was, to dally for years on the shores of possibility, imagining that what one assumed was a phase at thirteen is still only that at seventeen —though make no mistake, people continue to place their burgeoning sexuality in holding patterns while they zip around being star athletes or holy do-gooders (Brandon Clark is a good example). Still, it can be safely said that many gays and lesbians are coming out to themselves earlier than they would have twenty-five years ago.

After decades of decrying silence and exhorting people to come out, we can perhaps be excused a moment of applause. The more thoughtful might wonder where these adolescent gays and lesbians are going for support; the less attentive assume that compared to our own experience of not knowing if there was one more like us on earth, the teens of the '90s are better off. After all, now there are films and books and newspapers and MTV. For those who find media representations impersonal, there are lots of rap groups. A staffer at a large agency for gay youth said to me without irony, "There are one hundred and seventy groups nationwide. Any kid could be in one. I can't imagine why anybody in this day and age wouldn't join a group. My God," he concluded, "there's even a group in Little Rock!"

You are flying a small plane through heavy fog. You have no passport, no country, no home. You're alone in the fog, without destination or direction. You can't go back, and there is no forward, not down on the ground where people live.

If, ten minutes later, you discover the gay equivalent of Gilligan's Island, and you touch down and emerge to the cheers of the crowd, will you remember how it felt when you had no place to land? Once you know there's a somewhere, it's impossible to forget. Unfortunately, for the majority of gay teenagers, the fact that there are gay communities in the universe does not translate as knowing somewhere exists. This means those early risers, the kids who come out to themselves sooner, spend a longer time lost in the fog. The underlying reasons are linked to the nature of adolescence, of kinships, and of community itself.

It's 1992, at the gay youth group in Berkeley. A young African-American man, bejeweled and dazzling, listens to a dozen complaints from a dozen different teens, and then voices what might be the anthem of young queers everywhere: "Get the fuck out of high school."

Too many take this advice literally, and drop out, drug and drink themselves into oblivion, cut classes until their grades plummet so far they flunk out. Only a year or two later, they find their behavior baffling. "I can't understand why I dropped out," one will say. "I'm bright. I should have finished." Or, "I just pissed that time away. I was . . . I don't know. I just couldn't manage."

What's astonishing is how quickly we forget. Not the terrible experiences themselves, for their sting will linger forever, but the impact of those experiences on a self we can no longer pinpoint. We remember ourselves isolated, harassed, hiding, depressed, frightened, unable to talk even to our closest friends. But once we've found others who are capable of seeing and accepting us as we see ourselves, we can't imagine being without that source of strength. Eventually we believe that we should have held on, stuck it out, thumbed our noses at the bigots. Many of us emerge from the crucible of high school feeling like cowards (if we've hidden), failures (if we've escaped), or exhausted martyrs (if we've come out). Those are the options, and none of them is good.

Something else besides loneliness and alienation is going on during those years, something that demands an enormous fund of energy that might otherwise be directed toward school or friends. In his 1963 book *Stigma*, Erving Goffman calls it adjusting to a "spoiled identity." And this particular adjustment is carried on internally (usually in utter secrecy) and without the familial or cultural supports that provide a bulwark against racial, ethnic, or religious discrimination. To discover—and this is when most of us realize, in junior high or early in high school—that we are members of the most stigmatized group in American society is about six parts despair leavened with one part relief. Suddenly all bets are off. We're up in that plane headed for nowhere. The natives on the ground are calling for our heads. No use wailing for Mom. She probably hates us too.

The sooner we figure out who we are, the more quickly we're exposed to the killing fields of stigma. Almost always it means we're cut off from parents, siblings, friends, and social or ethnic groups—either because we are hiding, because we came out, or because we are found out. As D.A. Martin says in his paper "Learning to Hide: The Socialization of the Gay Adolescent," homosexuality carries such a charge that by itself it can discredit all other aspects of a person's identity. Researchers have long found that the sooner a child realizes he or she is gay or lesbian, the more difficult his or her life becomes. The difficulty has nothing to do with the condition of homosexuality per se, and everything to do with being forced to assume a "spoiled" identity.

Holding on to an inner sense of being a good person—holding on to ourselves—while living in the midst of total condemnation or enforced invisibility is wrenching, exhausting, and ultimately, if we survive, strengthening. Later, when we've met the pariah and seen he is us—when we've found hope and fellowship among gay and lesbian friends, we harbor a secret disappointment that we should have been

stronger. We don't remember we were often blind, igno-
rant, and judgmental; we don't remember we were fighting
for our lives.

What would ameliorate this painful process, obviously,
is destigmatization. Instead we are witnessing polarization,
with the gay community providing a zone of comfort and
acceptance for those within its purview. But outside those
borders exists the usual ignorance combined with increasing
levels of fear, intolerance, and violence directed at both the
gay community and at those gays and lesbians who are, by
reason of youth or circumstance, trapped on the wrong side
of whatever wall of safety we can sustain.

As the gap widens between how we perceive ourselves
and how we are perceived, the leap becomes harder to
make. Gay teens are steeped in a heterosexist reality—most
know nothing else, and what they *think* they know about gay
life is derived from a sarcastic language of stereotypes and
jokes, often expressed by their parents or friends. No wonder they're ambivalent about scaling that wall—and that
when they finally do reach the other side, they're eager to
leave behind memories of their own confusion and hurt. It's
tempting when you've "landed" to forget that there are
plenty more who have not.

For youth especially, there is a terrible irony: keeping
intact that wall of safety has depended upon denying them
entrance. By proclaiming we are innocent of "recruiting," a
charge we all agree is bogus on its face, we acknowledge
such a concept exists, thus handing those who hate or fear
us the ability to define the parameters of the argument.
When the religious Right trots out their false language of
"lifestyle" and "recruitment," we scurry like frightened rats,
responding to what we see as a breaching of the wall. In our

panic we hardly notice that shoring up the barrier means we cede the field to stupidity, that we abandon those who need to see us as real people, not as newspaper figures heaped with scorn, shaking with fury, or ravaged by disease. Because of ignorance and malevolence on one side, and an instinct for self-preservation on the other, we have both—straights and gays alike—left kids in the fog, bearing the brunt of much of the violence, ostracism, and pain that are visited upon the stigmatized in this society.

This pain is borne in almost complete invisibility. Most people cannot imagine gay kids exist because they do not believe children have an incipient sexuality. They conflate homosexuality with adulthood, bemoan early heterosexual behavior ("dating at ten?"), and pretend that we protect our kids from sexual knowledge in spite of the fact that we live in a highly sexualized culture. In this worldview, all ten-year-olds are "soft straights"—malleable innocents who would grow up heterosexual if given proper direction and shielded from the wrong information. Homosexuality twists the template; it's a distortion of what was cookie-cutter perfect, but uncooked and therefore bendable.

What are we to make of kids who insist they are gay and lesbian, or of kids unable to hide the truth? By identifying sexuality of all stripes as an "adult" behavior, and homosexuality in particular as a species of depravity, we preclude the possibility that a child can be both gay *and* innocent, which is why gay and lesbian kids who haven't a clue sex exists can look in a thousand mirrors and never see a reflection. If they're innocent, they're soft straights; if they become visible as gay or lesbian, either through gender nonconformity or their own desire to tell the truth, they're cast aside as damaged goods.

The soft straight theory, while it wreaks a vast amount of damage, arises from an inability to look beyond one's nose. People in the religious Right, however, have a political and social agenda to enact, and gay kids, vulnerable and powerless as they are, put the lie to that agenda. To these folks, gay kids don't just not exist—they are *not allowed* to exist. Children do not have a "lifestyle"—and therefore do not have a life. The Right has discovered what politicians have known since time immemorial—hook into mother rage, and you'll have a nation of soldiers on your side. That these "culture wars" with their "pro-family" emphasis turn those same families into mini-Gettysburgs, with close to ten percent of the children MIA or worse, killed by friendly fire, is political exploitation at its most cruel and cynical.

Growing up hidden—coming of age not only invisible but embattled in that invisibility—is hard to describe to someone who has not experienced it. A phrase like "a wolf in sheep's clothing" takes on special meaning to a gay kid—at least it did for me. Was I hiding because I was bad? Why didn't I feel bad if I was so bad I had to hide? What I should have asked—why do I have to hide?—was too obvious to require an answer, and yet it turned out to be the real question.

I don't remember ever not knowing who I was. For a while I revealed myself, saying I wanted to be strong ("Girls don't need to be strong"), that when I got married, my wife and I would have a wonderful house ("You won't have a wife, you'll have a husband"). By the time I went to summer camp, at age seven, I was already trying to tone myself down: people told me I was too raucous, too wild, and I had to drop that damn fool idea about getting married to a woman. I decided to shut up—not that I'd changed my mind, but it was easier than trying to explain myself to people who'd never met a girl like me.

In the closing days of camp, we were supposed to say who we were going steady with. No one was actually going with anybody—we were all too young—but I was still thrown into a quandary. If I were going to pledge my troth, it certainly would be to Stacy, with whom I'd been sneaking off all summer to plan our life together. Ken snagged me after dinner one night, just before campfire. "Look," he said bluntly, "you want to go with Stacy and I want to go with Roger. So what we'll do is tell everybody you're going with me and she's going with Rog."

God, what a mind! Such duplicity would never have occurred to me. It made me feel a little funny—wasn't it like lying?—but it wasn't a long stretch from the silence I'd been cultivating for a time anyway. As I became older, I edited myself more and more, especially after I realized that it wasn't that people hadn't known about girls like me, but that those girls were so horrible no one wanted to ever talk about them.

By then, I knew what I was called. I'd been risking my life balancing on my father's office chair, snatching books off the uppermost shelf as I rolled by. Richard von Krafft-Ebing's *Psychopathia Sexualis*. Havelock Ellis's *Sexual Inversion*. Freud. Erikson. I'd also been haunting the paperback rack at my neighborhood grocery, ripping off the romances of the '50s—*Beebo Brinker*, Ann Bannon, *Women on the Edge of Twilight*. Krafft-Ebing made me popular on the playground—I was the Susie Bright of Hilltop Elementary School—but my knowledge was a mixed blessing. I was glad to know people like me existed, but I also knew from my dad that a psychopath was the worst thing you could be. Finding my sexuality among those who fucked chickens or corpses made me feel—well, a little queer.

Still, I figured I was hiding successfully until the day my Girl Scout troop leader threw me out for being "too masculine." My world fell apart. I had believed censoring my thoughts was enough; I hadn't realized my manner and my body—the very way I moved—were betraying me daily. Something drastic had to be done.

Something was. I dropped out of the athletics I loved, wore nylons and makeup, carried my books in front of me, shortened my stride. I developed an imperious persona to go along with my new look and pretended an interest in boys (a breach of ethics I tried to mitigate by not letting them come too close). It was like learning a foreign language—and not coincidentally, I began drinking to blackouts.

From seventh through twelfth grades, I functioned as another person, someone I became in the morning and shed in the evening when, safely in my room, I could pore over my romances and daydream about kissing my own raven-haired beauty. It never occurred to me to look for her; my dreams ranked alongside my classmates' fantasies of becoming famous actresses or politicians. That I was labeling illusory the most important stuff of life—my identity and my relationships—didn't seem odd. Staying undercover was job number one.

My life as a spy reached a pinnacle of the absurd during my first year at Sarah Lawrence. I received a visit from several of my elementary school friends; they had traveled from Smith, from Brandeis, from Boston University, certain that I, the amateur sexologist, could set their minds at ease.

They were worried, they explained haltingly, about those sailor/whore games we had played at slumber parties. Wasn't it weird for thirteen-year-old girls to practice kissing each other? Was I concerned that we had lesbian tendencies? Not at all, I replied heartily, and proceeded to regale them with a lot of assurances they wanted to hear. They went back to Massachusetts much relieved, and I lay on my bed and stared at the ceiling, wondering who was the bigger fool. Two years later, I didn't lie when the college president asked if I was a lesbian, though it meant leaving the school I loved; I would never lie again—not about that anyway.

Those of us active in the gay community would like to believe my story could not now be repeated. That is probably true, though I suspect the differences are not as easy to identify as we might think. Being a reader, I would now have access to a broader—and less condemning—range of books, though depending upon where I lived, my choice might not be that much improved. Perhaps I would search for my raven-haired beauty, though I'm not sure of that, and the people I've interviewed for this book would not support that conclusion: what it means to be gay can seem as fully make-believe now as it did in 1960.

It's also hard to predict the effect of a visible gay community, even one so large as that in the Bay Area; Queer Nationals who'd grown up in San Francisco said that when they were in their early teens, Gay Freedom Day was the critical time to appear at the mall or the beach, because absence at the usual haunts would raise suspicions. Hiding or not, I probably wouldn't find much camaraderie up on Castro Street; as I discovered from my interviewees, hanging on the fringes while those inside the wall look right past you or are openly hostile is not pleasant. I might try to find some people my own age—join a gay and lesbian youth group—but then again I might not, for reasons that will soon become clear.

Depending upon my social class and circumstances, it's likely I wouldn't have the option of attending college. I might not even be able to finish high school—maybe I need to work, or maybe I'm getting beat up so much I can't take it anymore. Leaving my neighborhood probably isn't an option, either, be that the Bronx, Chicago's Southside, or the barrios of LA; in fact, I probably won't leave my parents' home for quite a while. Which means that whatever contact I have with the gay community will be restricted, and I'll try not to let my day life and my nightlife intersect.

One thing is certain: no matter who I am, no matter what my race or ethnicity, I would be growing up in a world that is far more violent and lacking in compassion. Almost a quarter of the kids in this country live below the poverty line. Youth violence is endemic; in a survey conducted in 1994 of fifteen-year-olds at three Bay Area high schools (two in the "safe" suburbs), almost three quarters knew someone personally who had been injured or killed as a result of violence. In a 1994 nationwide survey of twelve- to seventeen-year-olds, thirteen percent carried a weapon to school for protection and seventeen percent had been robbed at knife- or gunpoint. Children are brutalized in this society no matter what their orientation—by their peers, their families, their neighbors, and by do-gooders who do no good. For gay kids, the problem is multiplied: in a study done by Joyce Hunter at the Hetrick-Martin Institute, forty percent of gay and lesbian kids had been subjected to physical violence, half of it gay-related, and sixty percent of that gay-related violence occurred in the family.

Another difference is that the heterosexual assumption of the '50s and '60s made it easier for me to pass. Just as gay and lesbian teens are realizing the truth earlier, so are the rest of the kids in the schoolyard. According to studies done across the country in the late '80s, between thirty-three and forty-nine percent of gay and lesbian teenagers had been harassed, threatened, or attacked in junior high and high school. In a study conducted at Yale in 1986, twenty-five percent of gay and lesbian students had been threatened physically, sixty-five percent verbally harassed, a quarter had been followed or chased, and five percent had been punched or beaten. Considering that many gays and lesbians *can* pass, these are monumental figures. The perpetrators aren't just a few bad apples, either: in a study of college freshmen, thirty-seven percent of men reported verbally harassing gay men, while nine percent of women had harassed lesbians. Fully nine percent of the male students had hit, kicked, or beat gay men. Violence rates are rising—supposedly from panic over AIDS coupled with increased visibility. I'll buy panic as the culprit, but I believe the scum at the bottom of this well of hate has more to do with fears over sexuality and gender than disease.

Speaking of visibility, this new me growing up in the '90s has probably read in my better brand of books about how *I* need to come out—if only because there are so many like me who are hiding. They're hiding for good reason, I admit, but if everyone continues to hide, nothing will ever change. I go to school and think about coming out to this boy or that girl or the guidance counselor and then I think that once I'm out no one will ever look at me the same way. And if I *am* out, who will help me? There's no school group, no out teachers, no official acknowledgment gays and lesbians even exist. I don't know if I'm ready to put my life on the line, but then maybe I'm just a coward.

My debate about coming out assumes I *can* pass. Gay-bashing in the schoolyard is not based on which sex one might take to bed, but upon being unable or unwilling to conform to one's gender role. Vic Edminster, Tom Winters, and Brent Calderwood are examples of teens who did not conform to gender role stereotypes from early childhood, and who suffered mightily as a result. Sissy boys have a harder time of it than tomboy girls, both within the family and on the streets, and some are thrown out of their homes because they are unable to satisfy societal gender expectations. The fact that gender, like sexual orientation, is a continuum of possibilities is a relatively new idea, and not one that appeals to those who count on scapegoating queers as a means of ensuring that no blurring of gender boundaries will threaten male hegemony. Why is it more difficult for boys? Think about it this way: no one's surprised if the slaves want to live in the big house, but imagine how revolutionary it is for the master to move to the slave quarters. Spurning power that is a birthright brings the inevitability of that power into question, and ambiguity is exactly what those who depend on inequity want to avoid.

I hadn't grasped the implications of much of this to flesh-and-blood human beings when I flew to Portland in January 1994 to interview three young men who are about as different as they can be. But they do have something in common:

they had been cast out in some fashion, survived through sheer grit, and each is now engaged in a search for kinship, definition, and meaning that, through changes and complexities, will occupy the rest of his life. The gay community forms no more and no less than a backdrop to that search, a venue in which to function. An important part of that community resource for those under 21 is an all-ages gay and lesbian nightclub called the City—the club was Brandon Clark's point of entry, there's a special night every week for street kids like Paul Johnson, and bartender Tom Winters ups his pride and professionalism every time he shines a glass. But a place like the City exists nowhere else in the country—and the club itself is under siege.

I also received an important clue when I met a woman named Tia Plympton, who had just finished writing her dissertation on Portland's street kids. Plympton explained to me that the kids formed complicated family units, taking on the roles of fathers and mothers and sisters and brothers. The families didn't last long, and Plympton noted there was a lot of lip service paid to how well these associations worked when they usually didn't work at all. Plympton was dismayed; why would the kids want to replicate the nuclear family, the system that had failed them in the first place? But I came away thinking that a family is pretty much what everyone, street kids or not, is looking for. You look for what you know—and for what you feel you lack.

In fact, that's what adolescents are supposed to be doing. By making links with our peers, we gradually move away from our dependence on our family of birth. With a push-pull ambivalence, and usually lots of fireworks, we declare our allegiance to a power greater than Mom and Dad

—our friends. Depending upon what economic corner of the culture we live in, what racial and ethnic tensions we face, how we like and value ourselves, that road to social autonomy can be simply unpaved or downright treacherous. Our friends and lovers become both teachers and pupils, and we conduct experiments about trust and loyalty and what is fulfilling or just window dressing. The more authentic those relationships, the more we learn.

Of course, it's only adults who put such emphasis on learning, on gaining knowledge that will lend weight to some future decision. Teenagers need friends to survive *at that moment*, and this is exactly where gay and lesbian kids are at a disadvantage—and where k.d. lang magazine covers and movies (the few and far between), gay freedom days, and the gay community itself offer precious little solace. Few gay teenagers can have authentic relationships with friends or with lovers, since they cannot be open about who they are. If they are out, they are forever after seen as something less.

As I continued interviewing across the country, family loomed large. It explained why Vic Edminster, who spent her adolescence in San Francisco's Noe Valley, chockablock to the gay Castro, would feel isolated from the gay community but avoid youth groups like the plague: starting at age fourteen, Vic constructed her own family of friends and lovers. Youth groups carried a therapeutic tinge she found offensive. As she put it, "I didn't want a support group. I wanted *friends*."

Caroline Anchors loved her youth group. They went to clubs together, danced, dated each other, made a splash on the Philadelphia gay scene by demanding to be taken seriously. Then Caroline went off to college and became a pariah. End of family. It was particularly painful because Caroline chose a black college so she could explore more of who she is. She figured black superseded gay, but she discovered that in collegiate New Orleans, black supersedes gay only if you keep your mouth shut.

John Swensen's problem is that he has no family. He's lying to his mom, lying to his dad, and spending a ton of money on the Internet so he can talk to *someone*. John's daydreams take precedence over his real life, even to the point of spurning a budding romance with a college-bound partner because consigning himself to a long-distance relationship is too close to the agony he's been enduring for years.

But maybe the best example is Lee Garrett, who has made the emotional break with her nuclear family to dwell in her family of friends. Trouble is, her friends are straight, and Lee, who isn't too concerned about being gay, *is* concerned about leaving her pals behind to join a community that so far seems hostile to her. Lee's friends accompany her to gay bookstores and pretend to gag when she talks about boys, giving her a gentle nudge out of the heterosexual nest, while Lee wonders why she has to fly away from them at all —a question everyone might ponder.

Vic Edminster says, "In this society, at this point in time, I don't think you can be a member of two communities at once." Yet all of us belong to many communities. The trouble is that some communities are stigmatized to such an extent that being a member marks you as not being whole— in large part because that belonging takes precedence over everything else, forming the entirety of what people are able to focus on. Says Martha Carroll, a minister I interviewed in Missouri, "You're seen as someone else the rest of your life. That's what's so terribly hurtful."

At least you're *seen*, even if that reflection seems cast in a funhouse mirror. Paul Gibson, who wrote the report on gay youth suicide for the federal government, says, "What struck me most was how very, very little had been written about young people being gay or lesbian. To me, one of the biggest insults you can make to a group of people is to pretend they don't exist. Of course, if they don't exist, they don't have these issues or problems."

Gibson himself is responsible for the only measure of visibility—or notoriety—gay youth have achieved. No matter where I traveled, people reacted the same when I explained the subject of my book. "Oooh," they said, faces crumpling with distress, "it's so sad about them committing suicide!"

Published in 1989, Gibson's piece blamed high suicide rates on societal stigma, and called for passing antidiscrimination laws, recognizing gay marriages, and presenting "homosexuality as a natural and healthy form of sexual expression" in family life classes. These suggestions drew the ire of many, including then-California congressman William Dannemeyer, who wrote letters to George Bush and Department of Health and Human Services Secretary Louis Sullivan, asking that Gibson's report be denounced. In fact, the book was produced in such limited numbers that it was almost impossible to obtain for years.

I learned of Gibson's report late in '91. Pam Walton, finishing up her excellent documentary *Gay Youth*, sent me copies of her copies of someone else's copies. Until the spring of '94, I was still copying my copies to give to other journalists. Luckily Alyson Publications brought out Gary Remafedi's *Death by Denial* in June '94, which includes Gibson's paper as well as Joyce Hunter's "Violence Against Lesbian and Gay Male Youths" and a report from the Massachusetts Governor's Commission on Gay and Lesbian Youth, thus ending my cash drain at the Xerox machine.

Now a senior psychiatric social worker for San Francisco County's Department of Public Health, Paul Gibson doesn't look like an activist. A big, cheerful man in his early forties, he seems somewhat bemused by the attention he's received. He turns down radio and TV talk show spots ("I'm not inarticulate, it's just not something I want to do"), and it took more than two months to cajole him into talking to me. "I hate interviews," Gibson confesses at the conclusion of ours, as if I didn't know—"oh, except this one, of course," he adds gallantly.

We are sitting in his home office, perched on a hill above San Francisco's Castro District. Gibson's cream- and wheat-colored office is comfortable but so uncluttered—not a notepad or magazine or knickknack in sight—that it makes me nervous. But the room seems to mirror Gibson himself, who is equally uncluttered; clear-thinking and straightforward, he speaks with a courteous, quiet voice and listens thoughtfully, his head tilted slightly to the side. Once ensconced in his chair, he doesn't fidget, and he chooses his words with care, occasionally punctuating them with a shy smile.

"I was surprised at the controversy," Gibson says, and I believe him—he's the sort of guy who'd tell you the car he's trying to sell once overheated on the freeway. "I didn't write the paper from a political perspective. I wrote it based on my own experiences working with gay kids and based on the limited data there was. And I wrote it in a sincere effort to bring attention to the real problems those kids face. It's unfortunate that some people chose to make it into a political issue." He pauses and then smiles. "On the other hand, I believe the controversy helped to bring it attention. People who did not agree politically with the report may have done it a favor."

From 1977 to 1984, Gibson worked at Huckleberry House, a runaway shelter in San Francisco that was started in Haight-Ashbury in the late '60s—the first such runaway program in the country, Gibson notes proudly. "By the late '70s, we realized we were seeing a lot of kids who had problems relating to their sexuality. Gay-identified kids were coming to San Francisco in increasing numbers, and we wanted to make services available to those kids."

Gibson helped develop those services, and in the process, he conducted hundreds of intake and assessment interviews. "We started asking kids about their sexual behavior—who they were having sex with, males, females, or both—and about their orientation. About twenty-five percent identified themselves as lesbian, gay, or bisexual on intake. That was a surprise to all of us, that just by asking the question we were able to identify that many kids who had this as an issue in their lives.

"There was a time not long ago," he says, "where we didn't ask young people about suicide, we didn't ask them about child abuse, we didn't ask anything about sexuality. A gay kid is often not going to identify himself unless you ask. I always tell people don't be afraid to ask. To miss that information for a gay or lesbian kid is oftentimes to miss the single most important issue going on for them."

Meanwhile, concern was mounting over skyrocketing youth suicide rates (rising two hundred percent since 1960 compared to a seventeen percent rise for all ages), and studies had begun to point to the high suicidality of gay and lesbian kids. In 1978, Alan Bell and Martin Weinberg found that thirty-five percent of gay men and thirty-eight percent of lesbians had considered or attempted suicide, with the majority of the attempts taking place before age twenty and one third taking place before age seventeen. In 1979, Karla Jay and Allen Young found that two fifths of their large sample of gay men and lesbians had considered or attempted suicide. Eric E. Rofes's book *I Thought People Like That Killed Themselves* came out in 1983, stating that "taboos surrounding free and open discussion of lesbianism and male homosexuality are impeding people concerned about youth suicide from facing a major factor that is often involved." Shortly thereafter the Los Angeles Suicide Prevention Center began a study that revealed that the attempt rate for gay youth was more than three times higher than the rate for heterosexual youth.

"It's been stated as a fact now that thirty percent of completed suicides are by gay and lesbian youth," Gibson says, explaining that a *New Yorker* piece criticizing his report did raise some legitimate concerns. "Truthfully, we don't have a way of knowing that, and I didn't state that as a fact. Let me restate what the facts are. It's consistently accurate that between twenty to thirty-five percent of gay and lesbian youth will report that they've made a suicide attempt. If you look at studies that have been done with general adolescent populations, consistently you find between seven and fourteen percent. So that's where I extrapolated the figure that gay and lesbian youth are between two and three times more likely to make a suicide attempt than the general adolescent population. That's also taking into account that the general adolescent population *includes* gay and lesbian youth. If gay and lesbian youth are three times more likely to make an attempt than other youth, the extrapolation was made based on the fact that perhaps as many as ten percent of youth are gay, lesbian, or bisexual."

Studies since then have supported Gibson's figures. In 1991 Gary Remafedi found that thirty percent of his subjects had attempted suicide, with the mean age of the attempt occurring at fifteen and a half. In Curtis Proctor and Victor Groze's 1994 study, forty percent of respondents to a questionnaire sent out to gay and lesbian youth groups had attempted suicide. In T. L. Hammelman's 1993 study, twenty-nine percent had attempted suicide, with the majority of attempts occurring before age twenty. Hammelman identified several risk factors: 1) discovering same-sex preference early in adolescence, 2) experiencing violence due to gay or lesbian identity, 3) using drugs or alcohol in an effort to cope, and 4) being rejected by family members as a result of being lesbian or gay.

Remafedi found that a third of the attempts in his study took place in the same year the youth had discovered he was gay and that, in fact, an inverse relationship existed between self-identification and suicide attempts—the later you know, the better. "With each year's delay in self-labeling," Remafedi wrote, "the odds of a suicide attempt declined by more than eighty percent . . . Compared with older persons, early and middle adolescents may be less able to cope with the isolation and stigma of a homosexual identity."

Which, Gibson points out, is a blessing in disguise. "I think that in comparison with some of the other contributing factors to youth suicide, gay kids might be one of the easiest groups to help. We know that once people get some acceptance and support around being homosexual, those suicidal feelings are largely reduced." Helping suicidal gay kids is thus more a matter of altering consciousness than, say, trying to make vast economic changes or eliminate alcoholism.

Gibson is optimistic. "I've been really pleased with the attention the issue has gotten in recent years," he says. "There's been a proliferation of services for these youth. One area that I've seen more support is from the gay and lesbian community itself."

"In what way?"

"There's been an increasing number of stories in gay and lesbian newspapers and an increasing amount of attention to the problems these kids have. That greater awareness won't go away. It's not a reversible process. But there is a need for constant vigilance," he cautions. "A frustration I've had in working with HIV issues for the Department of Public Health is that it took us so long to realize that most cases of HIV in youth involved gay youth. I can only assume that the reason it took us so long to respond to that is because of our reluctance to admit that kids are gay."

"Aren't you dismayed that being suicidal is the first association people make?"

"Well, the unfortunate truth of the matter is that those problems are real for most gay and lesbian youth. Until that's not the case, I think we have to look at that and talk about it and prevent them from trying to take their lives."

"You're not worried it will be used as a tool for further stigmatization?"

"There will always be people who use a study for their

own purposes," he says, noting that his report was cited during the gays-in-the-military debate by people who claimed gays committing suicide would raise havoc in the barracks. "But that's not the message in the report, and I think people are clear about that. The message is that these kids are real, they exist in large numbers, and they have some very serious issues we have to pay attention to. No one likes to see a young person take his life, regardless of his sexual orientation. So it's helped develop empathy for these kids. Also, for people to recognize gay youth are at risk for suicide is at least to recognize gay youth exist."

Why is it easier for older adolescents? The less reliant we are on a family that is likely to reject or to abuse us, the better. As we become older, we are more capable of ferreting out the truth about ourselves rather than accepting other people's ignorance as gospel, and we are independent enough to search for our own families—ones that are supportive and nurturing. But how can we ease adolescents past those years of being lost in the fog? How can we help those who are hiding, or those who have been "found out," who don't gender-conform, who are left to fend for themselves in a storm of abuse? How can we help young men protect themselves from HIV infection during those early months of ignorance, despair, and self-hate? In a 1993 study performed by the San Francisco Department of Public Health, ninety percent of youth (ages twelve to twenty-five) with AIDS are gay or bisexual men, while those under age thirty comprise sixteen percent of AIDS cases. Given the lengthy incubation period, virtually all were infected as teenagers. Gay teens no longer need a gun to commit suicide, but it is surely a tragedy that by the time death comes, they will have fully embraced life.

We must first understand that a community is not a family and cannot be substituted for one. A community provides a public arena for discourse and a marketplace for goods and services; it is the boards upon which we stage the play, not the play itself. This is a great deal more than we used to have but less than we might hope for or expect. For too long, we've been indulging in a double dose of wishful thinking: believing that the mere existence of a community can satisfy the longing every kid has for a family of his or her own.

A larger and more active gay community cannot ameliorate the isolation and loneliness of teens who are not part of it; in some ways the community exacerbates that isolation, by seeming to make coming out a ticket to entry when in fact it is often not, when it is more likely an invitation to rejection by one's family and friends. Teens who manage to find the gay community—runaways, throwaways, or those who just hang out—are confined to the margins, where they are ignored, shunted off to social service agencies, or viewed as sexual objects. Far more teens, of course, have no contact whatsoever.

Believing an enhanced gay visibility is a wonderful boon to kids misses a very large point. Kids are as lonely as they ever were, and are more embattled to boot. What they have is a body of literature we did not, but not all kids read and not all find companionship in the written word. We simply have not come far enough to help teens, especially the younger ones; our partial advance down a path to acceptance has, if anything, put gay and lesbian kids at greater risk—their very existence is viewed as an affront by the Right. Newt Gingrich has pledged to hold Congressional hearings on withdrawing federal funds from school districts that mention gays and lesbians in curricula or that refer gay students to youth groups or counseling services, a punitive and financially disastrous measure similar to the Robert Smith-Jesse Helms amendment that passed the Senate in August 1994 but then expired in committee. These amendments would effectively ax the very few school-based programs that teach tolerance and foster self-acceptance.

Unfortunately the only group that seems to *have* an agenda is the Right, and people feel more comfortable following a map than not, even if they don't much care for the direction they're heading in. This is a fact of human nature to which Democrats and progressives have not paid sufficient attention. Gay youth may seem small potatoes compared to a national slide into fascism, but through no wish of their own, they've been assigned to combat duty, and they're showing the strain.

We can pray that we're now at an uncomfortable stage, that the increasing presence of gays who have come out in their private and public lives will cause a gradual lessening of stigma that will eventually seep down and benefit the kids. But what can we do in the meantime?

I've made specific suggestions in the conclusion, but suffice it to say that playing ostrich in the Castro or Greenwich Village doesn't work, nor does explaining over and over to an unreceptive audience that no one needs to be recruited. Simply opening up the walls isn't enough; most kids don't live within hailing distance of gay enclaves, and more than that, kids need acceptance from their peers, not from forty-year-old pals, no matter how well-meaning.

On a personal note, I want to say that during the writing of this book, I vacillated between hope, fury, and admiration. I was struck by the sensitivity, intelligence, and courage of every person who allowed me into their lives. Often the pain they'd endured seemed insurmountable, and yet they had emerged with a wiser idealism intact, in a testament to the human spirit that never failed to buoy me with optimism. But when I returned home and read through their transcripts, I was overwhelmed with a black rage that any of it should have happened to them at all.

Incidents stand out, as when Tom covered the microphone to tell me his "news," or when Caroline described her schoolmates' nighttime visit to her room. I remember the shifting quicksand of Neely's realities and Evann's rapturous realization that he was capable of being happy. In truth, I remember it all, and it makes me proud they shared themselves with me. How wonderful if they made everyone proud, if being gay did not obscure straight vision, if being black did not obscure white vision, if being black or gay did not demand an allegiance that obscures our own vision—if all of us, in Greg Fowler's words, could simply be who it is in our nature to be.

ABOVE LEFT: Paul Johnson
(Linda Kleiwer)

ABOVE: Brent Calderwood
(Phyllis Christopher)

LEFT: Vic Edminster
(Phyllis Christopher)

joining the tribe

ABOVE: Brandon Clark
(*Linda Kleiwer*)

RIGHT:
Brandon Clark at
Pride '94 (*Linda Kleiwer*)

the boys of portland

a tale of three cities (and one more)

In the penny paper in Portland, Oregon, every third personals ad has a C in front of the ubiquitous SWM. I puzzle over this for a good five minutes, sitting in my motel miles from downtown. Surely it doesn't mean cut, I think, influenced by too many ads in the gay press. Catholic? Well, close: Christian.

"If God's leading you, please call," directs one woman who wants a cowboy as well as a Christian. I picture a sweaty-palmed man hovering over his telephone, trying to determine which 900 number God wants him to dial. Apparently fundamentalists have as much difficulty trying to connect as we do.

There are other similarities. Members of the religious Right feel misunderstood, martyred, at risk. They compare themselves to Jews during the Third Reich, a besieged minority harried at every turn by swashbuckling ACT-UP members cast as Nazi storm troopers. If you think I'm exaggerating, read *The Lambda Conspiracy* by Spenser Hughes, a novel of high paranoia that portrays gays as fascist Typhoid

Marys; propaganda like this leads to shouting matches of the "No, *I'm* the Jew, and *you're* the Nazi" variety. Of course, members of the Christian Right have no doubt they occupy the moral high ground, and they suffer mighty humiliations to bring enlightenment to the rest of us. *The Lambda Report*, a newsletter purporting to keep an eye on gay radicalism, has even included a column on gays who bash straights.

The distinctions that render comparisons between gays and fundies moot—homosexuality is neither a belief system nor a lifestyle—aren't accepted by the Right. Nowhere does this clash of conflicting realities hit such ear-shattering decibels as in Oregon. Since the beginning of the decade, Oregon gays and members of the religious Right have existed in a state of siege, each emerging from their bunkers at intervals praying for more help, more money, a little rest. When I saw activist Donna Redwing at the March on Washington in 1993, she was shaking with exhaustion, her eyes red-rimmed and haunted. The Oregon Citizens Alliance (OCA) lost with their antigay Measure 9 at the state level, she said, but now they're coming to the counties and the towns and the school boards, and we don't have the energy or the resources to put out every fire.

Redwing was right; though antigay initiatives failed to qualify for most statewide referendums in 1994 (only in Oregon and Idaho did statewide propositions make it onto the ballot), Oregon counties and towns have continued to pass discriminatory legislation by increasing margins. Yet even as they rack up victories, the OCA worries over its image. Labeled religious fanatics or mean-spirited thugs, they try to explain they're just trying to fix a world gone to hell in a handbasket.

Signs stating otherwise are plastered all over Portland—in every other cafe, spray-painted on walls, in bookstores, in gas stations: HATE enclosed in a circle with a big red slash through it; HATE-FREE ZONE in a big triangle. OCA members respond by staffing tables in suburban shopping centers and asking, "Would you like your child to be taught that homosexuality is an acceptable lifestyle? No? Do you think that makes you a hating person? We don't either, but that's what they're calling us!"

There was other skulduggery afoot (or askate) in the malls during my visit to Portland. Tonya Harding was practicing for her Waterloo every morning at the behemoth Clackamas Town Center, which is why I—foolish me, not imagining Portland would be a popular destination in January—ended up in a motel miles from town. Folks were far more interested in Tonya than they were in the shooting war between gays and the religious Right. Ducking into Radio Shack to buy tapes embroiled me in a half-hour Tonya dissection, every waitress wanted to tell her Tonya story, the maids at the motel talked Tonya and Nancy as they stripped beds. It only underscored how important image—and dirty tricks—can be.

Portlanders seized on the story partially because it was small-town gossip, and there was a relief in that. The population has jumped almost twenty percent in ten years, to 438,000; this is an area undergoing growing pains, with the live-and-let-live tolerance of its citizens being challenged by big-city problems. That these dilemmas are occurring in a spectacular valley, with the Pacific ninety miles to the west and Mount Hood to the east, with the Columbia River to the north and the Willamette bisecting downtown, masks the sting but doesn't lessen the swelling. I don't spot Mount

Hood as I crawl through traffic up and down Sandy Boulevard (the peak plays hide and seek behind overcast and rain), but I do start awake almost every night, as the intermittent wail of sirens throughout the day comes to a crescendo in the late hours. The contradictions multiply close to city center: take San Francisco's Tenderloin, Castro, and Financial District, add a dash of the Oakland Coliseum, stir together in about twelve square blocks, and you've got downtown Portland minus Old Town, which briefly tried to gentrify but now serves as a hangout for the homeless.

In what has become an Oregon tradition (Rajneeshis and ranchers, rednecks and lesbian separatists, lumberjacks and hippies), strange bedfellows abound. Jake's Famous Crawfish (since 1892) tries to shield its view of the gay bar across the street by stringing green curtains on fancy brass rods, but almost all the customers have pulled open the drapes so they can gawk at the street scene outside. I duck into the bar to watch videos the OCA would love to hate, guys caressing their pierced cocks or dropping their 501s to moon the filmmaker. We all want to look, I think, but who knows what we see?

"I was such a *good* kid."

It's just turning dark when I meet Brandon Clark, a first-year student at the University of Portland (first year is a less sexist term than freshman, he tells me). Brandon's about five foot eight, with a dazzling grin that transforms his face so he's almost unrecognizable as the coolly good-looking kid I spotted a moment earlier striding up to the restaurant we'd chosen for our rendezvous. But it's not his miracle smile or his all-American-boy looks that strike me first: Brandon arrives for his interview dressed in a kilt, a formal white shirt complete with tartan shoulder sash, and a beret.

No one blinks an eye, not the waiter, not the other patrons. Downtown Portland is like downtown San Francisco—anything goes so almost everything does. But I suspect no one would give him a second glance in Cheyenne or Little Rock. Brandon has cultivated his conventional exterior for so many years that he would be presentable in a tutu and football pads or a business suit and a flowered hat. No matter what he's wearing, he looks exactly what he is: a wholesome young man. That he has plenty of moxie under the surface is all to the good, because Brandon is not going to make it easy on himself.

"You know popcorn?" he asks.

I admit I've heard of such a thing.

"I love popcorn. It's just about my most favorite food. So I don't eat it. It's like a test. See what I mean?"

I shake my head, confessing I go to a movie sometimes just to eat popcorn.

"But so would I! That's what makes it such a good test."

Okay, I think, the kid must be a bit of a zealot, but in the nicest way. And in fact, at the same time he was a Bible scholar and a Christian youth group leader at his high school in Salem, Oregon, he was causing the town cops to tear out their hair. He's a bundle of surprises, but above all, he's ethical to a T, which means he's gone from being the bane of the Salem PD to enlisting as a reluctant warrior in the war against the religious Right. In Oregon, war is not too strong a word.

I met Brandon through an online computer service, where he uses an obviously gay screen name. You'd call him *aggressively* out—an activist—something that surprised me because he seems so frustrated by the cliques, posturing, and nitpicking that go hand in hand with small-group political organizing. That was before I understood how Brandon thinks.

Via e-mail, Brandon told me he'd been elected senior class president at McKay High School in Salem, and also named class clown. "That last I don't understand," he wrote. But as we sit sipping miso soup, he regularly interrupts his narrative with tales of elaborate pranks he and his pals pulled during high school, on the order of chopping down landmark trees and hand-carrying cars from one block to another. As he tells me these stories, he cringes at appropriate parts (the tree), but his eyes are shining with fun. I can well imagine that bright, handsome, madcap Brandon was a hit in high school.

He was also a thinker. In his sophomore year, Brandon became a Christian and spent hours studying the Bible and theological texts. He was a church leader in his junior year, and then, as if he didn't have enough to do, he joined the Army that spring. Basic training occupied the summer between junior and senior year. It was during basic that the issue of sex first raised its head—at least consciously—so it wasn't until the fall of his senior year that he "started to wonder."

"In junior high there was lots of talk about queers. And I was right along in there, very homophobic myself. There were these people, and all they did was have sex. And they dressed up as women and wore makeup. That's all.

"Then in my sophomore year, I'd go over to this guy's house and have Bible studies with him. I was like, wow. I thought he was really cool, I wanted to be like him. I didn't realize that meant I *liked* him. Looking back, I see I had a big crush on him, but I didn't know that. I was really blind and stupid. I mean, I was sneaking downstairs to watch [gay-related] stuff on TV, and if I heard anyone coming, I'd change the channel really quick, and I *still* didn't realize."

One advantage to being a church youth leader, Brandon says, is that it gave him an excuse to fend off girls. "Though it didn't help *that* much. Some of those girls were really aggressive."

"So you taught people and held groups?" I ask, not sure what a youth group leader would do.

"And recruited," Brandon says. "In school."

"It was a nondenominational church?"

"Yeah, so I could get anyone," he laughs.

Then it was off to the Army where he discovered this thing called sex might actually have something to do with him—something more than fending off girls, that is. "I went eighteen years without doing *anything*. I've got a lot of catching up to do."

"Are you sorry it took so long?" I ask.

"Oh, no, it's kind of a cool story. Everybody else is like, wow, I was seven years old, or when I was in high school me and my best friend . . . and I'm like, I didn't even masturbate until I was eighteen years old."

After honing in on the fact of sexuality in the Army, Brandon began to concentrate on who might be his partner. About that same time, at the beginning of his senior year, he was chosen to star in a school production of *The Wiz*. "I had this major crush on this guy, so I quit the play in December. I just couldn't handle it. He was the first person that I had a crush on that I knew what it was."

With an inkling of what he was facing, he embarked on a Brandon-style offensive, cramming in lots of reading and thinking about homosexuality all in a few weeks. By the end of December, he'd come out to himself, then to his mother and his favorite teacher. In February he started driving up to Portland to go to the City, an all-ages gay nightclub.

That summer, he went back into the Army, to Fort Sam Houston for advanced training. While in Texas, he met Richard, his first love. It was idyllic (if making love in broom closets and on golf courses could be termed such), but Richard got scared they'd be caught and ended the relationship. Distraught, Brandon headed back to Salem only to discover that the rumor that he was gay had spread like wildfire among his friends.

"Well, you were such a popular kid," I say.

"And I was such a *good* kid," he affirms. "I called one of my friends, and she says, 'You don't dress up as a woman, do you?' and I say, 'No,' and she says, 'You don't strip at a bar, do you?' and I say, 'No-o,' and she says, 'You're not like this drug addict, are you?' and I say, 'No-o-o.' These were the rumors people were spreading about me."

"How'd you feel?"

"Oh!" He laughs explosively, then looks down at his tempura. When he looks back up, his face has again unmasked, this time with an agony that's hard to take because it *is* so naked. I realize his bland exterior is not defensive, that he's unaware his wholesomeness can be a kind of armor. When he lets himself be revealed this way, it's impossible not to plunge into his anguish right along with him. "How could people *think* that?" he asks me. "A couple months later was Christmas, and I went back down and tried to visit people. No one wanted to see me. It was like, Brandon, that queer. Here people consider themselves your friends and then they find out . . ." He stops. When he's able to go on, he says, "I've always been really concerned about what people thought of me. Completely. And that's why it's funny that I came out so fast . . ."

"Why do you think that is?"

"Well, I'm also like really truthful. This is who I am. And when I get involved with something I like, I get into it completely. When I became a Christian, I was a super Bible study person, I was completely devoted to it. Now I'm completely devoted to being gay." We both laugh, and he adds, "Well, it's true. About as true as it gets."

Brandon tries to help out where he can. He's an active member of the Oregon Sexual Minority Youth Network (OSMYN), meant to address the isolation of gay, lesbian, bisexual, and transgender youth. "One thing we really need —'cause if you live anywhere else but near Eugene and Portland, forget it—we need an 800 phone line and advertising in every high school and campus newspaper. And we're not doing it. I was like, 'Please hurry, do this!' "

"That sort of visibility seems the essence of OSMYN. What's the objection?"

"No objection, it's just not a priority. With ten people and twenty projects—we need to have one focus and get that done. If we had a phone line when I was in high school, it would have made things so much easier."

"Would you have used it?"

He nearly explodes. "God, yes! To talk to another gay person . . . just to *talk* . . ."

Brandon has also been trying to start a gay and lesbian group at his Catholic college, the University of Portland. According to Brandon, the administration has denied standing to the group several times because " 'it might be construed as advocating homosexuality and it's against Catholic doctrine.' " Brandon has attacked these objections on several fronts, altering the nature of the group so its purpose was simply to promote tolerance, contacting other Catholic colleges to discover about half have similar groups, and finally, doing some undercover digging about the sexual orientation of administration members. "What it ends up being is that some people are gay and not out at all, and they're very uncomfortable. They see us, these young kids, twenty years old, we're out and young and happy about it, and here they are, still trying to deal with it—it's just really really hypocritical."

When I asked Brandon if he'd been hassled much, he shook his head. Well, once when he was DJing at the campus radio station, this huge guy came up yelling about queers, but the dyke security guards took care of him. But other people aren't so lucky, he notes. He tells me about a guy who was HIV-positive who was beaten up and had his car vandalized, and a woman who was hounded out of the dorm.

"Why do you think you're not hassled?"

" 'Cause I . . . I don't really know. Probably 'cause I'm out and really don't care about it."

But when we're safely on another topic, he slides in the information that he was kicked out of the dorm just a few weeks earlier. "I got this letter on a Thursday that said things like I didn't care about building community, I didn't fit the image, and I marched to the beat of my own drum."

Sent by the director of the residence hall, the letter said that if Brandon weren't out of his room in twenty-four hours, a locksmith would be called and Brandon's clothing would be removed and stored at his expense. "This was right as finals were starting. So I thought, 'I can't deal with this now,' and I just moved my stuff out and never said a thing about it."

I was not pleased to discover that people were still being booted out of dorms twenty-five years after Stonewall, nor was I surprised by Brandon's attempt to slip it in unnoticed. In a situation like this, there's always the underlying suspicion: did I do something to cause me to be singled out? Am I at fault, culpable in my own exile?

But he's eager to expound in defense of someone else. He tells me that a black student who had written about racism in the campus paper was kicked out as well, and explains that he's so much luckier 'cause he could move in with Mike, his boyfriend of eight months' duration. Maybe the black guy is *really* in a fix.

"What do you plan to do?"

He shrugs, then perks up. "You mean in my life?"

"Sure," I say, since he so wants to be done with the dorm incident.

"Well, I wanted to be President, but then I switched to First Lady, so that means Mike has to be President." Then he turns serious. "Until everybody has equal rights and all the sodomy cases are repealed and we have domestic partners—" He's drumming his fingers on the table, and I realize we're back to Brandon not eating popcorn. "I could be a graphic artist and have an easy life. There's a lot of things I could do, but it's kind of wasted, because I have the potential to be this agitator. I'm like the gay agitator at the University of Portland, and it's done a lot of good. So that's what I'll keep on doing, 'cause not everyone can do it, and it needs to be done."

"there *is* such a thing as gay street kids."

A day later I'm back downtown, this time to interview kids on the street. Portland has a high population of street youth, and estimates of how many street kids are gay and lesbian range from ten to fifty percent, depending upon whom you ask. I'd already talked to two street youth workers and a woman who'd written her dissertation on street kids. Brandon had offered to take me around to introduce me to people. I was looking for one girl in particular, a girl I'd heard about in San Francisco.

Grace was brought to my attention by seventeen-year-old Lynn Duff, who works at the street paper in San Francisco, the *Tenderloin Times*, and who survived her own version of hell after being shipped away to a Mormon-run institution in Utah where she was drugged and harangued for being a lesbian. Lynn publishes a newsletter called *24-7: Notes from the Inside* for kids who are institutionalized, and she knew I wanted to talk to someone who'd been institutionalized for being gay. "It happens all the time," she told me grimly. "When I was there about half the kids were in 'cause they were gay."

Lynn had run into Grace when she was doing an article for the *Times* on street kids. She discovered that Grace, in Montana, had been kept in a sister institution to hers. I made several attempts to track Grace down in San Francisco, at one point spending a disheartening New Year's Eve trudging around Union Street asking questions of kids who didn't trust me and who couldn't understand why I was looking for Grace, who, it turned out, had several hours earlier gotten on a bus for Portland, accompanied by her girlfriend and two Stanford students who were shooting a video about her. "What's so fucking special about Grace?" one of the kids asked me bitterly.

Having never met Grace, I didn't know, except that her story had set me thinking. At age fifteen, Grace had either come out to her parents or been caught with a girlfriend, and been sent to the Montana institution for "treatment." After several months, she'd escaped and hightailed it to San Francisco. Where else would young queers run? Unfortunately, there is little help for kids in San Francisco, and no specific help for homeless gay kids. Within a few weeks, Grace was living in a parking garage and selling drugs to survive.

Grace knew I wanted to talk to her. First she agreed. But then Lynn relayed to me that Grace had decided she was doing too many drugs and was incapable of telling the truth. Grace figured it'd be discourteous to tell me a pack of lies. "You gotta respect that," Lynn said.

Respect it but take it with a grain of salt, I thought. I'd listened to plenty of self-hate brought on by substance abuse, including my own, and I knew Grace might change her mind in a matter of days. But then she and her San Francisco girlfriend got on that bus to Portland with the Stanford students—apparently Grace hoped she could clean up in Portland, and her girlfriend had pledged to help her.

I picked up her trail two weeks later, by calling the street youth center run by the Salvation Army. Grace had been there, all right, with her girlfriend. She'd enrolled in the school the Salvation Army runs and come to classes every day. Real responsible, the worker said. Bright and motivated. Then she'd disappeared. No one knew where she'd gone. Maybe to Seattle. Maybe back to San Francisco.

Or she might be found murdered. It happens with these kids, a few a year, especially the girls.

If Grace were straight she'd probably be home with Mom and Dad, not running around the West trying to clean up or lying dead under a train trestle halfway to Seattle. Could she go home to Montana? Could she turn herself in to get help? In each case, she would rightly fear that she'd be sent back to the institution with its drugs, restraints, and aversion therapy. But does the gay and lesbian community offer someone her age any help, even in the Bay Area? No. Because she is a lesbian, Grace is a write-off at age fifteen, and that's what's special about this kid who probably never wanted to be special at all.

Now I was about to meet another kid society has written off—and who has in turn written off society. Paul Johnson just turned twenty-one, a bad day in his life because it means he can no longer go to Voices, a support group for gay and lesbian street kids. He wasn't even supposed to go last year, but the facilitators made a special dispensation in Paul's case. "He needs it," street worker Mark Stucker says simply.

At age fourteen, Paul made a pass at one of his mom's foster kids, a boy two years younger. "I wanted to touch him, touch his genitals," Paul says. "I didn't end up getting to touch him, because I finally gave up. Everything got out the next morning."

The boy told Paul's mother and Child Protective Services (CPS) what had happened. Paul was removed from his mother's care and put into a group home. "After I'd been there a couple months, I asked them how long it would be until I could go live at home with my mom, because at this point I was really missing her. They said, 'It will be a year, but you have to attend a sexual offenders' group.' "

"Did you understand why they took you away?" I ask. "Did you feel like you had done something wrong?"

"No," he says softly. "I was curious. I attended the sexual offenders' class for about a year and two months. And I said, 'I thought I could go home in a year.' But they said I hadn't made enough progress."

"How were they measuring the progress?"

"I guess they were measuring it on my being able to freely admit that I am a sexual offender."

"Did your mom want you back?"

"Yeah."

"So they were really keeping you," I conclude.

When the home wouldn't let him go, Paul began acting up, fighting and running away. Once he went to Seattle and called the home after two weeks, wanting to come back. "They said, 'You can't, we give up on you. And you can't go home.' "

"How could they enforce that?"

"CPS. My mom was taking care of foster kids still, and if I would have gone back to live with her, she would have lost her license."

Paul was sent to a youth shelter, then to another group home, from which he ran away. At age seventeen, CPS threw in the towel.

"You mean they stopped chasing you?"

"Um-hmm." He grins. "And they weren't supposed to till I was eighteen."

Four years later, Paul is street-scarred and battle-weary. His face is ravaged, his voice and his laugh loud and raucous, and his clothes are torn and covered with graffiti. He walks erratically, with big motions, and since he's tall and skinny, the big motions look even bigger. When he's trucking down the street, he looks like a hyperactive spider or a windmill with a broken vane. People step off the sidewalk as he approaches. It's hard to believe he ever tricked.

"I was standing outside a gay bar, wondering what the fuck is going on in there. I thought, 'Oooo, those are faggots.' Then I was thinking, 'Wait a minute. I'm sitting here, watching them. I must like this shit, or I wouldn't be watching.' But I couldn't get into a bar. Then I see these guys up the street, standing on corners. 'Might as well try.' So I started pulling dates. My first gay experience was through a date."

"What'd you think about the guys who picked you up?"

"They are slobs. But I'll do anything to make a buck."

"So it was just business?"

"Except for Fred. I liked him. One of the reasons I never really got friendly with any of them is because none of them treated me like I was an actual person, they always treated me like I was a sex toy.

"First time I ever actually went down on a man, blow-job-wise, I thought, 'Ickkk.' Didn't really like it. But I kind of grew to like it. It was really weird to me."

"Weird that you liked it?"

He nods, engrossed in the Chinese dinner I've treated him to at a downtown restaurant. "Um-hmm."

"Did it seem to have any connection to that kid, the twelve-year-old?"

"It had to be."

"But you didn't want to think about it?"

"Not until I sat down and thought real hard: 'What the fuck am I doing?' "

Paul went home with a man who offered him beer and drugs. "He asks me if I want to go fuck, and I was like, 'What's fucking?' I mean, he asked me if I wanted to have anal sex, and I'm like, 'Huh? What's that?' Then he explained it, and I was thinking, 'Shit, I've tried everything else, might as well.' He stuck it in me, I was like real uncomfortable. But then again, I grew to like it. I still go to Seattle and see him once in a while."

But Paul hasn't tricked for more than a year. "I pulled dates for a year and a half. After that, I'd be standing on the corner, cars would just pass me. Finally I said, 'Ain't going to get no date, might as well just give up.' "

He loves Voices, and I can see why Mark let him stay an extra year. "I mainly turned into one of the mega-powers," he tells me proudly. "We have something called Street Friends. What they do is go out and talk to other gay, lesbian, and bisexual street youth and try to get them to come to the group. I was the one bringing in the most people, so they named me Powerhouse of Voices." He smiles and scoops up some more Kung Pao Chicken.

"How else has it helped?"

"When I first came to Portland, I knew I was gay, but I wasn't proud of being gay. I started going to Voices, and they taught me it is okay to be proud of who you are. And from that day forward, I'm proud to be gay. I'm proud to be bisexual now."

Paul says he's bisexual because for the past week he's been involved with a woman. "We're already thinking about marriage, and we're already thinking about kids. We've only been together a week. This has got to be a very serious relationship for me to be thinking about that stuff."

"Do you feel bad that you can't get married to a guy?"

"I've *been* married to a guy, Steve. Me and him were married for a year. I was the wife and he was the husband. Till he died. Died of HIV. It really hurt me bad. Because he only died like two months ago. And I promised him before he died that I'd never go out with another person. Or get married again. And now it's kind of like hurting me even worse because I want to marry this woman. Because to tell you the truth, Steve and I were in love beyond love."

"Maybe it seems like less of a betrayal to be with a woman," I suggest.

"In a way it does," he says. Then he assures me that he's HIV-negative. "I don't want to infect my girlfriend," he says as he scoops up another mound of rice.

"Do you feel more a part of the street community or the gay community?"

He answers by telling me he recently asked some drag queens for money. "They stick their noses in the air and go, 'No!' I go, 'Well, I'm gay too!' One of them goes, 'I doubt it, or you wouldn't be asking people for change.' I said, 'Have you ever heard of gay street kids?' She goes, 'There's no such thing.' That right there pissed me off. You're not supposed to hit women, and drag queens like being treated like women. But I get right in her face, say, 'Yes, there *is* such a thing as gay street kids, and if you don't know that, you haven't been paying attention.' And then I hit her. Because she kicked me. With her heel right in the knee. Still hurts to this day." He chuckles and pulls up his pants leg to show me.

As we get ready to leave, I ask what he plans to do with his life. "Get married and have kids. Settle down."

"What kind of work will you do?"

"At this time I would not know," he answers. His girl-friend wants him to join a program that would pay him $200 a month to study for his GED. "I flat out told her, I don't want to get my GED. If I'm never going to work, what's the sense in having a GED?"

Paul has another persona, his female side. "Sometimes you go by the name Tony?" I ask.

"Tawny," he corrects me. "I changed it to Tawny. My drag mother is Victoria St. James, so my drag name is Tawny St. James."

"You took Victoria's last name?"

He skewers me with a look. "No. I didn't take it, she *gave* it to me. She said, 'Now you're a St. James girl too.' That's why I call her my mother."

"You like drag?"

"I love drag. I don't think I would have been able to hold myself together if it wouldn't have been for drag."

"How come?"

"Sometimes life got too hard for me to deal with, and so I'd have to escape into what I like to call a fantasyland."

As we leave the restaurant and whirl through a couple gay bars looking for Victoria, with Paul hyper and loud, the reception is hostile or dismissive. Paul doesn't seem to no-tice. "Where's my mother?" he keeps asking people who ignore him. "Where's my mother?" I cut this off after the second bar by offering to take him partway home, back to the house he and his girlfriend have been living in for the past few days, with an unrelated older married couple they call Mom and Dad, and Mom's daughter and her husband, whom Paul calls his stepsister and stepbrother. "I enjoy my family very much," he says. "We all support each other. We're a very supportive family."

But first he has to show me the Embers, the bar where he's performed in drag shows. He almost sprints down the sidewalk, taking long steps and then spinning around every few seconds to see if I'm following. We leave the bars and clothing and leather shops of the gay area and head down toward the Willamette River, to the seamy side of town where the homeless congregate in the evening. All the while Paul is talking at me in gusts over his shoulder, trying to explain why the Embers is so important to him. What emerges from his roil of words is that the bar is the only place he's ever been where he can find what's deep in himself and lose what is shallow.

We finally wind up at a nondescript, down-at-the-heels building. "This is it," Paul says, staring at the entrance as if willing it to speak. But the door is padlocked and silent; the bar isn't open yet. As we walk away, Paul keeps looking back, wanting to catch a last glimpse, then another as we're about to turn the corner. I let him off at a bus stop on the other side of the river and give him a few quarters for transportation. He carefully counts the change, hauls himself out of the car, and stands at the stop, watching for a bus. I wave but he's not looking at me, and after a moment, I drive away.

"It's the only place they feel safe."

Everyone I talked to told me about the City, a gay and lesbian all-ages club. Brandon described it as "a real scary place." The street youth workers were full of praise—the club, open seven days a week, offered kids a chance to be with their own, and Lanny Swerdlow, the middle-aged owner, had a reputation for hiring and finding housing for those who really needed help. Not only that, but Lanny often staged benefits and special shows to highlight community events and organizations—a Voices benefit was only a couple weeks away.

The worker at the Salvation Army was less enchanted—she said the place was a hotbed of chickenhawks cruising young boys (and women cruising girls) and it was such a shame that kids had to be exposed to that kind of thing, and particularly horrible when it seemed to confirm all those awful stereotypes about gay men (and women). I assumed the parenthetical remarks were added because equal-opportunity villainy is essential to PC-speak, not that there were really a lot of forty-year-old dykes after innocent sixteen-year-olds.

The big building that houses the City is near the corner of Burnside and Thirteenth, in the warehouse section of downtown Portland, a few blocks from the gay area. As I turn the corner on Friday night, I spot a crowd of people standing across the street from the club. When I get closer, I see not the scene I expected—kids smoking, chatting, flirting, and indulging in horseplay—but twenty homeless men standing in tight, tense groups. "What's going on here?" I ask one man, but he doesn't answer.

Then a station wagon pulls up next to the men, and then another. The drivers, both middle-aged women, hop out as the crowd begins to stir. They open up the tailgates on the wagons to reveal paper bags full of clothes. But just as people start toward the cars, a Jeep tears around the corner, shoots past the crowd, then reverses and slams back up on the sidewalk, forcing several men to leap aside. If these are people helping the needy, I think, they're sure going about it in a nasty way. A grim-faced man piles out of the Jeep and hurls a paper bag on the ground. People approach it tentatively, as if the man might change his mind and grab it back.

"Do you want some shampoo and conditioner?" one of the women calls to me.

I look over my shoulder to see whom she's talking to. "Me?" I cheep. Gee, I just washed my hair this afternoon.

"You're welcome to join us," she tells me.

"But what are you doing?" I ask.

"We come here every Friday and Saturday night to distribute clothes and spread the word," she says.

"Ah," I say. I retreat back over to the City's side of the street.

"They used to stand right in front of the door, proselytizing the kids, telling them what a sinful place this is," City owner Lanny Swerdlow tells me. "Then they had to move across the street. To entice the kids over, they began handing out clothes and coffee and sweet rolls. Then transients heard about the food and started coming up from Old Town. Now they're stuck feeding the homeless whether they like it or not." He snorts with amusement.

Lanny is tanned, rough-hewn, and stringy, kind of like a bald Marlboro Man. If I'd run into him on the street I would have pegged him as a car mechanic. Instead he's sitting on a stool at the front entrance taking money; a big kid with long hair frisks everyone who comes in the door, while a girl with even longer hair stamps their hands. "Okay, here's how I started the club," he says as a girl in a black slinky dress hands him a five-dollar bill. "I was a member of the Central Police Chief's Advisory Council. I was the token homosexual, right? Every meeting people would complain about these kids hanging out at Third and Yamhill. They never did anything wrong, really, but if you put a hundred teenagers on a street corner, everyone panics. Well, a lot of these kids were gay and lesbian. They didn't have anywhere else to go, and the guys on the committee would say to me, 'Hey, Lanny, do you approve of this?' and what could I say, right?

"Then these six young people came to me and said they wanted to open a club. So I checked around and I found our first place, this ballroom that wasn't being used for anything. I put up some capital, and the kids spent fourteen-hour days for a month cleaning it and setting it up. The night we opened, I told 'em I was taking fifty-one percent and spreading forty-nine percent between the six of 'em. Later I bought 'em all out. They made some nice money."

More girls seem to be coming in than boys, but Lanny insists that percentage-wise it's sixty/forty boy-girl practically every night. Maybe my perception is skewed because I notice the girls more, or because they make such a dramatic entrance—almost every girl checks a weapon at the door. Switchblades, stilettos, nunchaku sticks, Mace, and brass knuckles with inch-long steel spikes all get carefully labeled with the owner's name and stowed in a box under the counter. After watching this parade of hardware, I wonder why I'm walking the mean streets of Portland without a Doberman and an Uzi.

"We get an average of a thousand kids a week, everywhere from a hundred to three hundred a night. Fridays and Saturdays are the most popular. As far as age, seventy-five percent are under twenty-one, twenty-five percent over, with the vast majority of those under twenty-five. The big difference I've seen between today and when we started in '77 is the kids now are much more cautious about sex. I attribute that mainly to AIDS."

"Have they changed since the OCA and Measure 9?" I ask.

Lanny screws up his face. "Well . . . I won't say they're more politicized 'cause what teenager is, know what I mean? But they're more aware."

They've run out of room in the weapons box, so another container is found for the overflow. I haven't laid eyes on so many switchblades since a visit to Tijuana in the '60s. I ask Lanny about the weapons. He misunderstands my concern. "Oh, the girls don't mind turning them in. They feel safe in the club. They're always telling me that it's the only place they *do* feel safe."

I repeat what the Salvation Army worker had said about the plague of older men, and he heaves a big sigh. "Well, look at the source," he says. "The Salvation Army! Have they ever bothered to stick their noses in here to find out the truth?"

I tell him Mark Stucker claims he's never seen anyone here over twenty-five.

"Oh, well, that's not true either," Lanny says. "I'll tell ya, a few older ones come by, and sometimes they're trolling. But nobody's ever gone outta here with a gun to their heads, know what I mean? You gotta recognize that some guys are interested in older men and some girls in older women. Also, lots of the older people in here are recovering alcoholics who come to dance where they won't be tempted by alcohol. We also have a big group of deaf kids. Some of 'em are gay and some straight. I'd say on some nights close to half our clientele is straight. This is often their first exposure to gay kids, and they keep coming back 'cause they love the club.

"Here's the one big controversy," Lanny tells me, trying to be helpful since the chickenhawk contention has turned out to be a bust. "No heterosexual behavior is allowed. What that means is if a boy and girl are making out, they're told to stop, and if they won't, they have to leave. People say that's discrimination, and I say, yeah, you're right." He smiles. Lanny is one of those people who has always made his own way, doesn't give a damn what other people think, and as a consequence is very at home with himself.

He returns to the discussion after selling a pack of Camels to a girl wearing a suit jacket. "Here's why: this is the only place the kids can go to get away from the constant heterosexuality that surrounds them. If I allowed heterosexual behavior in this bar, the gay atmosphere would be destroyed. It'd be like any other club in the whole country. I tell the straight kids they've got a million places to make out, while my kids only have one."

After I make my way inside, I can see why the straight kids put up a fight: not one of those million places is like the City. Pounding music blares out of speakers mounted everywhere, the dance floor pulses underfoot with flickering squares of colored lights, the strobes work in a rhythm rather than just blinking mindlessly, and a big mirrored ball overhead sums it all up, pulling the fragmented colors and reflections up into a circling whole. Underneath the ball, a hundred or so young people writhe to the music.

White T-shirts with rolled-up sleeves and shades are

the informal butch dyke dress—who says we've moved past the '50s? The more formal gals wear ties and jackets, and some of these have long hair, the ones who can pass during the day. Femmes get to be more playful; skin revealed in varying amounts and surprising ways seems the object, with slinkiness at a premium. Punks in ripped jeans dance with smart girls in uniform; women hug and pound shoulders and then stand around in big clots shouting over the music. I would have given twenty years of my life to have come here just once when I was a teenager. Watching the girls tease and fondle each other, comparing it to my own alcoholic, lonely, closeted-to-the-nth-degree youth, I'm so envious I could spit.

The boys seem more divided by class. We've got preppy guys in short-sleeved shirts and Bermuda shorts(!), guys in partial drag with pouffed hair and glittery blouses, guys in Chicago gangster gear, each one looking as if he ought to have a machine gun hanging off his shoulder. Some boys have blue hair, some have piercings, most look like your average American male dancing with your average American male.

The girls crawl all over each other, the femmes giving the butches light slaps across the face each time they get fresh, which causes both to keel over with laughter. One girl in a green jumpsuit and aviator glasses climbs up on a countertop and grinds the night away, raising her glasses on occasion to check out the talent underneath her. The boys are more tentative with each other, standing a careful foot apart, eyes cruising as they're dancing, though a few are as tangled as two bean plants crawling up a pole.

I spot one person over age twenty-five, and he sticks out like the proverbial sore thumb. So do I, of course, and a young African-American woman comes over to check me out. "Everybody's afraid you're a reporter," she tells me. "Are you?" Not a bad supposition, 'cause there I am, taking notes on my little reporter's pad.

"I'm writing a book on gay and lesbian youth," I tell her.

She heaves a sigh of relief. "Oh, good, we were afraid you were a reporter." Reporters might be aligned with the religious Right; reporters might want to close the club down. I ask her about the people across the street handing out clothes. "Oh, they tell people it's a bad place," she explains. "Christians, ya know?" Then she gives me a wink and announces, "But I'm a lesbian and I can do whatever the hell I want," before she punches me on the bicep and walks back to inform her pals I'm not dangerous, only ancient.

"What's ironic is that Christian's become a bad word to these kids," Lanny tells me later. "They'll say, 'Oh, don't be a Christian.'"

The following night I decide to hang out with the Christians. At least I won't spend all evening bemoaning my disadvantaged youth. This time more people are willing to talk, both homeless and helpers. I am scooped up by one woman who introduces me to all the workers, including the grim-faced man who won't look at me when we shake hands. He gives off such negative vibes they should pay him to stay away, but I guess it takes all kinds. That, in fact, is the message I receive from my tour guide the moment I tell her I plan to go to the City later. "We're completely nonjudgmental," she says. "God loves every single one of us."

I wonder aloud why they happened to set up their distribution station right across the street from the club. My guide tells me it's coincidence. I look skeptical. One of the other workers leaps in to say, "Oh, no, it's because of that club and those kids—"

"No, it's not," my source counters her. "That's not true. We are completely nonjudgmental—"

"But I thought . . . someone's son—" She points across the street at the kids who are waiting for the club to open at 10 P.M., and who are arranged in a neat little line against the wall, looking everywhere but at us, talking in low, strained voices. The Christians have accomplished one thing: the kids are too embattled to flow into the street to smoke and fool around as young people do in front of clubs nationwide.

"Lin plans on going over there later," my guide says meaningfully to her colleague, indicating me with a nod. What more can she do to telegraph the enemy is in their midst, send smoke signals? When light finally dawns, the worker emits such an exaggerated "Oohhhh" that we all start laughing. "Look," I say to my guide later as we trade quips with a pair of alcoholics who claim to have escaped from a mental institution, "it's absurd to pretend this is coincidence that you're camped out here."

"Well, to be perfectly honest," she starts, and draws me aside to tell me how God loves all of us, and she's sure those kids are good kids and she really hopes they'll find the Lord. I tell her probably some of them *have* found the Lord. "I'm sure you're right," she says, and then tells me about sin and adultery.

"I don't see the connection between homosexuality,

which is about love, and adultery, which is about broken promises," I say.

"I'm sure you're right," she says, and then tells me more about sin. After a few more exchanges, I realize what a clever tactic this is. She appears reasonable and objective (though illogical), while I seem intractable since I refuse to agree that homosexuality and sin might have anything in common—and just when she's being really sweet by admitting she's a sinner too.

"Look," I say, "here's what really burns me up. You guys aren't parked in front of a high school gym trying to save heterosexual kids." I don't use the A word because she's got me feeling unreasonable enough already, but abuse *is* what's happening here—the presence of this group of adults, who claim not to be part of either the OCA or any one church but simply individuals who have been "called" to this particular location on this particular evening, is emotionally abusive to the kids standing across the way. "For a lot of these kids, this is the first time they've broken through years of isolation to find a community," I tell her. "This club is the best thing that could happen to them. It's the only place they can go to be themselves."

I glance across the street at the kids still waiting for ten o'clock to roll around, so they can get inside and not have to stand out here pretending to ignore the fundies. Most have their backs turned to their tormentors, their shoulders high and stiff as they talk to each other softly. Even in this one little slice of paradise, they have to stand with their faces against the wall, surrounded by waves of disapproval.

I head over to the line of kids, feeling the stares of the workers behind me. A girl says she doesn't care about the

Christians. She won't look at them as she says it. Then she lights a cigarette, draws on it, and throws it to the ground. "They shouldn't be here," she says. "Why do they have to be right here? They want to close this place down. They hate us. I wish they'd go up a couple blocks . . ." She waves her hand hopelessly. No one's budging, not the kids, not the Christians.

As I start the long walk back to my car, I realize I would be less disturbed if my tour guide had been the grim-faced man, hate radiating from every pore. Hate I can understand. But why would a nice woman like her want to make kids feel terrible?

I try to console myself with platitudes about how the religious Right needs enemies—us, unfortunately—to feed their paranoia, while we don't need them. I tell myself what a good joke it is that they've been forced to be Christian to the homeless. But it doesn't help, because we're not talking abstractions. Real people are standing against that wall, kids whose self-worth is as fragile as a still-wet butterfly emerging from a cocoon. It seems so obvious they should be able to have an evening out without running a gauntlet, yet try proposing a seven-nights-a-week club for gay and lesbian teenagers almost anywhere in the country and watch the firestorm descend. Saying we have a long way to go doesn't begin to touch the reality; we haven't even started.

"If they were dreams, why did they seem so real?"

On another night, I run across Tom Winters counting paper cups behind the bar at the City. If Lanny ever thought employing Tom, who has lived in a maelstrom of horror and betrayal almost from birth, was an act of charity, he's been amply repaid. Pure poise, resplendent in a silver cowboy shirt and navy-blue handkerchief knotted at his neck, Tom siphons me a soda, raps his knuckles on the bar when I try to pay him, and leans forward to give me a wink when I crack a joke. Even though I'm certain he's devoting every ounce of attention to me, suddenly he's up at the other end of the bar getting some guy a Diet Coke. Never mind—here he is back again, all ears. I suspect he's all ears to the Diet Coke drinker too.

His professionalism's all the more welcome because he wouldn't have to try—with his slicked-back dark hair, deep tan, and dreamy brown eyes that can turn devilish in a half second, he could launch those thousand ships before last call any night of the week. "I get good tips," he confides. "Sometimes twenty dollars on a dollar drink." He's come to expect that kind of largesse, though he claims it'll end any moment now. "Turning eighteen was a big change," he mopes. The big event is only a couple weeks past. "Now I can't capitalize on my youth anymore." He droops dramatically across the bar, eyes sparkling.

Tall and graceful, Tom glides down the boards to slice a lime and then a lemon. He grins at me over the lemon, then pretends to toss back hair that's plastered so flat to his skull it couldn't move an iota. Eyes glittering with amusement, Tom manages to look ironic and angelic at once. Not only does that equation begin to seem reasonable, the paradox never lets up—he emits a laugh that leaves nothing to the imagination while simultaneously bubbling over with enthusiasm.

When I meet him at his apartment the following day, he bounds down to let me in wearing bedroom slippers. As he pads ahead of me, threading through a maze of fire doors and hallways, he explains that he's spent all morning gathering costumes for the annual Rosebud and Thorn contest, various stages of which will be presented on Saturday nights at the City for the next five weeks. He can't decide whether he should take the female—Rosebud—role or be the male Thorn. He's got a lot of costumes to choose from. "My boyfriend Mark has like, oh, three thousand costumes in his basement."

"He must have a big basement," I observe.

Tom steps aside for me to enter his apartment, bare of furniture except for a mattress, on which two kids are lying, one fast asleep, the other sleepy. A skinny teenager sits with his knees drawn up in front of him, glaring at me as I sink to the floor nearby.

Tom begins to move a stack of dresses from one corner of the room to the other, complete with running dialogue: "This'd be perfect if I did Rosebud." He stares at it critically, then grabs up a vest. "This'd be good for Thorn." He chews on his finger for a moment, undecided, though it's clear he won't turn down the chance to wear one of these spectacular gowns. He brightens as he points behind me at the wigs for Rosebud, which I manage to knock over as I shift position to look. Three Styrofoam heads lie topsy-turvy on the floor, their blond locks draped disconsolately across another pile of clothes. Tom's roommate Sue shouts from the next room as Tom holds a balloony dress in front of his slender figure: "I like the black one!"

"Which black one?" Tom asks. If the dresses aren't all black in the first place, they're as close to black as red can get.

"You know, the wispy one."

"That's a slip!" He rolls his eyes at me to convey the

depths of lesbian fashion ignorance. Sue's doing better than I am—at least she can tell the dresses apart. But I'm devoting a lot of attention to Tom's fashion show because the boy with the drawn-up knees has been shooting knives into my back since I walked in.

When Tom and I leave to go have breakfast nearby, I comment on the boy's hostility. "I don't even know who he is," Tom says. "Sue invites these people in, and then she's pissed off they're there." He shrugs philosophically. The three crashers—and Sue's irrationality—are just another blemish on the face of human nature.

Tom's seen his share of blemishes. "When I was six months old, my real father left the house after he and Mom had a big fight. He spat in my face and told me I was never his son."

"Did your mother tell you this?"

"No, my grandma, so I know that one's true."

Seven and a half years later, Tom's father found him wandering outside the bars downtown looking for his mom. "He was a cab driver. He sees this kid at like three in the morning so he pulls over and asks who I was looking for. When he heard who I was after, he gave me a really surprised look. He took me to my aunt's house that she used to live in before she moved. I said, 'How'd you know about this?' And he told me he was a friend of the family."

Tom ran into his real father again when he was sixteen, and both recognized the other from when Tom was eight. "He said, 'I didn't know you were hanging around downtown,' and I said, 'I didn't know you were still driving a cab.' He took me for coffee and then he dropped me off at the apartment I was living in. I mentioned him to my aunt, told her the name of this friend of the family. And she says,

'Yeah, he's your dad.' I thought, 'Why didn't that asshole tell me who he was?' "

He raises his eyebrows above a survivor's half-grin. "It kind of upset me, you know?" The waiter asks what we want, but Tom hasn't decided. "Just coffee for now," he says, and he waits for me to order. "Anyhow," he says, "I started running away from all the group homes when I was eight—"

"Wait. Why were you in group homes?"

"My adopted father—the one my mother married after my real father left—never did like me, let's put it that way. I was abused a lot, mentally, physically, and sexually. But one of the main reasons he put me in a group home was I threatened to kill him. He was beating the shit out of my mom, and from when I was five to like six and a half, I had to watch it every single night. So one time I went in the living room and picked up this pistol and went upstairs and I said, 'If you don't want to see your butt fly through the air, get your hands off my mom *now*.' So he told me I wouldn't do it and I aimed at the floor and fired. It knocked me flat on my back. The look on my mom's face . . . She took the gun from me, and I ended up going to a group home. Then they split up and visits became a constant battle.

"He wanted to put out the image that he was the warm, loving, caring father, and that was never true. I still have school pictures from when I was in the first grade and my face is all tore up from a rag with a rock in it he had rubbed all over my face. He was also sexually abusing me."

Tom's mother "kidnapped" him from the home, which ended in a custody fight as his adopted father tried to prove his mother unfit. "When it went to trial he and my grandma and about four other people said I was a habitual liar and that I exaggerate. How can you exaggerate at that age being beaten with a leather belt as hard as he could possibly hit me, how could you exaggerate the scars that were on my face, or the medical report? And they still believed my dad was good. They sent me back with him. After that my dad locked me up in the garage with no bed, painted the windows, nailed them shut, and completely put me away from everyone else in the family. I was like a pet. I had figured out how to unlock the door with a paper clip so I could get out to get food. The only food I ever got was lunch and breakfast at school."

"He let you go to school."

Tom nods. "I was always daydreaming about what it would be like to live a better life, so I never did my schoolwork. Every grade I got was an F, and for every F I was beat fifty times . . ." And here he slows down, until each word is an effort to wrest from his throat. "For him it was a big . . . *game* . . . a power trip. I was there so he could scare me and still have me around to say, 'I love you, Dad.' And I said it just so he wouldn't beat on me." He shook his head. "Then my mom and dad started seeing each other again, and he started beatin' on her, and I went back into the group homes.

"It was around that time that I figured out I liked boys. It scared me, so I denied it. Whenever the kids would call me fag, I'd tell 'em all to fuck off."

"Did you look different from the other kids?"

"Oh, yeah, I definitely did. I used to have a big bouffant wave in my hair. I wouldn't dare wear it that way now. And the girls and I looked at guys all the time . . . My first girlfriend, we went out behind the bleachers. She told me she wasn't a virgin, and she was nine years old and that freaked me out, and then she put my hand down there." His eyes widen in feigned horror as I laugh. "I said, 'That's it, get away, we'll be friends.'"

Tom's grades went to As and Bs as he adjusted to life in the home. He realized a couple things: that being beaten was not his fault, and that his mother's difficulties were not his responsibility. "Things were easier in a sense, but I still felt like I was pushing everything away. What hurt most was Mom and Dad fighting over who got the right to visit me."

"He kept saying she was unfit?"

"Constantly."

"And I guess you'd given up on anyone believing you by then."

"At that point the truth held no meaning for me. I figured if they believed my dad's story, then they didn't really care about me." He pauses, thinking. "This psychologist told me she cared, but in a way she didn't because she said [the abuse] was no longer relevant to how I was now. I told her, that's the biggest lie I've ever heard out of you. It was one of the *big* obstacles to my feeling good. I just had to block it out." He shakes his head. "The people who did believe me were my teachers. That confused me. My teachers believed me, why didn't the people I lived with?"

It's a rhetorical question, but I take it seriously, imagining bouffant-haired Tom—who was cross-dressing by age nine—telling people about this homosexual abuse he had suffered. "Do you think," I ask tentatively, "that because you were so obviously non-gender-conforming they might have thought you were fantasizing it? In other words, do you think they might have believed you if you'd looked straighter?"

Tom nods. "I think that's probably true. They knew I

was gay. They knew I did drag. They kept telling me it was fantasies or nightmares. But—" he says, pinioning me with insistent blue eyes, "if they were dreams, why did they seem so real?"

To this question I have no answer, so we sip at our coffee for a few moments. Finally I ask, "Did the group home people try to stop you dressing in drag?"

He laughs. "No, they were the ones who bought me all the clothes I needed. And my shoes and makeup. I actually ran away in drag. I'd tell people I was a thirteen-year-old girl. I had a boyfriend named Travis. He thought I was a girl, and he'd try to get me in the sack, and I'd think of every excuse to get out of it. When he found out I was a guy, he said, 'I don't care, let's do it,' and I was going, 'Duh, duh, duh—*what*?' He was thirteen and here I am, ten years old. He said, 'Damn, you look good. Stay like that,' and I'm going, 'No way, thank you, adiós.'

"I was using the name Jeannie. My mom knew I was dressing as a girl so the police wouldn't find me so easily. But then the police found out, so they started picking me up. Every time I went to JDH [Juvenile Detention Home], I'd get embarrassed totally, so I quit doing it."

"Was it pretty hairy in there? Did you get taunted?"

He nods. "Teased, threatened. Every time they'd threaten me, I'd say, 'Okay, do it, don't just talk about it,' and they'd back down. I may have been gay but I was going to back down to no fucking person. They said I was the first cool homosexual they'd ever met. I'd sit there with 'em and they'd talk about girls, and I'd talk about guys and not gross 'em out."

"Did you know any gay guys at this point?"

"No. Well, two guys, but they never told me they were

gay. I didn't find out until years later when I bumped into them at a pride parade downtown."

When Tom ran away, he stayed with older women friends in an apartment complex or with his boyfriend Travis and Travis's dad. Finally he was put in a foster home outside the city, but that didn't stop him. "I grabbed a ten-speed and started running away again. I'd go to downtown Portland and party, and that's where I met my first lover, Mikey."

Tom was fourteen and Mikey was nineteen, and the two were together for a year and a half, though occasionally the cops would pick Tom up and bring him back to the home. "Did you live with him?"

"Yeah. Him and his parents. His parents were great."

"Why couldn't you just live there? Social services wouldn't allow it?"

Tom nods. "The last three months we were together were awesome. I rode horses for the first time with him, did a lot of neat romantic things, wine and candles on the beach. Then I started hanging around with his friend Marcy the last couple weeks of our relationship, and he thought I was going to take off and be straight. I don't know where that idea came from, but he stopped taking his insulin.

"I knew he was diabetic, I knew he took shots for it. As long as he kept his sugar level and his shots within the parameters that his doctor had set, he was fine. I told him, never ever commit suicide on me, and what does he do? Went out and committed suicide on me.

"I was really scared to meet anyone else. I was like, what if they're gonna die on me? Then I started thinking, well, if that's what happens when you fall in love, why do it?"

"He was the first out gay guy you knew?"

"He wasn't out. His parents knew, but no one else. He was a butt-rockin' kid with a hotrod car."

"Not involved with the gay community."

"Nope. And neither was I. I knew about it, but I didn't want to be around it."

"Why?"

"Denying it."

"Denying you were gay?"

"Umm-hmmm. After Mikey, I met Gineen and tried going straight."

"So how long were you with her?"

"Oh, God . . . about three weeks. It was fairly disgusting," he muses, "almost like it'd been before with the girl behind the bleachers. She put my hand down there and I went, *bleeeah*!"

He lets out that devilish laugh. "I quickly went back to being gay, though I was still denying it. I was sitting around, and these guys were talking about going to the City, and I said, I don't want to go where a bunch of faggots hang out. And this one guy said, you better watch your ass, little straight boy, and I went, whoops! I ended up going out with him two weeks later. That relationship lasted about three months. After that I was a total slut. It was like pretty easy to get to me. Guys were getting away with it 'cause I didn't feel secure."

"Did they give you stuff?"

"Yeah. Drugs or money or clothes or a place to stay. Then I kind of quit being a slut and settled down and started going to school. Got a job at a gas station. Rented my own room."

"So at that point you started going to the City and hanging out with other gay kids?"

"Yeah. I moved away from my family completely, put my mom and her problems out of my life. Then about a year after I moved, there was a picture of me going to the junior prom in drag in the newspaper."

"Who'd you go with?"

"Pete. He's down in LA now, HIV-positive. Actually he has AIDS. His T cells are down to like three. That kinda hurts. He doesn't want any help, no help at all." He raps the table with his fingers. "My mom called me. I don't know how she got my number, except from maybe the reporters. And she said, 'What the hell is this picture doing in here? Your grandma and your aunt are all upset about this!' And I went, 'Yeah, so?' I didn't care. I thought it was funny. She said she wanted to see me, and I told her my apartment number, and she came over and we talked.

"It kind of pisses me off 'cause now she wants to be friends, but where was she earlier? When I needed her, she wasn't there. I mean, I love her, but you don't need your mom around all the time when you're eighteen."

"What do you think about the guys who gave you stuff when you were younger?"

"Trash. They're trash. I mean, they wanted something from me, and I wanted something from them too, but I think it's wrong to do that. I don't feel good about it. Ultimately I don't care about them and they don't care about me, so that's all it was, not caring."

"What do you imagine you'll be doing in five years?"

Without a pause, Tom says, "I'll have an interior design shop. I'll do buildings so that the insides are totally different from the outsides. See that brick building over there? Inside I'd make it like a log cabin or a Victorian or something."

I grin at him, remembering the dresses. "You're really into exteriors and deception, aren't you?"

He laughs. "That's right. I love the whole drag scene."

"Does romance come into this picture?"

"Well, I still want to be with Mark." He pauses, thinking. "And with Eddy." Tom had mentioned to me earlier that he had two boyfriends. His relationship to each was so unique that he despaired at someday having to choose between them. "I mean, I'd like to be with both of them, but I guess that isn't possible."

"They know about each other, right?"

"Oh, yeah. And they know about my health problems."

"Health problems?"

"That I'm—" He covers the mike on the tape recorder, tells me something, then says, "Fuck it," and uncovers the recorder to say he's HIV-positive. "I found out about it on August 18, 1990. It was the worst day of my life. Right there I felt dead." He stares out the window, the first time he hasn't been able to look at me. "Here's what I'm really afraid of." He names a string of men he knows who have died horribly. "I want to go like Raymond. Three days and he was gone. That's how I want to go. Fast." He nods affirmatively, as if saying the words will make it happen. This, then, is the real five-year plan. "But who knows? I might still be around, ten, fifteen years from now." He says it as if it's one of those Bette Midler torchers he likes so much. True romance is living to age thirty-three.

"I tell everybody," he says. "People are afraid to tell, because they think no one will sleep with them. I don't want to be responsible for people dying. And I've had more sex than ever."

"Have you changed much of yourself to fit in with the gay community?"

He explains that in certain situations he used to try to be more straight-appearing. "Now I'm just a femme submissive all the way. My mom says I'm worse than she ever was."

"Did you feel you had to take on a role?"

"No, it's just more who I am. The gay community has let me be more myself, in the sense that now I'm proud of who I am. I like myself now. I care about people, and it's important for me to be able to show that, because I was never able to do that before."

"What don't you like?"

"I don't like how gay men are mean to lesbians. Lesbians are cool, I like to talk to lesbians. Straight women are even better 'cause I can talk to them about men. I tell them I've got PMS. And they go, 'What do you mean?' and I go, PMS means Putting up with Men's Shit. Either that or Pretty Miserable Sex. If women think we don't get it, let me tell you we do."

Brandon knows Paul because of his work with OSMYN and Voices. Tom's seen Brandon's name in the newspaper. Paul remembers Tom from the bar. The gay community draws interstices between groups and people that resemble a fine lace tablecloth. Follow one thread long enough and you'll encounter the pathway to everybody else. It's our greatest strength, yet one difficult to penetrate for those under twenty-one.

The threads of that cloth are woven together by thousands of overlapping families of friends and lovers. For most of us, nothing is more important than the families we have created. Particularly for those of us who grew up feeling isolated, singular, and alienated from our biological family —still the majority experience for gay and lesbian teens— finding family is what we crave over anything else. Brandon was cast out by his friends but adopted a community of gay youth. When Tom found acceptance at the City, he stopped running away, got a job, and began to feel good about himself. Paul's still looking, and hopefully so is Grace. What help they got from adults, gay or straight, can be ticked off on the fingers of one hand, and much of the blame for that can be laid at homophobia's doorstep.

Can't get in a bar? Then forget it—or get in my car instead. By limiting kids' choices to sex or nothing, the community has abandoned them when they need us most, in the process lending weight to "recruiting" charges, for while the good guys stay away, scared off by the very implication of recruiting, the bad guys cavort in the vacuum. We of all people know the notion of recruiting is pure crap—if people could be recruited, we would all be straight. Yet out of cowardice and our own internalized homophobia, we conduct our lives as if such a thing were possible. Each time we choose to hide rather than help, we've hurt not only the kids who need us but diminished ourselves by acting out of expedience rather than from what we know is right. Honest people cannot appease a master who thrives on ignorance— it's as simple and as terrifying as that.

When I met Brandon, the first thing he told me was that the night before he'd had a nightmare about Lon Mabon, the head of the OCA. Lon was chasing Brandon around downtown Portland with a stick.

As I listened, I thought Brandon, the church youth leader and good kid, should be the one giving Lon Mabon nightmares. But then all these kids would. Because they weren't recruited, they're gay whether they like it or not, and they're as different as corn and marigolds and a redwood tree.

What connects them is that all three have suffered from the atmosphere that the Lon Mabons of the world have struggled to create. Brandon suppressed his sexuality for years, and when he finally did come out, he was shunned by the friends he'd been close to since childhood. His father, who is very religious, sends him literature about satanic possession. Yet Brandon, who won awards during high school for his garden designs (when he wasn't offing trees), has decided to spurn landscape architecture or graphic arts to devote himself to the fight.

Labeled a sex offender as an early adolescent, Paul was deemed damaged goods by the state and removed from his home, with the unhappy acquiescence of his mother, whose income depended on her fostering children. Paul's response —that the state can damn well take care of him forever— isn't surprising. But the physical and emotional manifestations of his alienation separate him from the gay community as well, so he searches high and wide for a family to fill a gap that must yawn painfully empty.

Tom, obviously gay at age eight or nine, was not believed. What would have happened if someone had listened? Tom refused to lie down and die, either emotionally or physically. When he connected with people who cared, he had the strength to find family in himself, but what few accomplish at such an early age didn't come soon enough. Tom needed help over the rough spots, and he didn't get it until after he'd become HIV-positive.

How different these three are, and how different is

Grace. The horror of Tom and Grace's stories—a boy emerging from a nightmare with a death sentence on his head, a naïve girl consigned to hell through no fault of her own—is that they were convicted by a society that would rather kill them than admit to their existence. Which is, to a greater or lesser degree, the dilemma faced by almost all gay teens.

In the fall of '94, the U.S. Senate overwhelmingly passed an amendment, cosponsored by Jesse Helms and New Hampshire Senator Bob Smith, that would cut off federal funding to public schools that "have either the purpose or effect of encouraging or supporting homosexuality as a positive lifestyle alternative." The amendment would also prohibit "counseling or other services on school grounds, or referral of a pupil to an organization that affirms a homosexual lifestyle." In language straight from the religious Right, this means no education, no groups, no counseling, no help for kids in trouble—in other words, making misinformation a priority. It translates to more kids at risk like Grace and Tom, more alienated outcasts like Paul, more reluctant warriors like Brandon—more people in pain from loneliness, abuse, and despair.

The bill finally died, but like a zombie in a bad movie, it will keep coming back. Choices will then be made. Will San Francisco schools, for example, lose $12 million in federal aid or will the board prohibit referrals to gay youth groups? If we pretend gay youth don't exist, that choice becomes easier on the wallet and the conscience.

"I don't think a lot of people realize homosexuals are people," Brandon says. "Those grandmothers in the shopping malls passing out literature are just doing what they're told. It's kind of like when you're in a war, and it's easy to sit back and fire your machine gun when you don't see anyone. But when you come face-to-face, then it becomes a little more difficult." Not difficult enough. In this war in which children are the primary casualties, both sides seem only too eager to ignore the wounded.

high school confidential

double trouble times four

If the four teenagers in this section were put into the same room, they would violently disagree about a great many subjects. Yet running through their stories is a plaintive song of separation—from their parents, their friends, their schools, their hopes and dreams, and most disturbingly, from a self free of the double-consciousness W. E. B. Du Bois describes in *The Souls of Black Folk*: ". . . this sense of always looking at one's self through the eyes of others, of measuring one's soul by the tape of a world that looks on in amused contempt and pity."

Allyson Mount lives by her principles; she came out at her prep school because silence is a form of lying. She makes excuses for the friends who abandoned her and worries over the reputations of the ones who have stuck around. John Swensen has no friends—he sits at home pounding his computer keyboard, talking to other lonely gay teens on the Internet. The most vivid fear of this reclusive sixteen-year-old is that another boy's parents will accuse him of ruining their son. Renee George decries at the superficiality of her relationships but doesn't let her friends get close because they might find out who she is. Lee Garrett is aided by a pack of friends willing to accept her—even when she doesn't want to accept herself.

Each is in that uncomfortable stage of adjusting to a "spoiled" identity, running away from the stigma of being gay and running toward who they know themselves to be at the same time. All have a heightened self-awareness, a fear that others now perceive them differently when they themselves know they have not changed. All carry the seeds of anger that they will no longer be judged for who they are inside but only for what they are seen to represent. Being gay or bisexual is the joker slipped in with the cards they've already been dealt: divorces, sexual molestation, privilege, poverty, a greater or lesser degree of social adaptability.

Three are sixteen, one eighteen; two are about to escape into college, while two are looking ahead to another year of high school. All are anticipating changes, though one, plunged from the predictability of Army life into the chaos of the inner city, has endured about as much upheaval as she can stand. All are bright and articulate, all have succeeded in school or with friends or jobs. They live at opposite ends of the country, in Massachusetts, New Mexico, the Bay Area, and conservative Orange County. None has a clear idea of how being gay or bisexual will impact their lives, because each is struggling to survive in a world where a straight ethos still rules. Since they've seen barely a hint of an alternative, the future is pretty hazy. Courage connects them. Or perhaps it's a form of faith, because they have so little idea what lies ahead.

"i wouldn't just go up and give someone a hug."

Deerfield Academy, a boarding and day school for grades 9–12, lies off a long, straight stretch that connects several towns in western Massachusetts—Deerfield, South Deerfield, North Hatfield—a stretch that was later flanked by State Highway 10 which was in its turn flanked by Interstate 91. But even as the fast lane is engaged in a glacial creep away from the venerable school, it is here, in the midst of those bright and comfortable enough to question everything, that I hope to find utopia—or at least acceptance—for gay and lesbian teens. But first I have to find the library, which would have been difficult without my student guide, since the almost two-hundred-year-old school did not anticipate cars and then, when they did come, fell all over itself to accommodate them, throwing capillary-like roads hither and thither across the lawns, as if playing a game of Connect-the-Dot.

The institution reeks of New England rectitude: the elegant decline that would have given it flavor in the South is absent here. There are no grandiose sweeping vistas or magnificent edifices held together by spit and sealing wax. Instead, the values of industry and sobriety are upheld by sturdy trees, no-nonsense brick buildings, and those twisting lanes, like the trails of very busy ants. The ants are indeed busy. Prep schools like Deerfield are springboards to the right college, and the pressure on both students and faculty to funnel a hefty percentage of a graduating class into the Ivies is anything but subtle.

As we enter the library, I'm astounded by the size of its holdings (fifty thousand volumes), by the number of computer terminals, by the huge list of periodicals to which the school subscribes. Comparing Deerfield's library to my high school's few bookcases is absurd, but poor Sarah Lawrence comes out a distant second as well. I later discover that Deerfield, with a student body of six hundred, has an endowment of $100 million, and gives out scholarships totaling $2 million to almost a third of the student body every academic year. What a difference being a boy makes.

Or made. To the dismay of many, Deerfield coeducated in 1988. When I told an old friend that I was going to interview a couple women at his alma mater, he was apoplectic. *"Girls at Deerfield?"* he bellowed.

Allyson Mount shrugs when I tell her this. She's the one who directed me through the maze of lanes, and she's now trying to chivvy me, as I gawk at racks and racks of magazines like a hayseed tourist, to a downstairs study room where her friend and fellow senior Trish Block will meet us. "The boys say we have it easy," she tells me. "Like in the dress code. They always have to wear ties, but we have more leeway."

Allyson is a rarity, a fighter without a chip on her shoulder. Eighteen years old, slender and attractive, with lanky brown hair she intends to chop off when she goes to Smith in the fall, she's shy but determined. Her integrity is so ingrained she never remarks on it, but her insistence on her right to be herself has exposed her to slurs, cold shoulders, and rejection. I found Allyson through Trish, whose name I'd been given by another gay writer; Trish told me rather mysteriously that she had rounded up her friend Allyson, because Allyson might have more to say. I wrote to the two in February, listing questions I was interested in: what stereotypes did they have about gays and lesbians; did they believe they would have to change to become part of a gay community; how would being gay affect them in the course of their lives. Trish called to say that she and Allyson had talked for hours after receiving my letter and had "gotten much closer." I thought this might be code for "become lovers," so as I follow Allyson into the study room, I'm not sure what to expect.

I'm arriving at a bad moment: it's college notification time, the second weekend of April, and seniors have been haunting the mailroom, waiting for the thin letters of acceptance or rejection. Allyson warns me that Trish has just been rejected by her top choices. "It's not fair," Allyson tells me. "Trish is really good. She's got better grades than I do." Allyson knits her eyebrows worriedly; she's a person who broods over inequities but tends to lay the blame on ignorance rather than malice. After puzzling over Trish's rejections, she shakes her head. "I don't understand it."

Just as Allyson begins to muse about her next year at Smith, Trish comes sweeping into the little windowed room, apologizing for being late. Tall, sandy-haired, and athletic—her tennis serve is feared in three states—she is as brash as Allyson is reserved, as bombastic as Allyson is understated. The two brush lips and seem genuinely excited to see each other. I'm none the wiser as to the nature of their relationship.

Between meanderings, switchbacks, and a lot of talking over each other—though a great deal quieter than Trish, Allyson won't let herself be bowled over—the two tell their very dissimilar stories. Allyson is from a middle-class family here in Deerfield, while Trish comes from scads of new money and lives on an estate in Darien, Connecticut. Allyson tries to see all sides of an issue, even when she's the injured party, while Trish expects malice, takes no one at her word, and is given to loud and frequent confrontations. She portrays herself as a fighter on the side of justice, but it soon emerges that it's been Allyson rushing the machine guns, partially because Trish, whom I would term "questioning," is not all that committed to a fight that may not concern her, and partially because Allyson is the one who believes a well-fought battle can change minds and hearts. I very soon decide to concentrate my interviews on Allyson, especially after I learn Trish has other commitments for most of the weekend.

Allyson grew up in this neck of the woods, splitting her time between Mom and Dad, who divorced when she was six. She's a day student, living at home with her mom and younger brother in a house a stone's throw from the Disneyland excesses and loudspeakered music of the Yankee Candle Company. "During the holidays, which start in October, we have Christmas carols until ten every night," she grimaces. But the company is a welcome neighbor in every other way, since it provides jobs in a community which at best struggles back to sea level after nearly drowning in whatever recession we're having at the moment.

Allyson depends on her dreams for insight: "I was in the seventh or eighth grade, and my best friend and I were walking along this dirt path. It was a very orange dream, and we'd just read Robert Frost. And she said, 'You like to take the road less traveled, don't you?' She said it really sarcastically; it was a very negative comment. And when I woke up, I remember thinking, 'Yeah, that's kind of true.' I've always felt different from my friends, but I've just never known why."

In the spring of her sophomore year, Allyson was going

out with a male student. "I knew the whole time I shouldn't be going out with him. And I didn't know why. I had a weird dream. He was hugging me good night, and I wanted to push him away so violently, it was a real intense violent feeling. I knew I should have done that in the dream, and I knew I wouldn't, and I was really mad at myself. It wasn't that I knew I was gay, I knew it was wrong for me to be there with him."

Shortly after this second dream, Allyson's classmate Leilani Lumen, perhaps given courage by the knowledge that she was about to transfer to another school, gave a speech at an assembly that was reprinted in the school paper and in *Speaking Out*, the newsletter Exeter alum Al Chase publishes every few months for sexual minority students in the boarding school community. "If there's anything I have to say about being a lesbian here," Lumen said in her speech, "it is *lonely*. Just imagine that you are a black American who was somehow physically turned into a white American and then dropped right in the middle of a Ku Klux Klan meeting. How do you think you would feel? All the Klansmembers would *assume* that you are part of the Klan. In that case, would you have the courage to voice your opinions, tell them that you *support* blacks? Probably not: you'd probably end up, out of sheer fear, just sitting there and letting all the Klanspeople make racial jokes and plan hate crimes right in front of you.

"This is how I feel most of the time here, and even anywhere. As a lesbian, it's *painful* to sit and watch while my friends, classmates, and peers tell gay cracks right in front of me."

Lumen's speech got Allyson thinking, and by the middle of her junior year, she had come out to herself. "Looking back on it, it should have been really obvious to me. There are things I wrote in my journal in the fifth grade. The people I'm describing are the same kind of people I would be attracted to now." Junior year was difficult, because her uncle, who had always attended family gatherings with his "roommate," announced not only that he was gay, but that both men were HIV-positive, and that his lover had AIDS. "The whole thing really shook everyone up. For a couple months, it was really, really tense."

Allyson came out to her uncle, and the two began corresponding. At the end of the summer she came out to her parents and her stepmother. "They weren't surprised, none of them. My stepmother had actually talked to [her uncle]. She asked him if he thought I might be gay. He was like, 'You'll have to ask her about that.'"

When school started again, Allyson was active in a new organization she helped found, a gay-straight student alliance called Get Rid of Homophobia! (GROH!).

"Is GROH! mostly gay people?" I ask.

"No," Allyson says, and Trish adds, "That's why I hate it."

"We have about forty people," Allyson expands, "but usually ten or fifteen at meetings. The assumption is that people are open-minded but straight."

"Yeah, right," Trish says sarcastically. She's not doubting the GROH! members' sexual orientation but their capacity for tolerance.

But Allyson *is* talking orientation. "It's a very, very strong assumption," she says.

Trish is shaking her head. "The people I see at GROH! often are homophobic, like so homophobic I don't understand why they're there."

"It's good," Allyson maintains. Where better to educate homophobes than in a stop homophobia group?

"It's good but it's not a place where you can feel comfortable saying things," Trish says. Allyson can't argue with this summation, and I'm thinking Deerfield doesn't sound like much of a utopia when gays are too frightened to come out in the gay-straight alliance.

Allyson shattered the tolerant-but-het supposition late in January when she came out at a meeting. "There were like fifteen people there. I kind of thought I might do it. I knew I needed to. At the beginning of the year, I had decided that if anybody asked me, I would not lie. But since silence is a kind of lying, I was on the edge of that . . . I just told people, and they all started clapping, which was very embarrassing. I was like, 'Don't make a big deal of it, I just want you to know.' "

"How many other out gay people are there here?" I ask.

"Just Allyson," Trish answers. "And Leilani, who's constantly made fun of to this day," and who, I remind myself, transferred from Deerfield almost two years ago.

"Do you think there are kids in GROH! who are hiding?"

"Oh, yeah," Allyson says.

"You think?" Trish asks skeptically.

"Of course," Allyson answers. And she's right, whether the people are known to her or not. There are plenty of reasons to hide at Deerfield, and not many to come out. Most decide it's best to postpone the revelation till college, when presumably there will be a larger group to ally oneself with, or off-campus housing, or a lover to buoy one's spirits. Facing harassment, violence, and isolation when you're unable to escape your tormentors, when they're living in your nest, is beyond the scope of almost anyone. As Trish says to explain her silence about her possible bisexuality, "I didn't want to deal with people removing themselves from me." After listening to her, I decide that in Trish's case, not jumping to conclusions is probably best: "When I came to Deerfield, I was trying to realize if it was programmed into me to like men, or if it was I really did or I liked women. And is it necessarily a gender you're attracted to or is it a person? I wasn't sure, it's really up in the air for me. But it's not overwhelming my life. I don't feel I have to resolve it this moment."

"So what's happened since you came out?" I ask Allyson. A lot, it seems. The senior girls are good, she says, but the senior boys avoid her. She's lost some friends. One boy slammed a heavy door in her face, knocking her hard against the wall, and then took off running. She knows she's a frequent subject of conversation in the dorms. In an essay in Al Chase's *Speaking Out*, she describes the aftermath: "The initial relief has dissipated considerably, and it sometimes seems as if all coming out accomplished was making others conscious of the distance I've felt between us all along."

Even more, it's made Allyson aware of her new status as a pariah and of the devastating consequences of that stigma. A volunteer child care worker at a shelter for battered women, she now worries that anything she says or does will be misinterpreted. "One day there was this four-year-old, he wanted me to spin him around, and then this eight-year-old girl wanted me to do it. My friends knew I was a lesbian, and though it never came up, the whole time I was thinking, if they wanted to make trouble for me, they could say, 'She has her hand across the girl's chest,' or whatever. It just got me really nervous. After that I either play with the really little kids or the boys. I shouldn't let myself worry about that, but I can't help it."

She is also concerned about the effect her coming out has on the friends who have stood by her. She tells me about a presentation she did for Diversity Day, during which members from a gay youth group in Springfield were supposed to speak. The Springfielders never showed, so Allyson and another member of GROH! took charge of two forty-minute slots, and Allyson came out again, twice. "After that"—she pauses, glancing at Trish—"well, she keeps telling me not to worry about this, but I'm just really worried about people seeing us hanging out together—"

"Aw geesh!" Trish explodes.

"It's automatically 'Allyson's gay, then *she* must be too.' I'm really afraid of that for you."

"I don't care!" Trish insists, growing increasingly agitated.

"Are your other friends concerned?" I ask Allyson.

Allyson fidgets. "Well, there's this one girl, she was my best friend for a while. She's really great, part of GROH!, but she's said things to me like, 'I don't really mind if people think I'm a lesbian, but I kind of wish they wouldn't, because I would like to go out with guys, and no one's going to ask me because they think I'm gay.' Just stuff like that."

Trish is rolling her eyes. "She gave up the friendship—"

"It wasn't her fault," Allyson insists. "It was just we didn't connect. It made me real conscious of what I say and do around her. And most of my friends. Actually almost all my friends."

"I don't think it was right she said that," Trish says. "Look at the effect it had on you."

Trish is so protective that I finally have to ask. "Are you two girlfriends?"

Silence.

Then Trish says, "Oh, no," and Allyson says, "No."

"Allyson likes Ruthie," Trish reports.

"No, I don't!" Allyson protests. "She's not my girlfriend." She pauses. "I like her a whole lot."

"Well, okay," Trish agrees. "We discussed it, and we decided we didn't want to put our friendship in any sort of jeopardy. We thought it would probably be best to remain friends."

Allyson breaks in with praise. "I really admire Trish for bringing it up, 'cause I wouldn't have said anything, I mean, it was something we needed to talk about—"

"I'm on a big communication kick," Trish says. "That's why I try to discuss and question. And anyway, you said you didn't know what was going on with you and Ruthie."

"I still don't," Allyson points out.

Ruthie goes to a school several states distant, which solves one problem but creates others. "Could you have a relationship with a girl here at school?" I ask, curious.

"Oh, no," Allyson says with certainty over Trish's waffling. Trish won't concede victory to the homophobes, but she does agree with Allyson that constant harassment of both parties would be the least of it; rape as a punitive measure was very likely. As fairy tale an environment as Deerfield is, with its huge endowment, privileged students, Diversity Days, and supportive faculty (Allyson says they have been almost unanimously sympathetic and helpful), the school can't escape existing on this planet. Boys were recently disciplined for taunting girls and publicly masturbating while a group of students watched *Basic Instinct*, fliers advertising GROH! are torn down as quickly as they're put up, and posters declaring Deerfield a school of tolerance were stolen from the bulletin board and pinned to the doors of students suspected of being gay.

"Okay," I say, admitting defeat myself, "you can't hold hands, you can't have a relationship with someone at school, but what would happen if you just *talked* to people about a girlfriend?"

Allyson ponders this. "I don't know. I think I'd get more things like getting slammed in the door. When I first came out . . . People have kind of forgotten about it, so as long as I don't do anything to remind them . . ."

"As long as you're not sexual," I say.

"Yeah," Allyson says, breaking into laughter. "We had people from the Gay/Lesbian/Bisexual Bureau at UMass come to speak at GROH! And people asked all these intellectual questions. The whole conversation was very political; no one was trying to get to know them at all. It was, 'You're representing something, you're not a person.' And that really bothered me. That's what people do here about anything. As long as you don't see it, as long as it's on an intellectual level, it's fine."

Allyson met Ruthie when she and several other Deerfield students attended a conference at another prep school for members of gay-straight alliances like GROH! "I liked [Ruthie] immediately, so cute. We spent the whole night together—that didn't come out right. The whole evening. But it *was* an overnight thing, there were all these people in sleeping bags, and it was really great. That's something I totally miss with my friends now, 'cause I'm so conscious, I wouldn't just go up and give someone a hug—"

"A lot of that happens because of people like your ex-best friend," Trish says darkly.

Allyson waves this observation off with a smile. "Anyway, the conference was wonderful, a really, really nice feeling. Not everybody was gay, but that was definitely the assumption. This girl I met wrote to me the day after, and I wrote back. We wrote back and forth and then she came up here. We had a great night, though it was uncomfortable with my mother. It was good my mom and I didn't know she was coming because—you can tell—she has a leather jacket, I mean, she really looks gay. When people stay over at my house, they just sleep on the futon in my room. So my mother couldn't really say anything, but the next day she was, 'I don't think it's a good idea if you have friends like that overnight in your room. I think it's very inappropriate.'

"I convinced her that she was just a friend, which was not true, because we did sleep together. I feel so bad because my parents trust me, and to lie to them like that . . . It really bothers me. I understand the point. If it was a guy, they wouldn't let him stay in my room, so why should they let a girl?"

"My view is that we're over eighteen," Trish says. "I don't find that to be my parents' business. I don't ask them about their sex life."

"What I was angry about was that my mother assumed she was my girlfriend," Allyson continues. "And that I really like her, which I did. But my mother had nothing to base that on, she just assumed it."

"It's a shame it had to happen at your mother's," I say.

Allyson is nodding. "I don't have a lock on my door, and I was like, 'Oh my God, my mother might come in.' What was really bad was that we actually slept on the futon all night; if I had gotten up and gone back to my bed, it would have been better. I didn't really care enough at the time, I'm afraid."

Given the two are in boarding schools states apart, it's not surprising that the relationship seems to be clunking along to an unstated conclusion. "When I saw her last weekend, we were just friends, and there was no tension there at all. She was with a straight friend, so it may have been that, but . . ." A wash of sadness has flooded her face, and she looks away for a moment. This isn't, I realize, a great time for Allyson either, and I'm grateful that the two have kept their appointment with me, made weeks before their hopes about colleges and romance were dashed. "So I don't know," she concludes. "I don't even know if she has a girlfriend. I've never asked her. It's none of my business."

Trish is staring at her with astonishment. It's clear she thinks Allyson is carrying New England reticence too far.

The next day, Trish is off to her parents' house, so Allyson and I decide to give the coffee shop in Deerfield a miss and journey seventeen miles south to Northampton, the town the tabloids (and even the *New York Times*) call Lesbianville, U.S.A. A huge banner proclaiming Breast Cancer Awareness Week hangs across Main Street. "That's been there for days already," Allyson tells me. We're cruising for a place to eat, but there's plenty to see on the way: joggers, lesbians, preppy college boys, lesbians, punky teenagers, and lesbians. The night before, I'd eaten dinner at the North Star, a gay club with good food. Several tables held Mom, Dad, and two young women with sharp haircuts. As I ate, I entertained myself by guessing the blood relatives, which, given lesbian merging, was more taxing than one might expect. This morning, before picking up Allyson for lunch, I'd sauntered through gift shops containing rainbow flags, T-shirts calling Northampton the home of ten thousand loving, laughing lesbians, and coffee cups claiming that in this town of thirty thousand the coffee is strong and so are the women.

"Straight people hate it," Allyson confides. "They were furious when that *20/20* segment came out." The popular television show had done a piece on the preponderance of lesbians in Northampton a year earlier, and everyone, gay and straight alike, still talks about it disparagingly. "You'd think nothing else was happening," everyone says, and lesbians add, "You'd think we were some exotic species." Plenty else is happening: Northampton serves as the hub for five colleges (Amherst, Smith, Mt. Holyoke, University of Massachusetts, and Hampshire), as well as for several prep schools besides Deerfield, and thus hosts a lively arts and political scene.

"Still," I say, after we've convinced ourselves that the Lesbianville thing is silly, "it must be helpful that you're so close to Northampton—"

"It seems like—it doesn't feel—"

"Like it affects you?" I've gotten into the Allyson/Trish habit of talking over whatever anybody else is saying.

"It really doesn't. 'Cause other than some concerts and a couple speakers at UMass, you have to be either twenty-one or have a fake ID. There's nothing—like where do you go? And I don't think I'd enjoy hanging out in bars anyway."

"Did you ever think of going to the gay youth group in

Northampton?" I ask. Allyson has known of the group's existence since she was a sophomore.

"No."

"How come?"

"I—I'm reluctant to talk to people I don't know. It would just make me very uncomfortable to do that. A couple of teachers even said they'd give me a ride there." She pauses. "I don't feel isolated. I mean, I do at Deerfield, but I have enough friends at other schools and adults and things that it's easy to say, fine, this is Deerfield, I hate it here, but it's pretty easy for me to get past that now. My mind's not there anymore."

We manage to find a parking place, no easy matter downtown. As we walk toward an Italian restaurant Allyson knows, we pass a number of her future schoolmates, Smith women out for a stroll around the town. Allyson doesn't look entirely happy. "I think Smith will be too easy for me. This whole area is like a fantasyland."

I know what she means. "Fantasyland or not, you still can't hold hands with your sweetie at Deerfield," I say.

"If I *had* a sweetie," she says with a wry grin. "I'm going to feel the same way at Smith, even though it'll be easier there."

"The trouble is you have to be hyperaware," I start—

"Against violence," she interjects. "And when you're walking with someone holding hands that's the last thing you want to be."

"Do you feel you've missed out on the stuff people do in adolescence? Dating and crushes . . ."

"Yeah, in a way. But in general I have a very negative attitude toward people at Deerfield. Basically anything they're doing I don't want to do. Even if I were normal. If I hear people gossiping about who's going out with whom—I just don't want to."

Kids are not a cake. It's hard to separate out, like eggs and sugar, what part is self-protection, what part sour grapes, what part antipathy bred by isolation bred by fear. "[Being gay] is something I'm very conscious of all the time," she tells me. "Trish doesn't seem to have that problem, she doesn't seem to think about it that much. Which I don't understand. In any conversation, it's always on my mind and I'm always on my guard. I am less since coming out—because I just don't care about this place enough—so if people here hate me, it doesn't bother me."

Allyson explains that now that she's the only out person at Deerfield, other students approach her, wanting to talk. "I'm totally willing to, but I kind of have to wait for her to come around . . ." she says about one girl who has twice asked to speak to her "sometime." "One of my teachers said that someone has come out to her, and he really wants someone to talk to, but he's really, really afraid that people are going to find out in his dorm."

We pause to examine the menu in front of a coffeehouse, but decide the Italian place will be better. As we walk, Allyson says, "Being gay changes how people look at you. Sometimes teachers call on me and then they space out while I'm talking, and I know it's because they're thinking about me being gay. It's so strange.

"I think there is a huge amount of political pressure to come out. I mean, huge. And in a way it's good. But it makes a lot of people feel guilty and that's no good . . ."

We pass another group of Smith students just as we get to the restaurant. "Going to Smith will be great, but I kind of feel like I'm running away from things."

"Like what?" I ask.

"Like the real world." She ponders this for a while, and then says, "And as much as I want to get away from this place where I've grown up all my life, I can see myself staying in Northampton. I don't want to purposely put myself in a position where I know I'll be uncomfortable. I don't know. I don't feel that need to know what I'm going to do with my life."

"If you were straight?"

She smiles. "I think I'd have more of an idea. I'd have a much more definite idea of my future and what I wanted to do. Now I just . . . I mean, I really would like to have kids, but I don't know. Everything seems really indefinite. I don't know what to expect. Sometimes it's just, 'Whoa, no precedent for anything here that I know of.'"

"I don't think people really appreciate how lonely it is."

"I love New Mexico. It's so spectacular, so wide open, so . . ." Words fail John Swensen as he gazes out the cracked windshield of his ancient station wagon at dark hills rising majestically over the bush-studded desert floor. I'm watching snowflakes drift past; my feet are propped up on the dashboard because the wagon's bottom has long since rusted out. I tell him it's freezing. He nods distractedly and sweeps his hand to encompass the area east of Santa Fe. "The air's so clean, there's no crime, the people are so nice. And the hills!" He's overcome. I might be too if I weren't shivering. John looks like the Pillsbury Doughboy in his puffy down jacket, while I'm more hip but chilly in leather.

After a moment he sighs. "It's so lonely, though. *I'm* lonely. People are so scared."

People are scared of all the other nice people? "I meet guys on-line," he explains, referring to the gay chat lines that more and more teenagers tap into so they can talk to other gay teens. "I talk to people right *here*, in Santa Fe." He glances over to see if I understand. "And they're too scared even to meet me for a movie." He stares out at the snow. "I ask them to come to the gay youth group. No one ever does."

"Why not?"

"Too scared," he repeats.

"But of what?"

He looks astonished at my idiocy. "Well, I guess they're afraid of their parents kicking them out, afraid of getting beat up in school, afraid of, you know, what other awful things can happen to someone their age . . . I get sick of hearing people say, 'No, I would love to do this, but I can't because somebody might find out.'"

That's exactly what John, a senior in a Santa Fe high school, said to me for quite some time before he finally agreed to be interviewed. "You're not willing to risk exposure either," I remind him.

He's willing to admit his own complicity. "Yes, and I'd be a hypocrite if I said otherwise. I'd love to be able to cut out all this pretense crap, but I'd hate to lose a job or something."

When I asked sixteen-year-old ("almost seventeen!") John if he wanted to participate in the interviews, first he said yes, then no, then yes with conditions: that I would alter his identity, that I would bring a letter from the publisher verifying who I was, that I would not send anything to his home address. He refused to give me his phone number, so one late afternoon in February, I arrived in Santa Fe blind, hoping he'd show up where and when he said he would—at a store near the Plaza, a central market square ringed by shops displaying Native American crafts like kachina dolls, black pottery, and beautifully fashioned heavy silver bracelets inlaid with polished stones.

John *was* at the store, all blown up in his down jacket, which should have clued me in to his plan for "a private place" for the interview. Now we're surrounded by hundreds of miles of empty desert and a lot of snowflakes while he assures me that he appreciates the reasons other teens won't meet him for a movie. "Just to talk," he adds, as if it's important to convince me of his harmlessness. "It makes it so lonely," he says. "I don't think people really appreciate how lonely it is."

Santa Fe's gay youth group isn't much of a bulwark against isolation. The sum total of the participants are John, one other boy, and two facilitators, one of whom is a straight man who wants to help gay youth and the other a lesbian. "We talk a lot about hate," John says. "About how we're so lonely 'cause people hate us."

Tall for his age at six-one, with a long face, a hint of a moustache, and antique-looking wire rims he keeps shoving toward the bridge of his nose, John could be called socially deprived. It's hunger in the midst of plenty; John's father has been a popular Santa Fe figure for several decades, and their eclectic house, a couple miles outside city center, is often full of visiting artists and writers. John intimates that his father is bewildered by him, and that sometimes puzzlement edges into frustration.

John was teased in school as a child because, he says, he wouldn't go along with the other kids. "I don't do things because other people do them," he says. "That got me in so much trouble. I never succumb to peer pressure." The teasing, he says, had nothing to do with being gay. "People didn't call me queer or anything like that. I just wasn't like a lot of the other guys, I was a lot more sensitive. I didn't like to fight."

It's hard to imagine him doing anything physical. He walks hunched over, his muscles tense and face tight, as if his own body is crushing him. I'd seen that beaten-down shuffle (the dancing bear syndrome, I call it), complete with flinching and ducking, at the gay youth group in Berkeley. It's painful to watch seventeen- and eighteen-year-old boys, who should be exultant and lithe in their bodies, folded into themselves as if they'd prefer to be invisible.

John sighs again and digs a lock of blond hair out from under his glasses. "The last two years before this one," he says, "Dad decided I needed something different, that maybe I should live with my aunt in Colorado Springs. So I was there during the Amendment 2 battle. It's funny—I really liked Colorado Springs. I thought it was gay-friendly." This in spite of one weekend when he saw a line of sign-holding Amendment 2 supporters that stretched for miles. "We kept driving and driving and they went on and on, standing there by the highway." He shakes his head.

"What'd the other kids think?" I asked, trying to imagine how this would strike fourteen-year-olds.

"The kids there, they wouldn't talk to you if you didn't recycle. They were very active in civil rights and whatever." He smiles to himself.

"So they must have been against the amendment."

"I think they were completely homophobic themselves," he counters, then debates aloud whether it's worse to be homophobic in your heart and liberal on the surface, or homophobic through and through. "I guess they weren't for it," he concludes, "but if anybody at school was gay, that person would have a hard time. *I* had a hard time, and they didn't even know." In other words, *real* ground zero is high school, and there, actions speak a lot louder than words.

It was in Colorado Springs that the rumor started. "Somehow it got out that I was gay. I don't know where that came from. I think it was more malicious than anything else." John is certainly gender-conforming; it wasn't that. Maybe it was girls—he gets a slightly panicked look whenever the subject comes up. "There were so many dances and so many social things, and it was really really tough be-cause—"

"You were supposed to have a girl to go to these dances with."

"Right. But I thought it would have been even worse if I had gone out with some girl, and she told her friends, 'Well, we were alone, and he looked repulsed.' That would have done me more harm than not to go out with anybody at all."

His few experiments with girls were not successful. "I asked this girl out, and she said yes, and we were sitting on this bench, and it was kind of time when you would ordi-narily start talking about getting to know each other better" —he glances at me to see if I'm understanding both the delicacy of his phrasing and of the moment—"and I sat there and as the time went on, I was getting more and more upset, because this was not something I wanted to be doing with a woman. So I said, 'I think we should break up.' And she said, 'Okay.' And that was that."

His dates with boys, while more adventurous, don't sound fun either. He's always on the alert for lurking school buses, acquaintances, parents. He's ducked around corners, into stores, and switched theaters at the last minute. "I met a guy and I went out to a movie with him, and um, it was kind of a shame, because we saw his brother there and we had to make up some cockeyed story about how I was some kid touring at a YMCA camp . . ."

"Why couldn't you just have been a friend?"

"Well, he said, 'Oh my God, if my brother . . .'" He twists the dial on his broken radio, then says, "He was the first guy I ever went out with. The very first thing that struck me was this overwhelming feeling of acceptance. Like all this time I'd been trying to hide this, and here was this guy and I could look at him however I wanted, and he would understand."

Since he returned to Santa Fe, dates have been few and far between. John used to answer personal ads in the local paper. "I'd throw my hope into it, you know, get dressed and do my hair up really nice. After a couple times, I decided I couldn't do it anymore. But I was just so *desperate*.

"For me, and for maybe ninety percent of other gay teens I know [through the Internet], getting out and meeting anybody is like hell, okay? If you're under eighteen, nobody over eighteen feels like they can touch you or even speak to you because of this big gloom of laws—"

"Recruiting," I supply.

"Or whatever morality there is, yeah. I met this person once, and I had this nightmare that his parents found out and were camped outside my house screaming that I'd taken their precious little darling and turned him into some kind of sick, twisted . . . and I'm thinking, jeez, that's all I need."

While this gumbo of fear, fantasy, and self-hate might

occupy space in John's head, it hasn't migrated south. "I should say right now that I don't ever run around. I'm still a virgin. If I had sex with people, I would get a nasty attachment to them. Some people don't, but I do. I'm damn proud of that, actually."

"I'm pretty cold," I tell him. This time he hears me, and he reacts instantaneously.

"Oh, I'm sorry! If the heater worked—" He fusses and fumes, and even manages to get it going. He promises to take me to a nice pizzeria where we can thaw out by a fire. On the way he tells me that a couple weeks ago he and a nineteen-year-old guy he was writing to on the Internet arranged to meet in Albuquerque for a day. His friend rented a hotel room, they took a long walk, came back to the room, and made embarrassed conversation for quite some time. Finally they began making out—"the first time I kissed a guy"—and spent a couple hours cuddling.

"Cuddling and making out?" I ask skeptically.

"Yeah. We didn't have sex or anything." The guy wanted to, but John refused, on the grounds that his friend went to college in the East, which meant he and John would never get to see each other. "If there had been the possibility of something, I would have said yes. Like if I were going to an Eastern college instead of staying around here. Well, I don't even know if I would, because I wouldn't do it without a commitment." We bounce along in his station wagon in silence, and I think that a long-distance relationship would be little different from the isolation John has already lived through for years. He needs hugs and wrestling and laughter to loosen the mind and muscles he's kept so long under wraps.

"But for the first time," he says, and there's wonder in

his voice, "I felt everything that I hadn't felt with a woman. It was great, I was just so excited about it." He smiles, far away, and then he suddenly remembers me and becomes unsure. "Is any of this usable?"

"Of course. It's such a revelation when you finally—"

"It is," he agrees, relieved to be understood. "But it sounds so crazy that the first time I kiss a guy is when I'm nearly seventeen. That's just crazy to me. Straight people—"

"Start experimenting from twelve on," I finish.

"Yeah. And this was the first go at it for both of us, and he's in college, and I'm in my last year." He shakes his head. "I've gone through my whole life not getting to know about relationships, not learning about any of this stuff."

John won't tell me about his relationship with his parents or about how school is, though he does say people don't suspect he's gay. He spends a great deal of time studying, so his grades are excellent, which allowed him to skip a year when he went to live with his aunt. And apart from his meeting with the nineteen-year-old, his social life for the ten or so months since Colorado Springs has been confined to the Internet, because anything else seems too fraught with danger or difficulty. When I ask what he thinks being gay will mean to him, he answers, "It will mean a lot more secrecy about life. Not being able to show my affection, having to lie to a lot of people, my friends not knowing as much about me as I think they should. Right now I'm worried that it will have a real profound effect, like what kind of friends I'll have and what kind of job I can get. And not to say the least, violence.

"If people would just let me, I would have no problems

being gay. I don't know what it does to a person who has to live in that kind of constant fear: 'Who might know?' "

By now we've managed to find parking and walk a frigid block to the pizza parlor. There's no fireplace, but John convinces the waitress we need a table near the wall heater. He keeps glancing furtively at the other customers, as if he expects them to suddenly leap up and denounce us. Once the pizza arrives, he relaxes a little, though he speaks more quietly whenever he thinks he can be overheard. "The older gay community is not willing to talk to younger people," he says. "That leaves me with much less knowledge about whether it's possible to have a more open life. There's this older guy I know, and he says, 'You can be open, there are places you can go, just wait till you're older.' I don't believe him, because I haven't seen it.

"The adult gay community thinks they will somehow ruin you or they will get booked on statutory rape for telling you what it is to be gay, or just taking you out to dinner. There's NAMBLA, and I don't know what their group is accomplishing in terms of changing things, but other than them, I don't know of any other group that's willing . . . See, in a lot of cities you have gay bars, but if you're under twenty-one . . ."

"There's a lot of controversy about NAMBLA," I say. I give him a brief rundown of North American Man-Boy Love Association-related news: barred from pride parades, from Stonewall 25, tossed out of the International Lesbian and Gay Association, because the tiny group favors doing away with age-of-consent laws.

"But people who are under eighteen are incredibly sexual," John cries, then quickly lowers his voice. "They have to learn about sex. If a sixteen-year-old guy and a twenty-year-old guy fall in love, if it's going to be mutually beneficial for them—I mean, what are gay teens supposed to do? What are you supposed to do when you want to learn about sex, when you want to learn about a relationship? You can't do it in school."

"You mean you can't have a relationship with someone in school?" I ask.

"Right. People will find out, and you'll get shit in your locker, and they'll tease you in PE. You can't meet anybody that way. And books only go so far. You can't kiss or talk to a book. So it's set me up for so much hurt, because they [the older gay community] are so afraid of some awful thing happening. Of course," he adds thoughtfully, "I have the same fear that some kid's parents would sue the hell out of me for making their kid gay." He sighs, his fire momentarily squelched. "I don't know that there's an easy solution. Still, if those parents came up to me and said, 'Look what you've done to our son,' I'd say, 'I was helping him.' He comes to me and says he can't stand being gay anymore, he knows his parents are going to kick him out, he's falling in love with all the boys at school, he doesn't like girls, he's going to commit suicide. What a lot of gay men will do in that situation is say, 'Go talk with some other gay kid,' and then they walk away."

How many gay men walked away from John? I can't ask him; I'm afraid he'll burst into tears in the middle of the pizza parlor. I rustle around with the check to give him time to collect himself. After the waitress has come and gone, I ask what stereotypes he had of gay men. He laughs. "Oh God, people who were completely promiscuous, who loved to mess around with children and who were into getting beat up, and who like to do any kind of raunchy, crappy thing you can think of. And totally effeminate. Every awful thing that I thought people could do, I thought these people did. And the more nasty comments I made about gay people, the less gay I felt, like further and further away from this horrible thing."

Until his body betrayed him.

He stares at the remains of his pizza, his brows furrowed, then he suddenly looks up at me. "You're going to have to do a very good job of changing things here. A lot of this stuff will point to me very easily. What if we say Phoenix instead of Santa Fe?"

I tell him no and wonder how I can explain to him that his isolation has constricted his vision. He sees so little of the world that he appears very large in it; he can't believe there are others like him, or that people have more important things to do than overturn every stone in an effort to identify him.

He nods, willing to accept my edict. "I'm really hoping life isn't going to be like it is now," he says. "I just cannot meet anybody. Sometimes I ask if being able to love who I truly love is worth it. I guess I have decided that it is."

John takes advantage of my presence to ask a million questions: Do I find men sexually attractive? How come the religious Right has targeted us? Do I read *Playboy*? Do all gay people have unhappy childhoods? (He refuses to tell me details of his own.) Can you get married in Holland—or is it Hawaii? He wants the advantages of marriage, including health insurance, but he's not interested in children. "Have some little rug rat taking up half my salary? And then if it's genetic or something, he could end up being gay too." He makes a sour face.

I explain that there are political implications to the gene research, in that the Right accuses us of "choosing a lifestyle." I tell him that when I went to a showing of the antigay video *The Gay Agenda* at a lesbian-owned restaurant in Berkeley, a man stood up and said, "How can the religious Right keep on with this choice shit? Who would choose to have all this difficulty?" John is nodding, nodding. "Sure," he chuckles. "I choose to have a horrible life. How 'bout you?"

"But then," I override, "a woman said she had chosen to be gay, and that she refused to be portrayed as a choiceless victim."

It's good John has finished his pizza because otherwise we'd be in for the Heimlich maneuver. He's stuttering so much he can hardly get the words out. "She said it was a choice for her?" I nod, and John is so agitated he grips the edge of the table with his fingers and rocks his chair back and forth. "Like I woke up one morning and I decided I didn't have enough people prejudiced against me," he says, biting off his words. "So I painted my face black and I cut off one of my legs and I painted lesions all over my chest." He slugs down his Coke and sits there for a while. Then he says, "You know, this guy suggested that part of my being teased in school *was* because I was gay. Like the kids at school didn't know *what* I was, but they knew I was different. That just honestly pissed me off.

"I don't like having to hide it. If I killed small animals, then that would be something I wouldn't want people to know, but why do I have to hide the fact that I'm not attracted to women?

"It's been real bad with my parents," he confides. "I just lie to them more and more. I can't even count the number of lies. I don't like lying to people. Here my mother is really showing concern about what I'm doing, she really wants to know, and I have to make up some bullshit lie. She deserves more than that. It would be so wonderful to bring home a guy I really liked, and say, 'Here is my boyfriend,' and have them be happy.

"I guess I'm lucky to live in a place like Santa Fe, which is a little more open—nothing like heaven, like San Francisco, mind you. I have never seen or heard of two guys holding hands, ever. It bugs me that I can't walk down the street holding hands in public. I shouldn't be deprived of these things, I recycle. Why can't I tell people that I'm in love?"

"straight people are different. they're better."

When Renee George walks into a cafe, no heads turn. In this society, we focus on flash, not substance. Soft and willowy, with an ageless serenity, she moves with seamless grace. But she doesn't shimmer above the surface, doesn't skitter across the floor. It's as if she's rooted to the earth, with her center way deep in her belly. Maybe that's why she thinks she's a klutz. "I drop stuff," she says, shaking her head. "I mess everything up." She has the look of someone who's had to live inside herself for a long time, who doesn't expect people to like or to appreciate her. Her resentment bursts out in tiny flames that she squelches quickly. She's desperate for approval but doesn't know it. She doesn't appreciate how special she is.

It's hard to believe she's only sixteen. How could she be so self-contained? "Growing up in the military," she says, "you've got rules to obey. It's not like these kids here."

Here is Oakland, California; Renee is a junior at Castlemont High School, most recently in the national news when a group of kids on a field trip acted up during a showing of *Schindler's List* and were expelled from the theater.

"I don't see kids carrying guns," she says. "Well, we had a drive-by . . . and there's these wannabe gangstas." She shakes her head. "When kids get that rough in the military, their parents ship 'em off to a private school until they learn how to be proper people again."

Being a proper person is more important to Renee than almost anything else. When she was fourteen a girl accused her of being a lesbian. People pinned signs on her back—DYKE QUEER LEZZIE. She carefully tells me the whole story—she complimented a girl on her jewelry within earshot of another girl who hated the jewelry-wearer, and that girl immediately spread the word that Renee was "after" her enemy—so I will understand she was falsely accused. "I was trying so hard to get a life and then somebody says something like that," she tells me, her voice shaking. "How dare they call me lesbian? I'm not lesbian. I'm not gay." Then she listens to what she's said and takes a deep breath to steady herself. "I just basically walked back in the closet."

"So the thought had crossed your mind," I surmise.

"Yeah. But after that I realized, if you *do* think about it, and especially if you *act* on it, that's what people do to you. They treated me like dog shit. My state of mind was, there's no way I'm going to be treated like this for the rest of my life. Before the lesbian stuff, they treated me like a geek. Well, I can take that. I can be straight and be a geek, but the other . . ."

Renee's mother is mentally ill. When Renee told her

mother six months ago that she was bisexual, her mother picked up the remote and changed the channel. Renee admits that maybe her mother was high at the time. "But I could see she was going to be really great about it," Renee tells me. Her voice is full of resignation; I'm not sure whom she's trying to convince. She means great in comparison with the horror stories she's heard at the gay youth group at the Pacific Center in Berkeley. Her mother didn't throw her out of the house, didn't scream and yell and threaten to shoot her. Maybe not noticing is worse.

When Renee was nine years old, her stepfather, who had married her mother when Renee was three and never paid much attention to her, suddenly wanted to play sports with her, take her to games, on walks. "We were just getting to be friends," she reports, "and then he molested me." She was a military brat; she knew he'd violated the rules, so she told. She gave details a child wouldn't be able to make up: her clothes hung in the wrong order was reason enough to have to play with Daddy. There was a trial, and he was released for insufficient evidence. Her mother, who had thrown him out, sneaked him into the house when she felt lonely. Finally Renee was asked to "forgive" him so the family could mend. Soon afterward, the family—Mom, stepfather, and Renee's younger sister, the child of her step-father—moved, and Renee, then eleven, went with them.

"Were you scared to go back with him?"

"I was terrified. Nothing happened after that, thank God. But I hadn't dealt with any of my feelings. I was numb as hell." Renee, an athletic kid who liked to swim and read and was interested in all things military, turned into some-one else. "I just sat, thinking about it over and over. I'd go to school, sit by the wall at lunch, come home, take a bath, lock myself in my room, watch TV, pass out, wake up, do the same thing over again. All I did was think about it." She stares at the hamburger she will end up taking home to her mother. "I still think about it, but not so much, thank God. It's just self-torture."

It was when the family was transferred again that the jewelry incident occurred, and Renee was labeled "the school dyke. See, here I was thinking of who I was attracted to and what that meant. I was starting to not beat myself up so much. That sort of ruined my spirits for a while." Renee's family bought a house in another neighborhood, and she took the opportunity to switch schools. "The rumors didn't follow me to the new school, but that I was a child of sexual abuse did. By the grace of God I was not known as a lesbian, I was known as an incest survivor."

Although the Georges now owned a house, they were further apart than ever. "It was just four people living together. He'd stay away all day and almost all night. It got so bad she moved into the spare room. But she didn't want to separate 'cause she'd finally gotten what she always wanted, her own home. About this time I stopped sleeping. I just lay awake hearing crickets, and I hate bugs. I was going to group counseling."

"To deal with the incest?"

She nods soberly. "Incest was my life. The only reason I'd leave the house was to go to school or to the groups or go to my counselor. My mother and I both decided I needed some mental help. We signed me into the mental ward in the summer of '92. My stepfather showed up at the hospital and said, 'I don't want her anymore, get her out of the house.' They discharged me after seventy-two hours, saying there was nothing wrong with me. Little did I know that during those three days my stepfather had taken my clothes out of my room, painted the walls, given away my furniture. He was basically saying I did not exist in that house. So we —my mother and I—left on a Greyhound to come to California."

A year and a half has passed since that moment her mother chose to stand by her. Renee's younger sister stayed with her father. "In that whole time, he hasn't given us a dime. What we're living on now is welfare. We ended up in a bad neighborhood. Every other night I hear gunfire. My mother started getting into crack cocaine. I thought, 'If she doesn't give a damn about me, why should I give a damn about school?' " Renee's mother is in and out of institutions, on and off drugs, on and off men. She depends on Renee to make sure the bills are paid and to keep a semblance of sanity in the apartment. Renee's resentment, never far beneath the surface, is riddled with guilt: Mom's drug addiction is Renee's fault; after all, didn't Renee lose her the house and the husband? Not to mention her other child. Renee picks up her hamburger and some mustard plops on the table. "Oh! I'm so clumsy!" She puts the hamburger back down and folds her hands in her lap, as if she can't trust them anywhere else.

During one of her mother's institutionalizations, Renee met a counselor who suggested that Renee might be bisexual. "She was asking me who I found attractive. She asked, 'Do you like strong guys?' and I said, well, I like men who are sorta soft. And then all of a sudden I said, I like women who are sort of strong but soft too. And she asked if I were a lesbian. And I said no, 'cause I liked men too. Then she asked about bisexual. I'd never heard that before. I thought, you have a selection?"

The counselor referred Renee to the gay youth group at the Pacific Center. It proved to be a revelation. "For the first time in my life I had something to talk about with people my age. Usually with people my age it was horrible, I had nothing to talk about except for school. In this group, we talked about literature, sex, MTV, clothes. I felt like a normal teenager. I was so happy. And the greatest part was I could be whoever I wanted to be. I didn't have to be the stereotypical black female, because the majority of the group was male and they were all queens. They weren't living up to who they were expected to be, so why should I live up to mine? I was free and happy."

She is smiling now, eager to explain. "I never talked about sexuality before. I never *felt* sexual before. I'd pushed it all aside. Now I was able to talk about it and feel it and be around it and accept it."

Renee hoped the group would free her from the dead-end lane she'd been stuck on for years, letting her rejoin the highway that led back to the athletic girl she was before the molestation and forward to the proper adult she knew she would become. But she quickly ran into roadblocks that caused her to drop out of the group six months after she'd joined in June 1993. She was put down for being bisexual. She was exhorted to come out. But most disturbing for Renee is what seems an insoluble dilemma: how can she be both proper *and* queer? The guys at the group weren't much help; to them, propriety is something they'd name a goldfish, and they insisted Renee wake up to the real world. Renee asks me now, a month after she left the group in December, what real world they're talking about. "These guys don't go to *my* school," she says. If they did, they'd understand what it would mean to her to come out: Renee's not willing to face the social isolation and torment she knows would be the result. After all, that's what she's been enduring for ages now; she doesn't need to bring it on herself.

And, as she explains to me carefully, she's got enough problems. For a girl who values order and discipline, the past eighteen months have been hell. Twice in that period, she and her mother have been in homeless shelters, each time for a month. For a three-month period, they lived in an SRO hotel with alcoholics and crazies slamming on their door at night, trying to break in. Renee's mother might or might not be around; it depended on the drugs. As Renee tells me all this, she keeps glancing down, deeply humiliated, then glancing back up (she is unfailingly polite and will not carry on a conversation with her head in a plate). She can't imagine, she says, how this has happened to her. "I'm no homeless person," she assures me, and she reminds me that she volunteered at a school for developmentally disabled kids near the base, and has a sheaf of recommendations. "And I'm only sixteen!"

Her life, she says, used to be sensible. "I never had any racial problems growing up 'cause I was in a secure environment. When I was in the seventh grade, I went to an all-white school except me and one other black kid, and a boy called me a nigger. That was my first and only experience with racism. See, I was raised on an Army base. You just didn't have it there. I never had to worry about robberies, drugs, gangs. Kids were expected to be good. There were certain rules you had to follow."

"It's almost like *you* were in the military."

She nods seriously. "I wanted to go into the military. I always was in ROTC. See, I didn't know you couldn't be gay. I mean, I never saw any flaming queens or dykes on base, but I never saw any Japanese either. Then I heard there were only two kinds of people who couldn't get into the military: homosexuals and the mentally insane.

"I remember when I let the dream go. It was after we'd moved out here, and I was parking cars at an event. I was standing at attention in my uniform right behind these pom-pom girls, and all I could see were those cute little butts under those little skirts. And I'm standing there in my uniform thinking, 'Okay, they got this policy, I gotta get out, I'm not going to do this to myself.'"

Renee is not the only person to tell me she abandoned plans to go into the military after the public hearings in 1993. A policy that supposedly made it easier for gays and lesbians (though that in itself is a cruel joke) has in fact had the opposite effect on a lot of kids. What Renee heard is "You are not allowed to join," and her response is a defiant "If they don't want me, screw them!" Unfortunately, the person most likely to bear the brunt of that defiance is Renee herself, who, with her appreciation for discipline and structure (and not least, equal opportunity), seems singularly well suited to a military career.

Renee then decided she should go into teaching. She has volunteered in the Oakland schools with younger children, but the programs are so overburdened, the teachers so overworked, that she feels unappreciated. "If only they'd once say something nice," she says. But her teachers take her for granted. Unlike that noisy squeaky wheel, Renee seems to need no oil. She doesn't cause problems, doesn't skip, giggle, or burst out laughing. She carries herself with a dignity that is far beyond her years, shows up when she says she will, carries out the tasks that are required of her. Who could guess that inside is a kid who's scared and sad and angry?

And hiding. "I have a really bad social life," she tells me. All she does, she says, is stay at home taking care of her mother. What about the group? Does she plan to go back? She shrugs. She hasn't been for a while, not since December. "They were dressing all in black and going to this club named after Edgar Allen Poe—the House of Usher—and talking about death and drugs. It was less like let's have a good time and more like who has the same Cure albums or can sing the most Morrissey songs. All the queens started looking older and trendier and one day I just exploded and yelled, 'Screw everything, I've had it with you guys!' and I walked home and smoked up a whole pack of cigarettes while I was walking. I was that upset."

But on the other hand, the group *is* her social life, because she can't talk to anyone at school. Every contact must be kept on the most superficial level in case she reveals something untoward, which is pretty much everything: her mother and the institutionalizations, her bisexuality, her gay friends, the SROs or the homeless shelters. Maybe, she says sighing, she should go back to the group so she'd have *some* kind of social activity. But then she'd have to put up with the razzing. "I was getting this weird vibe, like I didn't belong there. Every once in a while someone would look at me and say, 'Admit you're straight. Admit you're a lesbian.' There's only about one or two people in these groups who are bisexual. So if you're dating someone of the same sex, suddenly your bisexuality never gets spoken of again, and if you're dating someone of the opposite sex, you can't go to the group. But it would be denying half of myself to put myself in one camp or another."

"Most of your social contacts are with gay people now," I say, thinking about her two close gay friends. "It seems there's real pressure on you not to date boys."

She's shaking her head. "I talk about *nothing* but boys at school. I seem straight-straight-straight."

"But you aren't dating guys. What about boys who ask you out?"

"They're these macho straight guys. I want to date someone on the softer side, someone bisexual. If I tell these straight guys I'm bisexual, once we break up, that's going to give them something to gossip about. I've heard a lot of straight people call bisexuals freaks, and I don't want to be known as a freak."

Renee spends a lot of time talking about respect—how to gain it, how easily it can be lost. Her reputation is the most valuable thing she owns—maybe the only thing. The reputations of high school girls depend on walking a fine gauge wire between being too loose and too rigid, but in order to get up on the tightrope at all, you have to be popular, fun, and heterosexual. Plenty of fun queers-in-the-closet skitter over that latter requirement with hearty doses of opposite-sex dating, but Renee is too truthful and honest to go that route, even though she'd actually *like* to date boys. Dating boys is too dangerous. If she got close to someone, she might tell him about herself, and there would go her reputation. And if dating *boys* is too dangerous . . .

In May 1994, a couple months after I'd finished my interviews with Renee, I went to a play at Castlemont High about AIDS. Kids from another Oakland high school were putting it on, and the largely black Castlemont audience— Renee was not among them, as only seniors were allowed to see the play—filed into the auditorium full of good cheer.

They'd gotten their prom pictures back, and as we waited for the show to begin, people passed them around with elaborate courtesy and flattering remarks. When the play finally started—it was a multimedia piece in which each student took several roles—everyone watched with a minimum of coughing and giggling. But during the audience feedback, the questions had an agenda: Why did you do a play about AIDS? Did you know any of the people you portrayed? How'd you come up with these stories? Did someone—some *adult*—suggest to you that it should be about AIDS? It was as if the actors, fellow Oakland teens the Castlemont kids wanted desperately to embrace, had put on a show about elephantiasis, and wasn't that the oddest thing.

Finally one of the actors, no doubt frustrated, asked, "How many of you know someone personally who has died of AIDS?" Almost the entire audience raised their hands. People looked around in shock, not believing, and not willing to believe, what they were seeing. A girl broke the silence to say to the actors in an almost pleading voice, "But still . . . none of you is *really* gay, are you?" She had finally articulated the stumbling block: since nobody was gay (and surely they could not be, since being gay is so very heinous that none of these very talented kids *could* be), why on earth had they conceived a play about a *gay* disease?

The teacher leapt in to explain that a question like that is very personal, that while any of the actors could answer it, nobody had to. The audience didn't expect anyone to answer, and no one did. There was barely a pause before hands were again waving in the air, this time with a less gnarly query about how the video segments were integrated into the performance. And of the one hundred and forty kids in that auditorium, I knew there were at least 14 who were clenching their jaws, digging their nails into the palms of their hands, and breaking out in a cold sweat. Hearing yourself described as the ultimate horror by the person sitting next to you, a person who can't conceive that someone like you exists, *is* the ultimate horror, worse than people hissing dyke or faggot behind your back. It was a better demonstration than any why Renee has not been able to come out at this school—and kids at Castlemont are probably more tolerant than most, given that they live in Oakland.

Renee feels tormented by a demand to reveal herself, to take a stand. In an aggrieved, hopeless voice, she explains how ironic it is that in the group, in the very place she is supposed to feel supported and safe, her sexuality is trashed and she is encouraged to do something she feels would literally put her life at risk. "There's a *lot* of pressure. Every week a kid comes out to his school or to his friends or something. They say it's a big weight off their shoulders and they can be themselves now. And they say they feel a lot closer to the people at school." She considers this, but it's clear that these kids inhabit a different universe, where reputations aren't dangling by a single gossamer thread. "I don't *want* to come out," she says vehemently. "There's nothing in it for me. And I know about myself that when I don't have to do something, I won't do it."

Each time we meet—and we met five times between January and March 1994—Renee explains to me that coming out at Castlemont would be disastrous if not deadly. "There's this girl and I've spent afternoons with her the last two days. And just in that short amount of time, the things she's said . . ." She sighs. "Just because I'm in the closet doesn't mean I don't have feelings. If she knew I was bisexual, she wouldn't hang around with me. In order for me to come out, I have to eliminate all the people who I know are going to treat me like shit once they find out who I am.

"If I were to come out to another girl, she'd have to accept it and not be all edgy towards me like 'She's looking at my body.' That's just totally fucked anyway, 'cause once you find out someone's straight, you just let 'em go."

"It's hard if people act like you're different—" I start.

"Yeah. I don't want to walk through the halls and have girls say to me, 'Hey, what are you lookin' at?' And guys come up to me and say, 'Hey, you want her? You think she's cute?' if I just talk to a girl in the hallway. I might think she's attractive, but I'm not going to do anything about it, 'cause it's school. Don't do anything in school. It's sorta like a rule everybody follows."

"Straight people don't follow that rule," I point out.

"Straight people are different. They're better."

I laugh, she doesn't. She's staring at me with defiance, challenging me to prove her wrong. If straight people aren't better, how come they can do whatever they please? How come they're free to talk in the halls and laugh and rag on boys and look at anybody they want? She knows she's not supposed to say straight people are better—and she'd never say it at the Pacific Center—but she's breaking free of a restraint that's hemmed her in just as much as she's been hemmed in by everything else in her life. That this freedom is mired in her own self-hate and shame doesn't make it any less exhilarating.

The next time I see her, she reminds me that she *has* come out to a number of people, all the ones she came out to last summer, when she first started going to the group. "I'm just doing it at my own speed," she explains. She tosses their names on the table as if they were chips in a high-stakes poker game: Her mother. Two teachers at Castlemont. A boy who graduated so maybe he doesn't count but he should. A boy who's a senior now.

Will he divulge her secret? "He wouldn't waste his time spreading little meager gossip about me. He did tell me there were other bisexuals at school but he wouldn't tell me who they were.

"See, during the summer I told everybody in my life that I cared about, that needed to know the real me. And now I feel like . . ." She throws her hands up in frustration, trying to be brave, but actually she can hardly speak. "I guess I was expecting my life to get better. Because I'm freer, I'm happier, I'm not some closet person laughing at fag jokes. I don't laugh at them at school. I say, 'You know what? I have gay friends.' And they look at me like I'm crazy.

"I don't know. I was just expecting better. There are things about gays and lesbians that *are* so much better—there's a lot more color, lot more music, lot more energy, and I'm just not in it anymore."

"How come? 'Cause you dropped out of the group?"

She pauses, then hefts a huge sigh. " 'Cause I'm worried about my mom. I'm worried about her 'cause she doesn't have a life, so I feel like I have to end mine, whatever life I *did* have. I feel like I'm needed at home. It gets to the point where I feel like that guy in *The Shining*, like chopping everybody up."

"So coming out didn't save you."

"It *did* save me," she insists. She is sure about that. "It gave me an honest look at what gay and lesbian life is, bisexual life is. I looked at it and I liked it and I wanted to become it, but then somehow I got *yanked* out of it and thrown back to what I had. Now I have to go back to the group and start talking to the same people I used to talk to and get invited to places. I mean, it's fun and everything"— she is making a horrible face, as if being dragged through mud by galloping horses might be preferable—"but I thought I was past all that. At least before I was excited about everything. Everything was brand-new and beautiful and wonderful and free. Now everything's like, 'I've done it.' "

"And you still feel you can't come out in school 'cause you'd get your ass kicked."

She's nodding. "So I have to start all over again and at the same time I have to deal with whatever I've got now."

"Of course you're getting to the age when you can think about not being so tied to your mother, about moving away."

"Yeah." She doesn't sound thrilled. "Oh, my."

"What?"

"When I was growing up, all I wanted was me and my mom, and now that I got it, I'm gonna have to move out!" Her voice breaks and she has to look away. "I *do* want to move out. But here we finally got what we wanted, just me and Mommy all over again, you know, like when I was three years old, it was me and Mommy till she married that asshole and had my sister. So now I got my mommy back all by myself and . . ." She rolls her eyes, in obvious pain.

"Do you feel like your mother couldn't survive without you around?"

"She can't even walk two blocks!" Her anger is full-blown now; she tries to keep her voice down. "I keep telling her, get out, get a life. She has such low standards for herself as far as guys go. A woman should have standards."

The last time we meet, in March, we drive around the East Oakland neighborhood near Castlemont High. She's been pointing out the sights, which are few and far between: the bus stop she waits at, the little cafe where she goes sometimes to eat lunch. The houses are almost all single-family wood-frame dwellings with neatly kept lawns, while the school looks appropriately institutional, like a mini-city with its big auditorium and gym. As we cruise past, she gazes at the school with interest, as if she's seeing it through my eyes.

Then she reports that when she went back to the group at the Pacific Center a couple days earlier, for the first time in almost four months, a woman began putting down bisexual women. "If she'd said she hated hard-core dykes with short hair and deep voices, every single person, even the flaming queens, would have yelled at her and said she'd have no business. For her to say, 'I really hate bisexual women because—' and go on like that . . . And the other bisexual people just sat there. I thought, 'Well, no one else is going to say anything, so I will.' But then even the facilitator started making bisexual jokes, like why don't they make up their minds and get off the fence. I just felt it wasn't right. Okay, I'm not the best person in the world, but I shouldn't feel bad about my sexuality. If I came in here with the stereotypical lesbian look, if I was more hard-core, you guys'd love me, but since I'm not, you guys make fun of me." I glance over at her, but she's not talking to me, she's only repeating to herself what she wishes she'd said before she got intimidated by the facilitator.

She stuffs a Tracy Chapman tape in my car recorder and starts singing along. "I really like this one," she says. It's "Fast Car," which is, I think, exactly what Renee needs—escape from a place where she is never, ever right or enough. "Fuck the group," she says. "I'm just sick of it. But then I get sick of school too. I get sick of that whole world where nothing homosexual is ever spoken about and I have to talk about it in a really low voice and I can't say anything." She pauses, then sighs. "I guess I have to keep going to the group."

". . . doing the lesbian lambada."

Lee Garrett, a high school junior from Yorba Linda, California, drives with her left leg drawn up beside her on the seat, her elbow propped on her knee. In this gymnast's position, with her cheek resting on the palm of her hand, she tools her '71 Ford Fairlane—"a studly car"—through Los Angeles freeway traffic, past malls and palm trees and John Wayne Airport. Normally she heads in the other direction, toward West Hollywood and freedom with a capital G(ay), but today she has decided to "be my sister and go to Nordstrom." As she steers with the tips of her fingers, she speaks in a concentrated rush, which she interrupts at intervals with a low, bubbling laugh or a question directed at the radio: "What the fuck is *that*? Jeeeezus!" But mostly she talks about her friends or the horse camp she attends every summer in the Nevada high desert. "The camp is my real home," she says. "I've been going there since 1984."

Ten years is a long time in the life of a sixteen-year-old. Lee's parents divorced when she was five, and she lived half the time with her father, half the time with her mother until her father moved across the country. He's an artist, she says —a free spirit who wanted to smoke dope and sleep with other women. But he was stunned when Lee's mother announced she wouldn't put up with his girlfriends. Lee shakes her head. "My mom says that just because you're in a relationship doesn't mean you don't get attracted to other people. The problem comes when you think you can act on it." Lee whips around a slow car in the right lane, shading her eyes with one hand. "The way I see it, the *real* problem was she couldn't deal with it. Maybe that's why I'm not interested in being in a relationship."

There are more compelling reasons. Lee is teetering on the precipice of claiming a lesbian identity, and part of her just wants to crawl back into the safe world she's carved out with her friends, where she exemplifies the three b's: bright, bratty, and bisexual. The bisexual tag has worked for a long time, and it's got real cachet in this corner of conservative Orange County, but in the last six or so months Lee has realized it won't wash.

Still, accepting herself as a dyke has its problems. Besides implying that she's ready for a relationship that is more significant—and therefore more demanding and scary —than her casual rolls-in-the-hay with boys, lesbianism might mean leaving the family of friends she loves. Those friends, with Lee's happiness in mind and less to lose from the labeling game (they call themselves theoretically bisexual, but they fall in love with boys), are more willing for her to make the switch from bi to gay than she is. "They actually get mad if I say something about guys," she says. "Like I'll be talking about some boy being cute, and they'll say, 'Lee, it makes me sick when you do that.'" She stops to laugh. "They have an idea of the way I should be."

None of this emerges in a linear fashion. Interviewing Lee, I quickly realize, will not be like talking to some of the other kids. Start them off at birth and in four or five hours they'll have rolled right up to the instant they are sitting across from me, telling their stories. Like engines chugging along a track, they are impossible to divert. The younger ones haven't had time to reflect back analytically; everything is of equal importance, so nothing can be left out. Besides, if you don't tell the whole thing, you might get stuck back when you were twelve.

Lee's monologue is like a roller coaster ride at Disneyland: three-dimensional with a lot of bone-crunching right angles. After a weekend in the cruise ship Fairlane, browsing from freeway to freeway as she talks nonstop about her friends, I'm charmed but exhausted. She should have handed me a cast card when I got in the car. Mother, sister, stepfather—these three are offed in the first ten minutes, never to be heard from again. "How old's your sister?" I ask.

"Like thirteen?" She calculates. "Three years younger. Anyhow," she continues, "Yorba Linda isn't really a hell on earth, but it's close. We've got the Nixon museum"—at the time of my February 1994 visit, only Pat was in permanent residence—"and a lot of the parents are really wiggy, so the kids are in and out of rehab programs. And also, I don't know if it's the trendiness of it, there's a lot of bisexuals around me too. Hmmm, like basically hmmm," she ponders aloud as we roll through a parking lot the size of a small town, "I wonder where I'm going." As we pass Saks, I spot a sign for valet parking.

By the time we're safely through Nordstrom and seated on fake wrought iron chairs at a crepe place that has run out of crepes, we've dispatched mall food and the mall lifestyle, which brings us back to Lee. She leans back recklessly in the flimsy chair, now stretching out the rangy, slouching body she'd contorted to a compact rectangle in the car. Brushing back her bird's nest curls of dark hair with one hand, she says, "I decided to do my school project on gay and lesbian youth, and my mom is going, 'I'm wondering about your sudden interest in this,' and I'm saying, 'Look, Mom, I've been going to West Hollywood since I was five, and I've been hanging out with your hairdresser and his friends since forever.' So she was asking me all this stuff, and I was like, no really, DUH, and she was like AAAGH, and I'm like, I gotta do my homework. I went to my room and like a half hour later—"

"Wait. She asked if you were gay and you said you were?"

"Yeah. So my sister comes up and says, 'Mom's freaking out, she's gonna like kill herself or something,' so I just said whatever whatever, and she said, 'Just tell her you were kidding,' so I did." By now the chair's tilted toward me, and her elbows are planted on the table, the better to wave her hands around like frantic marionettes.

"So you feel like she really knows—"

Lee is nodding rapidly. "But she's way out there in mother denial land."

"And your sister?"

"Oh, my sister's whatever. She cares more about getting into Stanford than anything."

We fall into a rhythm, neither of us completing a thought, half the time losing the thread of the conversation. Every time we're talking about being gay, Lee lowers her voice and skirts not only specific words but entire phrases.

At first I think this is to ensure the comfort of nearby diners, but then she tells me how she and her friends love to upset people by crawling all over each other at the mall. Playing gay for shock value or making half-defensive jokes with friends is different from talking about it seriously with someone nearly three times your age.

When the omelettes come, she mentions a Wim Wenders film she has tried to see three times but has missed because of Marcelle and Jan one night, and Carol and Marcelle the other, and then they ended up the third night at the club on Santa Monica. No, there aren't any clubs for (sunken voice) *gay kids* in LA. They go to coffeehouses and bookstores or whatever, Tower Records. I tell her about the City in Portland. She's shaking her head. Nothing like that here. But Santa Monica Boulevard itself is like a vast club. This one new kid at school goes to the club on Santa Monica with this girl Polly, but what was the point of this story? Damned if I know.

Of course, I *am* using a tape recorder. Every five minutes I could play it back to try to unearth the beginning of the thought. I don't do it because I don't think it would help. After a while, as names recur, as activities jell in my head, I begin to make connections in a more organic way, filling in the blanks between Lee and her friends. She and her friends exist as a free-form unit, coming together in one pocket of time and separating in another, then grouping in a different configuration later. A couple times she interrupts a long story to say, "I'm just talking about my friends," but that's who she needs to talk about—her life *is* her friends, and she is defined in juxtaposition to them. It takes all of them to build the house that shelters each—one's the roof, one's the foundation, one's the walls.

Susan is the one Lee was desperately in love with for ages. Marcelle is a cohort in a lot of pranks. Sarah is the summer fling who has since been abandoned. Jan was interested in Lee, but Lee turned her down. Carol's the one Lee's really smitten with—maybe. Eddy is Marcelle's friend who says he's bisexual, but that means nothing because he's on the football team and they all say they're bisexual. My head is spinning. "The whole football team says it's bisexual?" Not in any lifetime of mine.

She nods. "They hated their girlfriends but they couldn't figure out how to stop seeing them so they just said they were exploring their gay selves."

"Hmmm. Does this cause problems for the boys who really are bisexual?"

Lee laughs. "Naw, everybody knows who's who, but it's made for some pretty funny couples."

"When did you start realizing?" I ask. I'm speaking in code too.

"Well, I could say it was really young, like I had a crush on my fourth-grade teacher, you know what I'm saying? But uhm, junior high. That's when I realized there's a name for this."

"Did you feel different?"

"Yeah, but it didn't have anything to do with that. I was like a crazy kid. I was like, 'Why didn't you send me to a shrink, Mom?' "

"Why?"

"Oh, I was always trying to kill myself before I was eleven. Like I'd get the knife out or try to drown myself. Up until the sixth grade." She laughs.

"What were you thinking of?"

"I have no idea. Probably I was just really upset. I'd

been told my entire life that I was so smart and I'd gotten into this program for exceptional kids, like my IQ was 170, and I wasn't doing well in school."

"You felt you couldn't fulfill your potential?"

"I don't *want* to fulfill my potential," she says, her laugh welling up above the canned mall music. "Damn this society! I'm not giving them me." She strikes a defiant pose but simmers down when she notices two women staring at her.

Then she tells me there's a curse on the male members of her family. "See, it's really kind of scary 'cause consecutively all the guys—do I identify myself as a guy? Well, no, but anyway, all of them—my great-grandfather, my grandfather, my father—had this tremendous potential and then they bombed out. So it's fate. Like my dad is saying to me, 'Oh, I did the same thing *my* junior year, don't do it, Lee!' "

"What happened that made you start thinking about yourself?" I ask.

"I don't know. It wasn't like this is who I am. It was more like this is okay—well, not even that, it's just another step in my life. I try not to make a big deal out of it, 'cause I think . . . I think I'm kinda avoiding it."

The waitress, with unerring timing, chooses this moment to ask if we want anything else. We both shake our heads, not looking at her. "It's just another thing about me," Lee explains, shrugging to show how unimportant this particular thing is. "See, in the past, I was not dealing with it properly. I was having all these complexes. I used to hang out with my mom's hairdresser and his friends. I was the stereotypical flamer. Last year I got kind of confused, like why am I hanging out with all these gay guys? And then with guys period. Like for a long time I was bisexual. And now I've pretty much decided that no, I'm not. Like it was a conscious decision 'cause I was starting to get sick every time . . . I mean I just did not feel okay with myself after I got together with guys. I have a lot of guy friends, and then we end up doing whatever sexually just because . . . for whatever reason."

"I know what you mean," I say. I had done the same thing for a short period of time, hanging out with men because I enjoyed their company and then ending up in bed with them. Once I'd made love with a woman and understood what sex was supposed to be, I realized how hollow and ultimately immoral this "friendly gesture" toward my male friends was. Lee had the same revelation, though it came from just sleeping next to Susan: "I had this biggest crush on her, like mass out of control . . . We slept in the same bed, and during that weekend I was able to separate my attractions."

"Have you had relationships with girls?"

She laughs. "Not good ones. Not real ones. Look, at the [horse] camp, people I've known my entire life, they started coming up to me in the seventh grade and saying, 'Have you figured it out yet?' and I'm going, 'Figured out what?' I was totally clueless. This summer my counselor knew I had a crush on someone. She said, 'I know you do,' and I said, 'Why?' and she said, 'You're doing your hair,' and I'm like, 'Good point.' Anyway, I told the counselor about Sarah and she was like dih dih dih"—it's too tiresome and painful for Lee to replicate the counselor's worried lecture, so she uses her shorthand for an emotion-laden confrontation—"and I'm like, NOOO. And everybody was telling me they'd heard the rumor and I'm going, 'What the hell are you talking about?' "

This is too muddled for me. "So what was the rumor?"

"Oh. That Sarah and I had been like really getting together. That we had basically been doing the lesbian lambada. So I was like, I'm not ready for that. I don't want to talk about that. I don't want to fuck up camp, see."

"If you were having a sexual relationship—"

"I wouldn't be allowed to go back there."

"So you haven't—"

"Oh! Well, there's this person, the person who flaked on me last night for the Wenders film?"

"Carol?"

"Yeah. It's just a weird thing. I don't want to think about it or deal with it." But as we pay the bill, parade through Nordstrom again, glancing at Levi's as we go, and load ourselves into Lee's car, she regales me with the story. Lee met Carol through her friend Jan. "Carol's going, 'I need a woman,' so Jan sets this up without our knowing each other. And we really hit it off. We had the same childhood and we're into the same things. In fact, I think we're a little too similar. So we get together a lot, have special encounters. But it's weird, 'cause she gets really moody." Lee knits her eyebrows together. "She keeps telling Jan, 'I love Lee, she's just so great,' and I'm like, 'Okay, why don't you just show it, babe?' "

"Maybe she senses your reluctance," I suggest. Lee told me over the omelettes that she can't handle a relationship, she has to concentrate on school and her SATs, and that she considers making a phone call too much of an obligation.

"I don't know," Lee says. "I don't get it." But moments later she's back singing with the radio. She has a date to see the Wim Wenders flick with Carol tonight. As she points the car in the direction of Laguna Beach, she tells me she wants to be a cinematographer. Sure, it's so LA, but it's what she really wants. On the other hand, she says, it shows how affected by her environment she is, like she's a map of all the influences she's been exposed to.

She tells me that when she was doing her project on gay and lesbian youth, she attended a youth group at the gay and lesbian community center in Garden Grove, a few freeway exits away from Yorba Linda. "I didn't like it there. It was a bunch of guys who were just, 'I'm really insecure so I'm going to vent it by making fun of people who are just like me,' you know?"

"Self-hate run riot," I say.

"Yeah. I made Marcelle go with me and she was, 'They are so pathetic.' So lately I've been going to West Hollywood a lot, and I really like it there, even if it's a guys' place. I like going to the bookstores and to Don't Panic [a gay retail store] and to Little Frida's [a coffeehouse frequented by lesbians]."

"And your friends come with you?" I ask. I could have said, And you drag your straight friends along for company?

She understands my real question. "My friends are pretty open-minded. They're like, 'I'm attracted to women, but not enough to act on it.' I don't see them as a 'straight' community if you see what I mean, but just a community of people."

Several times she and her friends have been told by older lesbians to tone it down. "This lady comes up to us and says, 'You guys are giving a bad name to the gay community,' and we're like, 'We're just kids, we want to have fun.' I think the older gay community tries to be as normal as it can. And if you're abnormal they assume you give a bad name to all gays, like you're evil or you should be in one of those sadomasochistic groups." She puzzles over this as we turn off the freeway into a pretty green canyon.

"See, right now I'm comfortable with things about myself and I don't want to change them," she says. "My anti-responsibility, for instance. And my flamboyance. Like we were in the West Hollywood area, and we're going, 'Fuckin' dyke!' like you do, and this lady turns around and she says, 'I don't know whether you guys are being weird or derogatory,' and I pull my freedom rings out of my shirt, and she's like, 'You!'

"Well, I don't think there should be a stereotypical anything, and I don't care about breaking all these rules. So I told this lady, 'I'm not you, deal with it.' I'm like, 'I'm gonna do what I want.' And I walked off, do, dah, dah!" She manages to mimic a triumphant march in her car seat, using her fist as a kazoo, then lets her hand drop back down to the steering wheel. "But I was really upset about that for a while." She pauses and then says sheepishly, "I mean, I know I'm really loud and obnoxious. I know that."

I'm thinking several things: that being comfortable enough to make insider, on-herself gay jokes in front of her straight friends is a quantum leap from my closeted existence in high school, that gay adults seem to feel it's legitimate to approach teenagers in a critical capacity but not in a helpful or a friendly one, and that it must be nice to be in an environment where people don't hassle you. "With the football team pretending to be bi and half the girls claiming to be attracted to other girls, sounds like kids at school wouldn't make homophobic remarks," I surmise.

"Oh, no. That's not true at all. It's a very anti-PC school, deliberately."

"So people make jokes?"

"I think it's more of a habit. Like this guy said, 'When I call someone a fag, I don't mean they're gay, I mean they're bad.'"

"But when someone *is* gay, they perceive it as a taunt."

"Yeah, but I take it into consideration when I hear someone say stuff."

"So you don't see it as a personal affront. You focus on what's positive for you."

She rocks her head back and forth, measuring what I've said. "Well, I'm not sure about the positive part. I'm self-destructive. But I don't take what people say personally. So I guess I *do* offend the gay community in that sense, 'cause I'm not promoting niceness, but I think if people were meaning harm in it I might be more rigorous."

She pulls into a back parking lot in Laguna Beach and we walk down to the main street, then wander around a bookstore for a few minutes before settling on a plaza with cups of tea. Laguna Beach reminds me of a smaller, seedier Carmel, though the townsfolk contradict this, since there are more wealthy residents than dowdy tourists. Pretend Clint Eastwood got hold of Stinson Beach instead of Carmel and you've got the idea.

To my surprise, since neither of us can seem to remember anything, Lee picks up where we left off. "People think I'm intimidating at school," she says. "I guess it's a good thing, 'cause then they don't bother me." They do, she says, bother other students. "People know they're not gonna get me."

No one, in fact, can get Lee but herself. When I ask what her fears are, she opens her eyes wide and says, "Oh, wow! I gotta have an Orangina. I think I'm in denial of fear.

Wow. The answer to life lies in that." When she returns, she says, "Okay. I take a nihilistic approach to things, and I'm scared I'll change my mind and not remember why I felt this way. And I have a problem with separating stuff, like my artistic approach with a more structured way of going about something, so that's caused difficulties with my writing. I was scared that if I learned how to write for the reader then I'd forget how to write creatively. And then, like when we were watching *Citizen Kane*, you know that movie is supposed to define American life, and I'm going, I don't want a definition, I don't want to understand."

"You don't want understanding forced on you," I say, though it is more than that: Lee senses that defining something eliminates all the other definitions that might attend upon that something if only we were open enough to see them.

She's nodding. "My biggest fear is losing creativity, which I think I've lost a lot of already. I have such a complex about being less than . . . This doctor wanted to give me Prozac 'cause my dad's on Prozac, and I said, no, thank you, sir. It's not worth losing parts of me."

She's thinking again. "From a very early age, I have never understood why one opinion is better than another one. I can see the flip side to everything. So that's a big problem to my feelings. Like I had this crazy crush on Susan, and I don't have that on Carol, and that's crazy, 'cause she's there and she's exactly what I want. Susan tells me about her sex life [with boys], and I try to deal with that. I think I'm saving myself the pain of having a more involved relationship with her."

"What would it be like if you were straight?" I ask.

"I don't know if I could imagine that." She tries hard

but can't, then finally says, "I guess if I were straight I'd understand what I was supposed to feel if I broke up with a boyfriend. Part of what was so terrible about going with boys was when we broke up I knew I was supposed to be upset, so I'd like go around trying to make myself cry, but I really didn't care."

She's gulped down her Orangina, so a few minutes later, we're back in the green canyon, and Lee is singing softly to the radio. "What's this self-destructiveness?" I ask.

She gives me a long sideways look. "Oh, I don't know. I don't want to talk about that."

"Okay," I say.

The green slides by. "I often . . . I have these really bad cycles."

"Where you feel depressed?"

"For lack of a better word."

"Suicidal?"

"Yeah. I can't help those feelings and I don't want to deal with them. Not with drugs. If I kill myself then I did it and it's done. I don't like talking about it 'cause most people have a fit, and that's not what I want. I just think most things are boring and stupid and cheesy." I almost chuckle because she is so obviously the opposite of bored. With her ebullience, her laugh like a geyser, her slouch that can turn into a high-flying jump at a moment's notice, her broad range of interests—physics, astronomy (she gives lectures to elementary school kids in stargazing), trail riding at her horse camp, the films she's making of her friends, the screenplay she describes that actually sounds good—the girl's a dynamo.

Sure, she's moody and concerned about losing pieces of herself, but what smart sixteen-year-old isn't? "Sometimes I feel compelled to show off around people, and that is not cool with me at all," she grouses. She hunches over the steering wheel, her eyebrows drawn into a frown. But even as she's telling me that Americans love TV because they're bored to tears, she interrupts herself to exclaim, "God, it's so beautiful today, so green! It's not like it usually is at all. I should come out here and shoot tomorrow."

The following day, Lee and I make a quick trip to a coffeehouse in Anaheim. She's exhausted, having intended to see the Wim Wenders film with Carol, except that Carol had a huge fight with her parents and once again opted out of the evening. Lee is frustrated, and in defense tells me a story about how she turned someone down. "This girl, she calls me up, and she says, 'Lee, I was wondering if you'd like me to be your girlfriend.' I almost dropped the phone, and I thought, 'Fuck you, I'm not gonna deal with this.' So the next day at school, I said, 'Look, as perfect as you are, and as much as I'd like to be with you, I'd say for you personally, put it off till you go to college.' I was being so mean to her, but it's like she's so open-minded she jumps into things without realizing what they mean. I told her, 'You can't handle it, you don't know what's going on.' "

"Does it seem scarier to think about a relationship with a girl than with a guy?" I ask, since despite all her bravado, Lee herself seems far from ready.

"Uhmm, I'm not too scared to *think* about it. Last night I kept driving past Carol's house over and over. I was like, 'Stupid bitch,' 'cause she flaked on me. And ya know with the girl I liked over the summer, Sarah, by the end of the summer, it was like 'Stupid bitch' with her too. So I thought, the Sarah Syndrome is coming back, and Marcelle says, 'Hey, it's not the Sarah Syndrome, it's the Lee Syndrome.'" She shakes her head at Marcelle's perception. "Wow. So what happens when I really get into someone is I cut it off 'cause I get scared."

"You're in this difficult place of being betwixt and between."

"Yeah. And my friends . . . well, they have these ideas of what's right for me." She sighs. "See, at the time I had the crush on her, Susan wasn't sure about herself. She was like a typical teenager who is questioning her sexual identity. Then after having sex with Frank this summer, she realized she's straight. But at the time, she left it open. And I had still—I had known no women who were available to me."

"You felt like everyone was straight."

"Pretty much. And I didn't want to go—all I could think of was the bars, like the Palms. And I wasn't—I thought, I don't want to go to a bar to *meet* people. So Susan says, 'Let's go to the Palms,' and I got really mad at her, you know? Like all my friends kid around, they're broadminded, it's no big deal—"

"It's not serious for your friends in the way that it is for you."

"Right. I have nymphomaniac friends." She pauses. "Orangina. I gotta have an Orangina."

She rolls her eyes when the surly waiter informs her they have no Orangina. "Anyhow," she says, turning back to me, "I'm very anti-separatist, but I think I'm becoming one now. I see people from my school or my mom and my sister in West Hollywood, and I say, 'What are *you* doing here? Go away.'"

Lee is on the crux of a dilemma: while she knows instinctively that being gay should not be a major factor in her life, as she grows older and begins to feel the stigma and the exclusion, she is realizing that what she knows to be true is not the same as what will happen to her in spite of that truth. And the course of romance cannot run smooth when the repercussions include adopting more fully a stigmatized identity; she and Carol are circling each other like wary tigers, unsure whether to fight or to play. Meanwhile, Lee's friends are as helpful to her as they can be, coming with her on her forays to gay territory, teasing her gently when she tries to edge back to a straight world she knows is wrong for her, but even all their support and perception can't erase the sting of her ambivalence and disappointment. Still, Lee's in it for the long haul—she won't compromise herself for other people's pettiness, and she and her friends believe if they create a world where everyone is taken at face value, other people will join in.

She's grinning at me while I'm thinking her friends are good people, and so is she. "You're quite the optimist," I tell her as we leave the Orangina-less cafe to return to the car.

Her whole face lights up, and she punches her hair back with her knuckles. "You can see that? I keep telling my friends that, but they don't believe me." She laughs. "I say, 'Hey, there's a big difference between being cynical and being pessimistic.'"

"So what now?" I ask when she drops me off at my motel.

"I'm going to pick up Marcelle and Susan and go ride around." She thinks for a minute. "Go to the beach? Kinda cold for that. Maybe we'll just drive."

a lesbian at a
women's college

"I've been called worse than chic."

Judging by the signs along Interstate 70, Missouri's famous for fireworks and military academies. What's more apparent to me and my skittish rental Sundance is a hell-wind from the south, grass gray-brown from one of the hardest winters in years, and skeletal trees not yet awake. Near Kansas City those trees look like midgets against the vastness of the slate sky, but closer to Columbia the land begins to assert itself, bunching up in craggy outcroppings and hills tall enough for canyons, caves, and tumbling creeks. Here the trees are broader, spreading, sheltering, their trunks twisted into spectacular shapes. Freed from the hegemony of a sky that goes on forever, they join with the land to orchestrate a concert fully as dramatic as that of thunderstorms rolling across the open plains.

But it's only stark up on the interstate. Columbia in late March is in bloom—Columbia is, in fact, hysterical. The trees along Broadway are sheeted with white blossoms, the

magnolias glow pink and purple and lavender, and everywhere forsythia blazes as yellow as flame tips in a campfire.
Few in this town of 72,000 are captivated by the floral
frenzy, however, because the Mizzou Tigers are off to meet
the Wizard in LA, enduring earthquakes, floods, and mud
slides to put the screws to the Syracuse Orangemen in the
NCAA tournament.

I expected Tiger mania. I also expected Portland-style
slash-hate signs or billboards decrying the religious Wrong.
In the spring of '94, Missouri is one of nine states facing the
possibility of a statewide antigay initiative; signatures are
being collected to qualify the measure for the November
ballot. Such an edict would outlaw antidiscrimination poli-
cies statewide and would overturn those already in place in
several cities, including Columbia, Kansas City, and St.
Louis. But there's no sign of strife in Tiger Town—I don't
even spot any mildly provocative Celebrate Diversity
bumper stickers.

I'm about to ask Victoria Edminster for an explanation,
but her attention has been caught by the street trees. "I
didn't know they did this," she says, staring at a fulsome
specimen, decked head to toe in white flowers which now
carry a pinky-orange cast in the setting sun. "I thought they
were just green." She leans close to see where the green
went and then she grins. "I don't know much about trees."

Vic, age twenty and a freshman at Stephens College,
stands five-five, with long hair sticking out in a ponytail
from under the bill of her backward baseball cap. She tells
me some kids just called her "sir" when they tried to get her
to buy a paper about the Tigers' trip to the land of Oz.
Rolling her eyes, half irked, half pleased, she admits she
looks "pretty butch." She's certainly got the butch bounce

down pat, that ground-eating motion that looks as if you're striding across ocean swells rather than sidewalks. Has she always been like this?

"Kinda."

Does she get in trouble for it?

"Kinda."

When Vic was eight, she and her mom came out to visit her mom's brother in San Francisco. Vic's dad was already long gone, a victim of divorce when Vic was two. Vic's uncle took them on a sightseeing tour of the city. As they crested the hills into Noe Valley, he said, "This is where the lesbians live," and Vic perked up, wishing more than anything she could live there too, with her people. "I thought that's where I'd fit in," she says. In her hometown of Columbia, she was sometimes hassled for looking like a boy. Once, a little girl she had a crush on decided Vic needed "therapy" and spent months trying to cure her.

A couple years later, dismayed by the lack of jobs in Columbia, Vic's mother moved to Pacifica, a bedroom community south of San Francisco. Vic hated it. She hadn't wanted to leave Columbia, where the summers were long and hot and she was pretty much accepted; the few disputes she'd had in Columbia escalated instantly to constant name-calling and beatings in Pacifica. "They thought I was weird in general. I'd made up this snake character, this creature I drew called Kobe. I had pictures of Kobe all over my room. I looked like a boy, I slept naked, and I drew snakes. So kids tormented me. They kept saying, 'Are you really a lesbian?'

"Then when I was twelve, we moved to Noe Valley, and I went to James Lick Junior High. And I was tormented there too, so there went that lovely vision of what would happen in Noe Valley." She shrugs and looks away, off across the street, and we walk along without saying anything for a few moments until she can talk again. She tells me about how bad the next few years were for her, about how frightened she was of the antigay violence she experienced —frightened for herself and for the out lesbians she saw around her. "I was getting beat up on the bus just for having short hair and dressing like a boy. I'd see women and think, 'They're holding hands—what's going to happen to them?'

"At the same time, obvious dykes made me cringe. I remember thinking, 'I don't know if I want to be like that.' I'd hear stuff from my family, stuff they probably don't re-member saying, but I remember every word. Once my uncle called someone a 'pear-assed dyke,' and later I'd see a woman with a pear-shaped butt and I'd think, 'That's not good.'

"I didn't want to see butch dykes. I wanted to see nor-mal people, women that looked like everybody else. I didn't want to see stuff that was considered bad. I liked to think there was a way I could be the good part and not the bad part."

In spite of a family she describes as "fairly radical," Vic says she doesn't remember hearing anything positive about gays. "What my family said meant more to me than seeing rainbow flags or watching Gay Freedom Day on television. I remember quietly squirming while someone would say something homophobic."

She sighs, then lights a cigarette from the one she's about to stub out. "A lot of my issues were physical, the gender stuff. When I was in high school, I said some of the most horrible bullshit. Like, 'If I'm going to be with a woman, then I want to be with a woman who looks like a woman.' I would date somebody who was femme—"

"Who hopefully doesn't have the same idea," I interject.

"Right. And from them I got, 'I love you as a *person*,' like, 'We'll just ignore you're a woman.' As if I could somehow transcend gender boundaries. You don't forget that 'You're just a person' thing."

In fact, it hurt her so much she's about to squeeze the life out of her coffee cup. After our tour of Broadway, we've ended up at Ernie's, a grungy steak and hamburger joint. Vic worked here for two years as a short-order cook, earning $4.60 an hour by the time she left. She abandons her painful memories when a woman sharing our long table asks her to pass the cream. Vic leaps to her feet and brings it to the woman with a half-bow. Unfailingly polite, with manners verging on old-fashioned, Vic reminds me of myself at her age: earnest, intense, and courtly. It's an interesting mix, the gentleman-butch/punk-scholar. Make a few adjustments in musical taste and slang, and she would be at home anytime in the past fifty years.

Though she *is* more precocious than most: Vic was seven when she first came out to her mom. "I said, 'Mom, I like girls.' She knew what I meant. And she said, 'We'll see.' Seven years later, I said, 'Mom, I still like girls.' And she said, 'Oh.' She didn't take it very well."

Compared to most parents, Vic's mom took it beautifully. Vic had already begun her first relationship, with another ninth grader at Lowell High School. "I thought my mom would be cool with it. But at the time I was doing a lot of drugs and being moody and uncommunicative. And Shelley, my girlfriend, was incredibly somber and depressed. My mom felt like there was this shadow hanging around us.

"I'd say, 'Can Shelley spend the night?' And you know,

it *is* kind of a conundrum 'cause now you know there's cunnilingus going on. So she'd say, 'Well, no sexual hankypanky.'

"One morning she had to leave really early for the airport, and she came in when we were having sex, and she pats around on the bed and feels one head and then pats up the bed and feels another one, and she goes perfectly calmly, 'Vic? Which one are you? Are you the one on the top or the bottom here?' And I said, 'I'm up here.' And she gives me this kiss goodbye. I thought later, what was she gonna do if I was down there, was she still gonna give me a kiss?"

Vic and Shelley were together for about a year before Vic began seeing Diane on the side. "We were all friends, and Shelley was pretty horrified that Diane and I had gotten together, especially since I hadn't bothered to share that fact with her." Vic rolls her eyes at her own bad behavior. "Around then I decided to transfer to McAteer, to the School of the Arts. Diane wanted to go too, so her father and my mother went over there to check it out. Her parents didn't like me. They said it was a dangerous school and wouldn't let Diane go."

Diane stayed at Lowell, while Vic transferred to McAteer, which she loved. But soon afterward, she came down with pneumonia and missed weeks of classes. "Then I didn't want to do high school anymore," she explains. "I was burned out." Her mother helped her negotiate the proficiency test, the equivalent of graduation, and then insisted Vic get a job.

So at sixteen she was finished with school, still with Diane, and labeling herself bisexual because being lesbian was too risky and isolating. "I felt totally ignored by the queer community," she says. "Nobody meant to do it. It wasn't like, 'We hate young queers.' It was more, 'You can take care of yourself.' Now I *can* take care of myself, but back then . . . I wanted to know I existed.

"I don't even remember much eye contact. I didn't get support from older dykes at all. You're on your own until you're old enough to be in the scene, able to be picked up. Part of it's that I didn't make an effort. But I felt it was other people's responsibility since I was so young and shy.

"I don't think there's anyone more isolated than queer kids. You don't see yourself anywhere. At least racial minorities have their families. With queers, oftentimes our families are who we're *most* alienated from. So what do we have? Maybe a room. A room and nothing."

Vic, who at twelve had cringed at the obvious dykes she saw around Noe Valley and the Castro, now wished she could be recognized for who she was, but she hadn't counted on the gay community's hands-off stance toward queer kids. Feeling an outsider, and with Shelley and Diane in school all day, Vic drifted toward a community that *did* accept her, the Haight Street youth scene. "My group was based on being the weird kids, not on being queer. Haight Street was supposedly free love with a '90s twist, yet very straight. I think a lot of alternative communities are particularly homophobic, the same way women's colleges can be."

Vic got a job panhandling for a community food program, but soon she was off to Oregon to live in a collective. When she returned, the collective came with her. "We got this apartment in the Tenderloin, eight people in a two-bedroom. This woman Sukie and I were the only ones working, so we paid the rent for everybody. What ends up happening is I can't stand it, I can't take fighting for where I'm going to sleep every night. They all go back to Oregon, and I move in with Mom.

"The Oregon people, we called ourselves a family. And it's not like I wasn't out to them, I *was*, but I wouldn't bring lesbian friends over. If I had dealt with them on the level that I deal with people now, I don't know that we would get along. Being queer didn't have the same focus that it does now for me—I wasn't letting it.

"Most of the people I hung out with would have considered me bisexual, and I wouldn't have disputed that. Being bisexual was very hip, but being lesbian was too far. Diane was the queen of Haight Street, and in certain circles we were this cool couple, but we were made acceptable by the fact that she was incredibly femme. If we had crossed that boundary between hip and too radical, it would have been uncomfortable. *I* was uncomfortable enough, 'cause I was pretty dykely throughout, no matter what I called myself."

Although she was aware of its existence, Vic never felt moved to join a gay and lesbian youth organization like LYRIC, the Lavender Youth Recreation and Information Center. "I didn't want a support group. I wanted *friends*. I felt basically okay. Something about the support group atmosphere was almost offensive to me . . . that an adult was there. I felt like, 'We don't need you to lend validity.' And there was the split between a group like that and my friends on Haight Street."

That rift would not have been only between Vic and her street friends, but between Vic and Diane. Diane's attitude was, "I like *you*, but that doesn't mean anything about *me*." In fact, when Diane and Vic moved to Columbia, Diane was gone within months, complaining that Vic had disappeared into a lesbian community that was foreign to her.

Yet that was precisely why Vic moved to Columbia. Unable to be fully herself on Haight Street, still squirming at the homophobic remarks of her relatives, too young to be accepted on Castro and Valencia, Vic left San Francisco on an odyssey to find a family in which she finally could be herself. In doing so, she flew in the face of the thousands of young gay people who leave smaller towns and cities to come to New York or San Francisco or Chicago.

Through her years in San Francisco, Vic had carried her memories of dreamy summer idylls in Columbia. Where better to start her search than in the place she'd once been accepted, that she hadn't wanted to leave? "But I was so scared I wouldn't find people," she says, stubbing out her last cigarette and crumpling up the pack into a little ball. "When I was a kid here, I didn't remember any visible queer community." She made an exploratory trip first, ran into a few dykes, and she and Diane moved within a matter of weeks. "I came here bent on meeting lesbians. When I was fourteen or fifteen, I wasn't confident enough to go up and meet women. Now people sought me out. In San Francisco, they still wouldn't make eye contact, but here they came up and introduced themselves."

Those same people were shocked when they discovered later that Vic was only eighteen. "There was some anger about that," Vic recalls. Because she's so at ease with herself and articulate, many people assumed Vic was older, and some felt they'd been tricked. Still, by the time her real age came out, she was well ensconced in the community, Diane was making going-away noises, and true to Vic's romantic modus operandi, new girlfriend Vanessa was already on the scene.

Vic arrived in Columbia almost bald. "See, I had this mohawk, and then I shaved it really narrow, and finally . . ." She sighs. "When I was living in San Francisco, I had this feeling that unless I was a definite dyke, with really short hair and Queer Nation stickers, I'd get ignored even more. I sure didn't want to be ignored because people assumed I was straight. Appearance is something you have control over, but at the same time it controls you, because who says what looks queer or not? I happen to *like* Queer Nation stickers, but what if we had to wear hula skirts or something? I'd be shit out of luck."

Vic decided to go to Stephens after she'd been in town for some months. Diane had already left—"great pattern here"—and Vic finally felt landed. She was happy with Vanessa, a woman nine years her senior; she was working at Ernie's; she'd helped start a political and social group, the Lesbian Community Project; and she'd made a lot of friends. It was time to move ahead. "I'm in an undeclared major, but it's something like twentieth-century studies, where I can concentrate on women writers and on history."

Stephens, a women's school of some eight hundred students, on a large and beautiful campus in downtown Columbia, has proved to be a mixed bag. "I've met some incredibly cool people, but I'm not willing to get close, 'cause I'm just waiting for people to say something racist or homophobic or gross. I get asked a lot of questions. 'How do *you* feel?'—in other words, I'm supposed to represent every lesbian on earth. But I don't mind so much. At least they're asking.

"There's a new trap to fall into, kids who think it's cool

but who are truly phobic. It can be really hard coming out and investing in people and getting burned, this time under the guise of people saying they're tolerant.

"But people now are more aware. All the attention on this stupid-ass lesbian chic stuff is creating new myths. At least it's not lesbian sicko. I've been called worse than chic. It's an exciting time to be queer. If we can steer away from being a novelty, there might be some serious stuff going on. There already is."

"Have people been weird to you? Avoided you in the hall?" I'm worried that Vic, emerging from the kiln of Haight Street, might prove at once too hard-shelled and fragile to survive in Columbia. She certainly won't keep her mouth shut.

She shakes her head. "I've been lucky that I have a whole other community so I don't need these people. And I don't live on campus." Although Stephens has a policy that unmarried students must live on campus, Vic convinced the administration that she shouldn't be financially penalized because she and Vanessa can't get a piece of paper that says they're married. "Living in the dorm would have cost me three times as much. I couldn't have gone to school."

I ask her what she'd change or if she feels she's missed out on anything. "I haven't been without a lover since I was fourteen, not even for an hour. I'm happy with Vanessa, but if it happens that we split, I'd like to see what that's like." She pauses, thinking. "See, I didn't ever really date. It's gone from friendship to being someone's lover. And maybe that means I've met great people but in other ways it means I haven't experienced . . . I think that whole straight ceremony of dating is not accessible to queer youth. Dating implies a certain amount of choice, the freedom to pick and choose. Well, pick and choose from who? A bunch of people who have to flash each other secret signals to be recognized?"

"You can't wink at someone in the lettuce aisle," I say.

"Right. If you wink at someone in the lettuce aisle, you'd probably get beat up."

She drums her fingers on the table as she listens to the music on the jukebox, then finally breaks down, digs in her pockets, and feeds coins into Ernie's cigarette machine until a pack of Camels pops out. "When I was little I thought gay men and lesbians actually lived in the closet," she says. "I imagined it was really dark and there were spiderwebs and you'd never get any air. So it seemed it was a life of fear or peeping out of the closet, screaming, 'Give me some air!'

"There's not so much people can do to me now. It's so much less scary when you're out. There's a lot less fear in having someone say 'dyke' aloud. The worst thing they can do is kill you." She shrugs. "No one here's gonna beat me up." But when I asked her what she feared, violence was her second thought—the first was having to be closeted.

Last summer, at an alternative music club in Vancouver, Vic was attacked by a man who suddenly grabbed her and began choking her. When she kicked him in the chest, he punched her between the eyes. As she tells me this story, she chokes up and wordlessly exhibits an inch-and-a-half-long jagged scar, running from the bridge of her nose up past her left eyebrow. "A friend grabbed me and took me into the bathroom. I was bleeding all over the place and crying and I said, 'You know, this is just fucking great. As a woman, I can't even come into this fucking bar.' And my friend was trying to say, 'Hey, it probably isn't because you're a woman.' I thought, well, why *had* he done it? There were only two reasons: either he was insane or he knew I was a dyke."

The next morning, I wander by the Peace Nook, a tiny store on Broadway that flies an upside-down rainbow flag. The store is the locus of a host of countercultures, and it is here, among herbal remedies, incense, and psychic healing brochures, that I encounter the first evidence that anyone has noticed the amendment at all. On a mounted piece of butcher paper is pinned a flier, which reads in part, "While the Amendment Coalition—a group of supposedly religious people—says it opposes bigotry, the recent experience of Oregon and Colorado indicates that gay and lesbian bashing and other hate crimes are part and parcel of anti-human rights initiatives." Numbers are given to call, and a marking pen strapped to the butcher paper invites comment.

"This hasn't been as fruitful as we'd hoped," an employee says to me as I crouch to read the five or six entries, each written in miniature script, as if modesty forbade their authors to write large upon such a wide expanse of paper.

"If a true representation of the populace comes to the polls, we shouldn't have to worry," opines one.

"We are in Missouri," reminds the next. "In Springfield, people are homophobic enough to pass it overwhelmingly. Be visible in Columbia, but don't do anything in Springfield. All you'll accomplish is to anger fundies. Fighting would be destructive. If we try to gain ground fighting, we're liable to lose."

No one has taken pen to hand to challenge this observation. Earlier, Vic had tried to reassure me that *something* was being done. Her group, the Lesbian Community Project, was holding a dance at Stephens just this Friday to raise money to help fight the coalition. She points out that while the queer community seems quiescent, the religious Right isn't exactly out there swinging either. "I'm hoping they'll have a harder time of it than they think," she said. "Maybe we can stop this early. Maybe we scared them off."

The guy at the Peace Nook has another theory. "It's true there's not that much fight against it, but they [the Amendment Coalition] really haven't been gathering that many signatures. They're probably waiting until the weather warms up and then they'll make a big push."

I suggest that perhaps they're gathering signatures in churches where their real power base is. I imagine them bounding forth in June, clutching piles of petitions covered with scads of signatures. I also picture everyone's wide-eyed surprise.

Vic agreed this was a possibility. "When we did Columbia's antidiscrimination clause a couple years ago, it was bad, and this is a million times worse because it's a direct attack against us. I mean, we've never attacked them or their stupid family values. It could get pretty horrible. The only thing I *don't* worry about is people marching down the street with semiautomatics. This town is not all of a sudden going to turn into a hotbed of Nazis."

"suddenly you're one of 'them.' "

Fulton may be only ten miles southeast of Columbia, but in terms of gay liberation, it's closer to Dresden in 1988—that is, behind the Iron Curtain. I breakfast at Mom's Kitchen and gain the impression that all Fulton residents under sixty are imprisoned under lock and key, but the town actually boasts two colleges—William Woods, a women's school affiliated with the Christian Church Disciples of Christ (the school's graduate division coeducated in 1994), and coed Westminster. Fittingly, Winston Churchill delivered his Iron Curtain speech at Westminster in 1946; wanting to memorialize the event, the school ferried the ruins of an English church to Fulton in 1961. The undercroft of the rebuilt church now serves as a repository for Churchill's letters and paintings. Fulton also provided the setting for Ronald Reagan's *King's Row*, the one where he loses his legs. "It's the quintessential Midwestern small town," says a friend of mine who grew up here.

It is also the home of Martha Carroll, a Disciples of Christ minister who until last year was the chaplain at William Woods. And it is the temporary stomping grounds of Lauren Dreyer, a senior at William Woods who's counting the days until graduation, when she will rejoin her high school sweetie back in Arkansas. Not that Lauren is a stomper; she describes herself as a lipstick lesbian. "Is that a real term?" Martha Carroll asks me, bemused.

Martha and Lauren are both charter members of what they call the "little group," a lesbian and gay support group for Fultonites. Pretty much everyone in the group of fifteen is a charter member. "I suggested that maybe we could make it known to the community that we exist," Martha says. She's talking about Fulton at large, not the gay community, which *is* the little group. "I'm sure we're missing people," she says wistfully. "But the group just isn't ready for that. They feel it's too risky."

Martha knows about risk, though she says her teenage daughter is frustrated that she just doesn't come out and be done with it. "She thinks I'm poky," Martha says. Poky Martha is now working as the director of a substance abuse treatment facility—"It's okay, but it's not my career"—because her contract as chaplain was terminated after she wrote an article about homophobia for the school newspaper.

"Of course," Martha says, "that was not the reason given. No reason was given. They were just going to cut the campus ministry. But the year before I had asked the vice president what the problem was, and I had really gotten it— my 'causes.' Well, I hadn't even done anything. All I had asked was if we could have a lesbian support group on campus and I said I might write an article for the school paper.

"The next year, I *did* write the article, and then when my contract came up, the job was gone. I didn't even come out in the article. It was about homophobia on campus and the fact that it was never discussed."

Martha had lost a job before, for similar reasons, in Lauren's home state of Arkansas. "I just figured, 'What the heck? I'm losing jobs anyway, why be quiet?'" After discussing the risks with her partner, she signed on as a plaintiff in a suit against the Amendment Coalition's initiative. "I thought it was a way to take a stand against this kind of stupidity. And as a minister, it just was a good thing to do. So much of the impetus behind the amendment is coming out of the religious community, the religious Right." Afterward, Martha and her partner removed their names from the mailbox "just in case."

One day Martha spotted an announcement in the local paper that the religious Right's propaganda video *Gay Rights, Special Rights* was going to be shown at the Fulton library. Martha called everyone she knew who was lesbian or gay—namely, the little group. They all showed up that night at the library. "This guy who was leading the group, I don't think he expected to have a crowd of lesbians and gay people there. There were about as many of us as there were straight people. So he does his little spiel after the movie, and we immediately started challenging what he said. It was pretty hostile for a while. But we just kept talking, and people started saying, 'I don't want to take any rights away from you.' "

Martha didn't declare herself that evening and neither did Lauren Dreyer. But Martha plans to do a devotional at a conference in a couple weeks where she will talk about her life. "I'm not going to use inflammatory words," she says. "I'm just talking about planting a garden. Because we do have normal lives. You start talking about lifestyles, and I wonder, what do they think we do all the time?"

Lauren Dreyer came out to Martha after the article was published in the school paper. "Lauren is very, very careful," Martha tells me. "She's afraid she'll lose her campus job." It is only in her senior year, when she's in the home stretch, that Lauren has let on about her life even to her closest friends.

"People are so cautious," Martha says. "My sense from the very few people I know is that there is just tremendous fear. From family, from school, about their jobs . . . For me at that age, it was just an unknown. But for these people the fear is just tremendous."

"They know and they're afraid of—" I prompt.

"They're afraid of what's going to happen to them," Martha says. "You know. And that people won't see them the same way. Which is true. Suddenly you're one of 'them.' A big frustration of mine is that we don't know each other.

We're so cut off from younger people, because you talk about any kind of support or counseling and people immediately . . ."

She pauses, her face undergoing a change as she remembers something that upset her even more than losing her job at William Woods. "After my contract wasn't renewed, I talked to the president who oversees all the church-related colleges—he serves as a resource to the various chaplains but isn't involved directly with the colleges—and I said, 'You need to know that I'm sure a part of this is the fact that I am a lesbian.' And he said he could see how a board wouldn't want a lesbian at a women's college." She pauses and shakes her head. "Just the assumption that that was okay to say . . . He wouldn't think there shouldn't be men at a women's college. My integrity, which had never been questioned before, was questioned in an almost offhand manner. He didn't *know* that's what he was doing."

"Did you say anything?" I ask.

"No, I didn't."

"Probably so stunned . . ."

"Well, I was. Because this man has been completely supportive of me. You know, what do you say? I don't think they even hear it."

"i keep wondering, how did i end up here?"

Lauren Dreyer meets me in the stairwell of her dorm at William Woods, and we repair to the TV room to talk. Lauren is as unlike Vic as she could be. With feathers of soft, dark hair framing her face, smooth skin, and a shy smile, Lauren does indeed wear a discreet amount of lipstick

—and eyeliner as well. Her voice is so quiet I have to strain to hear her, and she huddles inside a sweater big enough for someone triple her size. But I soon discover that Lauren's diffidence disguises both a sharp observer and a wit dry as a California summer. She touches her finger to her cheek and says, "It's quite a shock for people when they find out about me. After I'd come out to a few people, I thought, 'I'm the one who needs to come out to break the stereotypes that these people have.' "

In spite of the fact that Lauren has been in a relationship with her girlfriend Michelle for five years, she waited until her last year in college to tell anyone. "I was real worried about my job," she says. Lauren works at the campus library three evenings a week. Without that income, things would be tough. But she was also afraid that people would treat her differently. "Some of them I'm actually closer to now, because before I was like, 'I can't get too close. If they find out, they'll take things that I've done wrong.' Now that they know, they come up and give me hugs. I think it's kind of neat, because I was always standoffish before."

At William Woods, Lauren says, gay people simply do not exist—to the administration, the students, or the faculty. "People here are real close-minded," Lauren says in her soft Arkansas accent. "I should be at some bigger school." She sighs. "But I do like it being real small, and I got scholarship money. That helps."

Lauren occasionally runs into other William Woods students at the gay bar in Columbia. "I wouldn't have known anything about them before," she says. "But I don't blame them [for being in the closet]."

"What's the fear?" I ask.

"Well, it's just so small that within minutes, everybody on the whole campus knows all sorts of things."

Lauren figured out she was gay when she was sixteen. "It was such a relief," she says. "I thought something was wrong with me. I tried going out with boys and when we'd start getting close it would feel really weird, and I'd freak out and tell them I couldn't see them anymore. I knew my friends didn't have those problems. Then when I realized, I thought, 'Oh, there's nothing wrong.' "

She met Michelle in high school. "I kept wondering, 'Why do I want to be around her all the time?' I knew I had feelings for her, but I was so scared to let any of those out. I thought it would be weird to kiss a woman, and then when she actually kissed me, it was, 'What was I worried about?' "

While in school, Michelle and Lauren took pains to hide their relationship. "We avoided each other in the halls and the cafeteria, and we maintained separate groups of friends," Lauren says. "If we were out and saw people from school, I'd go stand away from the crowd we were with. But I never did anything to cover, like dating men. That's one of the things that started the rumors, that I never talked about men."

Lauren's been dogged by rumors since she was seventeen. "I don't even care, as long as they get it right," she tells me. "Just don't say I'm bi. That was the rumor about me 'cause I couldn't be a lesbian. After all, I wear makeup." Only a slight smile touches her lips, but her eyes dance with glee.

When she was a freshman, Lauren briefly broke off her relationship with Michelle. "I was worried about what my parents were gonna do when they found out. That's what scared me most of all. I started seeing a guy in Columbia. I thought I could change the way I am.

"It was a good act. Even Michelle said, 'Well, I'll accept this 'cause you seem really happy.' And I'd hang up the phone and want to sit down and cry. Inside I was just miserable. When I went home at the end of spring break and saw her, that was the end of that." She chuckles, then says more soberly, "I really regret those things. Part of it was that people were constantly telling me and her that I wasn't 'that way.'"

"She was the lesbian and you weren't?"

"Yeah. Even other lesbians said that. They said, 'Michelle got herself some straight girl,' and I'm like, 'Straight since when?'"

Lauren's come out enough to hang freedom rings from the rearview mirror of her old Pontiac. "Except no one knows what they are," she says, rolling her eyes. "One girl asked me if they were the Olympic rings. 'Sure,' I said, 'and they've added a sixth continent.'"

What's really bothering Lauren now, just a couple months before graduation, is the need to tell her parents. "They're Baptist," she says. "It's going to be interesting." She rat-a-tat-tats her fingers on the bare wood arm of the old upholstered chair she's curled up in. "I can't see them totally disowning me, but then again I don't know. They'll want to get me help. My mom says, 'It's just wrong, and it *is* a choice.'" Lauren rolls her eyes. "I can be me or I can hide and lie to everybody—*that's* my choice. But my mom will never understand that. She'll want to know how to fix it."

Lauren had planned to tell her parents during Christmas, so they'd have a few months to get used to it before she returned home from college, but it didn't work out. "They were having problems with my sister," she says, "stressing about some of the guys my sister's dating. My parents are going, 'We never had these problems with Lauren,' and I'm like, 'Clue number ten thousand!' " She shakes her head. "I don't know how much longer they'll use me as an example."

Lauren's sister, four years younger, once said, "You better not ever tell me you're gay."

"I've thought about telling her," Lauren says, "but I think I should tell my parents first. Only then I'm afraid they'll do one of those 'Never speak about this to your sister.' She'll say stuff like, 'There's not any that I go to school with,' and I'll say, 'They're there. You just don't know it.' She loves Michelle. She calls over to Michelle's house all the time. My parents love Michelle too. I just wonder if that's all gonna change when they find out." The rueful smile flits across her face again.

Thinking about the "information" her parents are likely burdened with, I mention the showing of *Gay Rights, Special Rights* at the Fulton library. "It disgusted me," Lauren says vehemently. "I thought I was going to throw up when I got out of there. Just about everything they showed was a very small part of the community. They tried to make the men out like child molesters. And they kept showing the march and the parade. Someone said, 'Well, what happens at Mardi Gras?' I thought that was a good point."

"Do you worry about violence?" I ask.

"No. But then again, when I'm walking down the street, I'm not so noticeable that people can pick me out."

"Is Michelle more noticeable?"

Lauren's eyes crinkle in appreciation. "Yeah."

"So when you're with her, it's more obvious?"

"Yeah, it probably is. So far I haven't run into those

problems. The first time I do, I'll worry about it quick." She laughs. "No, my biggest fear is my parents not accepting me. Michelle worries about that too. She says, 'Do you really want to tell them?' But I want to spend the rest of my life with her, and if my parents aren't going to accept that . . ."

Lauren says Martha Carroll's been a big help to her. "Before, I had a real hard time with my religious beliefs and how I was brought up. Until I met her, I didn't know anyone [gay] who had strong religious beliefs, and I didn't know where I fit into all that. She made me feel a lot better about myself."

Lauren is the youngest member of the little group, though she considered inviting another student who's even younger. "My fear was, she's a freshman, and I've had problems with freshmen not knowing when was a good time to keep things quiet, so I was afraid to take her. But I've talked to her quite a lot, and I think she realizes it could cost somebody their job. Then I went to each of the people who would be affected, the ones who work on campus, and asked them personally if she could come."

"It sounds like a cell in the French Resistance," I say. Lauren's too young for this analogy to hit home. "So did she ever come?"

"They said she could, but . . ." Her voice trails off. It seems that somewhere during the discussions, the freshman lost heart. The reasons this intergenerational group was formed—that gays in Fulton feel embattled and unsupported—are also what conspire to keep out those beyond the inner circle, those who probably most need the group. Martha Carroll's simple wish to help a younger generation instantly becomes mired in a quicksand of heterosexual assumptions that becomes deadlier each time we try to shift our weight. In this worldview, innocence and queerness are mutually exclusive states of being. Gay and lesbian kids need no mentoring; if they do, they must not be all queer, and it's even more important not to influence them in the "wrong" direction. What then could be the motivation behind wanting to help them? Something unseemly, no doubt, or at best ill-considered.

The same misconceptions underlie liberal thinking. Alice Stone Ilchman, president of Sarah Lawrence College, told a friend of mine who was concerned about lesbian students: "I'm not worried about them. I'm worried about these naïve kids just off the farm who don't know about any of this." It never occurred to her that lesbians, naïve and otherwise, also come off the farm—we must spring full-blown, tattoos and piercings in place, from gay baby centers deep in the Castro or Greenwich Village.

Lauren rouses herself to tell me about a skit that was recently performed on campus. "At one point, one actress leaned close to the other, and everyone in the audience started whispering, 'They're lesbians. She's gonna tell her she's gay!' I could hear it all around me, like a wave. I thought, 'Where is this coming from? This story has nothing to do with lesbians.' It made me realize how fearful people are. They're just terrified.

"And when the speakers come every year for the human sexuality course . . . it's always the men. This lady from the Lesbian Community Project said, 'I don't understand why they don't invite us given that it's a women's college.' Well, I do. It's 'cause they don't want any of us to feel like, 'Hey, we're normal, we'll all come out!' "

Still, Lauren is optimistic about the future. "I don't

think being a lesbian will affect me that much. Maybe my job. If I go into the theater, it's more acceptable in that type of community. If I went into business, that'd be another story. But I don't really worry about that."

"What *do* you plan to do?" I ask.

Lauren glances up at the ceiling for inspiration. When she looks back at me, she's gotten comfortable enough to flash me a big grin. "That's a really good question," she says with a chuckle. Just dealing with the chaos that her announcement will cause her parents is more than she wants to envision, yet she can't see beyond it, even to where she and Michelle might settle down. If her parents accept them, they'll stay in Little Rock; if not—well, they could end up just about anywhere doing just about anything, as long as they're together.

"Do you have close friends here?"

"I'm really close to the girls on the floor upstairs. They've gone to the [gay] bar in Columbia with me. And the other day I was talking about playing volleyball, and this one friend said, 'Oh, I want to play.' I said, 'It's a lesbian team,' and she said, 'Well, can I pretend?' " She smiles, proud of her pals. "Now how many people do you hear say that?"

At the dance the Lesbian Community Project is hosting, I hear more about lost jobs. "I think my coworkers tried to kill me," a woman tells me. She'd been working on a highway crew, a dangerous but well-paying job she'd managed to qualify for after losing another job when people suspected she was gay. "At the time, I couldn't figure out what was going on, but guys came up to me later and told me that what happened hadn't been my fault, that the others had ganged up on me. The ones who talked to me didn't join in, but they wouldn't stop it either." She pauses. "I have a child. We ended up on the street, but I was lucky to be alive. My girlfriend lost her job too. I can't afford to lose this job I have now. That's why I can't join the Lesbian Community Project."

We are having this conversation in a hall on the Stephens campus; a local band is playing on a foot-high stage in front of us. We each paid four bucks to enter and got our hands stamped with big script letters in purple ink: *Positively Queer*. Literature is available for free, and baked goods are being sold. All funds raised at this benefit, we are told, will "fight the Right."

The ex-highway worker asks about my book, but it soon becomes obvious she's interested in only one teenager—her sixteen-year-old daughter, who is straight, and now living with her father. "Nicole's just so angry," she says, shaking her head. "I keep wondering if she's angry about *me*." She indicates herself wordlessly, this earnest butch woman with an anxious girlfriend who hangs on every word but gives us room by pretending to listen to the band. The highway worker explains that things apparently aren't terrific with Dad, because Nicole runs away a lot. Mom is desperate for solutions and haunts bookstores for anything that will help. Do I think it would be better if Nicole stayed with her father and his conventional nuclear family? Should she *make* Nicole stay with Dad even though Nicole insists she wants to come home, even though both Mom and her girlfriend miss Nicole terribly?

I protest that I don't know Nicole, her father, or even my confidante. Well, could I think about shifting the focus of my book so it would address the problems of straight teenagers with gay parents? She needs answers in a hurry.

What she really wants to know is if, in spite of her tremendous concern and care, being a lesbian somehow prevents her from being a good mom. If it does, she loves Nicole so much she'll fire *herself*. After all, what can she offer Nicole, with never being sure she can hold on to a position or a home? Meanwhile she *has* to keep the job she's got now, can't lose it too, she has to work tomorrow even if it is a Saturday, otherwise she'd come to the reading I'm doing at the bookstore in Kansas City, maybe they'd have a new book about teenagers . . .

A tall woman in a wraparound skirt introduces herself to me as a Stephens employee. She shrugs when I mention the low-key amendment fight. Leaning forward to shout in my ear, she tells me that politics of any stripe barely cast a ripple on the smooth pond of Missouri placidity. "We've got such an educated community here," she continues. "I don't think it's going to come to much. We've made a lot of progress lately. The gay bar used to be miles out of town, with no sign or anything. Now it's right on Broadway where everybody can see it."

She tells me that when she first came to Stephens she hid her private life from the students she works with. "You know," she says apologetically, "lesbian at a women's college and all that. But then later I did come out to a few people, and it was fine." It was fine with the students, she means, not with the administration.

"The college is holding this dance," she says, as if trying to convince herself. "That would never have happened a couple years ago." It almost didn't happen tonight—the

Lesbian Community Project was not allowed, as the dance's sponsor, to put its name on the fliers. "Too inflammatory," an official decided, so the fliers simply announce a "Rainbow Rumble," using a code that hopefully only the initiated will comprehend.

But no such luck. Vic arrives with a gaggle of terrified-looking Stephens students. I smile as she uses the stamp to mark *Positively Queer* in a dozen places up and down her arm. By contrast, the students move as if they were all roped together at the waist. Vic herds them from place to place, trying to introduce them to people. "How will they ever meet anyone?" she wails to me when she steps outside for a cigarette break.

Later I see her dancing with Vanessa, leading her in a slow waltz around the floor. Vanessa is half draped against Vic, while Vic moves regally, with a sure grace. I remember what she'd told me earlier. "Look, I'm so happy to finally be with someone who says not only I think you're an incredibly attractive woman—not some nongendered human being, but *woman*—but that I think it's fucking great that you're butch.

"It's incredibly destructive to our community to have to constantly compare ourselves to the straight community in terms of man/woman. We're our own beings. I get disappointed when people ask if we aren't perpetuating patriarchal myths, 'cause I don't think we are. I think we're screwing with them entirely."

As I watch Vic and Vanessa dance, I ponder our own myths. One is that we're a tight-knit community, able to gauge what we need to survive. Another is that our best chance lies in proving that not only are we completely innocuous but that *we're just like you*. All we've accomplished is to hamstring ourselves, defusing the diversity that is our greatest strength. Gay agenda? Gay chaos is more like it. But then again, we're only living our lives, not feeding a belief system.

An organizer hops on the stage and shouts into a microphone that every day she runs into lesbians who haven't heard a damned thing about the amendment. "The Right is dumping its theocratic crap on my front lawn, and frankly it's pissing me off!" she bellows. No one's really listening. Why should they? Few believe anything will happen. They think they're so inoffensive that the Right can't say a damn thing about them. As several people have explained to me that evening, they're not marching around in leather like people do in San Francisco. They're not demanding anything or breaking windows or having kiss-ins at the mall. They're just trying to hang on to those ever-so-elusive jobs.

The next morning, I realize how little we know each other when I take a shower and discover that the purple ink on my hand is impossible to remove. I'm certain that at that exact moment Nicole's mom is standing in her own steaming cubicle, water pouring on her bent neck as she scrubs at her skin harder and harder, frantically trying to erase the stamp that brands her *Positively Queer* at that job she can't afford to lose.

A couple months later, on the very day Lauren is graduating, I receive the current issue of *Family Voice*, the house magazine of Concerned Women for America, a right-wing organization headed by Beverly LaHaye. Pink letters on the cover read, "Militants Penetrate the Mainstream," and a superimposed pink triangle adorns the jacket of a young boy standing among a group of demonstrators. Inside are articles like "The Mainstreaming of Homosexuality," "Gays' Revenge: Recruiting Children," "Sex in Media Too Tame for Gays."

LaHaye writes in her editorial: "Homosexuality is a tragic choice for any man or woman. It is destructive to those who choose it, to their families, and to society. It is not a lifestyle that fulfills or satisfies anyone. What's more, it is neither honest—nor loving—nor helpful to tell homosexuals that they were created that way, which gives them permission to make demands on our society."

LaHaye's husband Tim, in his book *Everything You Need to Know About Homosexuality*, offers helpful advice to parents, reprinted in *Family Voice*: "Don't blow up. Accept him while rejecting his lifestyle. Don't take him to a psychiatrist. Participate in a Bible-believing church. Contact an ex-homosexual ministry [offering counseling for change]."

In "The Mainstreaming of Homosexuality," we learn, "And because same-sex couples cannot reproduce, until recently they have been content to recruit. But now homosexuals have devised a plan whereby they can actually reproduce children biologically . . . Those homosexuals who do not participate in this eugenics experiment continue to recruit. And their most vulnerable victims are children and teens."

It's only too possible Lauren's parents have leafed through *Family Voice*, watched *The Gay Agenda* at their church, listened to their minister preach against "the gay lifestyle." Why else would Lauren's mother be repeating that tired rhetoric about choice? I try to imagine how her parents will react to the friends who are journeying from Arkansas to join Lauren on her graduation day, something

Lauren was concerned about ("I was just thinking how open they are. I mean, if they're with their lovers, they wouldn't hide anything. They might be real obvious"), and how we, as gay people, so often find ourselves in the position of monitoring not only our own behavior but that of our friends and lovers.

And now the stakes have been raised. Ten or even five years ago, discovering your child was gay would rank somewhere between a disappointment and a tragedy—but the letdown would be personal, and with it would come a sense that the upheaval could be mended with time and love, with assurances that neither the schism nor the challenges were insurmountable. Since we've become so polarized and gays are portrayed as heinous monsters out to destroy home and hearth, if not democracy and freedom, it must seem to parents like Lauren's that not only has she joined the armed forces of another country, but that even as she pleads for peace and understanding, she wages war. What will they now think of Michelle, a woman they've loved for years as if she too were their child? Will they believe Michelle has recruited their daughter? To my mind, one of the greatest sins of the religious Right is in driving apart families like the Dreyers, creating a tragic and too often permanent rupture when in earlier days respect and love could forge a path of communication even on rocky ground.

Ultimately, Missouri's Amendment Coalition did not receive enough signatures to qualify the antigay amendment for the statewide ballot. In fact, out of nine states, in only two (Idaho and Oregon) did these busy folk collect sufficient signatures—and in both those states, the measures were voted down, though in Idaho, the proposition lost by only four thousand votes out of more than four hundred thousand votes cast. Could it be people are growing weary of the nonissue of "special rights"? Are people in Missouri, as the teacher at Stephens said, too well educated to be duped?

According to an analysis by journalist Arlene Zarembka, the efforts of the Amendment Coalition were partially undone by the lawsuit brought by Martha Carroll and others. Believing a ruling on the suit was imminent, the coalition postponed circulating petitions, only to be told in May that the suit would not be ruled upon unless enough signatures were gathered to warrant a decision. The coalition also received less financial support than expected, and hotel and tourist industry leaders expressed concern about the economic impact of a Colorado-style boycott on Missouri's convention business.

With a Republican Congress, the emphasis of the Right is likely to shift to the federal level—along with a continuing focus on the grass roots. School boards, city councils, and county boards are prime targets for takeovers. The Christian Coalition, which claims a million members, distributed 33 million pieces of literature in the '94 November elections, much of it through churches. An exit poll by the organization claims that religious conservatives counted for one third of all votes cast, compared to eighteen percent in 1988 and twenty-four percent in 1992.

Those least able to mount an offense, particularly the threat of economic boycott, will be the first to feel the sword of a right-wing jihad. And those least capable, of course, are those too young to benefit from the protection of the gay community. With HIV on the rise among teen-agers, we can't afford to erase our already minimal educational efforts, but it's likely that's exactly what will happen. Missouri is a victory in a war that should have been won yesterday if we expected there to be winners at all.

# of bars, sodomy, and demon doctors

just another day in cajun country

The intersection of Bourbon Street and St. Anne marks the DMZ between straight and gay America. Barely fifteen feet wide, large enough for a horse and a buggy to pass comfortably on the way down St. Anne toward the banks of the Mississippi, by day the intersection seems little different from others in the French Quarter of New Orleans. But at night the crossing forms a barrier for both traffic and the imagination. On one side is a pedestrian mall spanning several blocks of Bourbon, where drunken tourists reel from bar to bar, their slack or contorted faces lit garishly by neon and street lamp. But they pause at St. Anne, because across the way, on the other side of the traffic cones, lie the forces of darkness in the form of two gay bars, both flying rainbow flags, both blaring disco music, both with bodies literally falling out the many doors that open onto Bourbon Street.

It's comical to watch from the gay side as tourists meander up to the barricades, squinting into the darkness, perhaps wondering why so many others are hovering here rather than crossing the street. Then awareness dawns.

Mouths turn to whisper into ears, eyes get brighter, straining to see across the great divide. Women goad their boyfriends to cross. Families hold UN sessions on their side of the barricade, the parents trying not to let the children hear, the teenagers rolling their eyes at dumb old Mom and Dad.

The families invariably turn right, down St. Anne toward the river, where they'll find Cafe Du Monde and Jimmy Buffet's Margaritaville as well as a measure of safety in an increasingly dangerous French Quarter. Some of the couples about-face and head back into the light. But a few cross St. Anne to drift slowly by the bars, looking in with such curiosity you think they might burst.

Of course, all this scrutiny does not go unnoticed. "How does it feel to be an animal in the zoo?" a man asks me as I lean against the door frame, returning the stares from people on the street.

I want to tell him it's chilling but strangely exhilarating. It makes something familiar and often tawdry—hanging out in a gay bar—seem like a revolutionary act. I've been a Real Live Gay Person before, stared at with openmouthed fascination, but that was during actions or marches when I was consciously being queer. Here just living my life makes me an object of amazement. It could go to your head, I think. And never before have I seen such a stark reminder of just how wide the gap is, of how tremendous the consequence of crossing that line.

"our kids are pretty much out here."

"How can they stare at us like that?" Tony asks indignantly. He can't be over sixteen, and I'm more amazed that he's been in the bars than that he's noticed the incredulous looks.

" 'Don't feed or tease the straight people,' " Caroline Anchors says. Caroline is nineteen years old, in her freshman year at Xavier University, a black Catholic school in New Orleans. She came here because people back home in Philly told her Xavier had an excellent pre-med program, and Caroline's wanted to be a doctor since she was three. "We used that line in Philly," Caroline explains. "When they'd stare at us, we'd say that to 'em."

We are sitting in the front room—the only room—of the Lesbian and Gay Community Center, at the Saturday afternoon meeting of the youth group: three facilitators, observer me, and a few young people. Caroline comes in late, saying she had a feeling she ought to show up. Lucille comes early, dropped off by Mom. Bob rambles in, followed soon after by Tony, who, at age sixteen, does volunteer work for several gay-related organizations.

Earlier, the facilitators had treated me to a person-by-person rundown of everyone in the group, which meets once a week, always on Saturday: thumbnail descriptions are easy because since the group's inception six months ago, only fifteen people have attended. After looking at a flier, I can see why—it says anybody from age fifteen through seventeen needs a signed parental consent to attend each meeting. "This rule would eliminate practically the entire Berkeley group," I say.

"Oh, our kids are pretty much out here," says Brad Robbert. Then he hears himself. "Well, I guess the ones who come would have to be, wouldn't they?"

All three facilitators—Brad, Stephen Dunlevy, and Joan

Ladnier—have argued against the policy since day one. And they've debated whether the proviso has to go on the flier, in what size type it must be printed, and if a person has to have the consent at the very first meeting he or she attends. They've gotten nowhere with the legal counsel of the center. "Louisiana has a sodomy law," Brad explains. "The lawyer thinks we'll get charged with contributing to the delinquency of minors."

Whether delinquency is being encouraged on this fine Saturday afternoon is a matter of opinion. Bob, who is eighteen and therefore "safe" as far as liability goes, says his best friend came out to him when they were both sixteen. "I didn't speak to him for two weeks," he recalls. "I was fighting myself, trying to deny it. His coming out hit home closer than I wanted. But then I met this guy." He smiles. "When I kissed him, it all fell into place. I knew then what was right." He looks up at the ceiling. "My mom says she can't disinherit me 'cause I'm all she's got, but she hates it."

Lucille, the sixteen-year-old girl who came early, is ready to talk now that Bob has broken the ice. "My mother went through my gym bag and found letters from my girlfriend. She's suspected for two years. That's why the letters were in with my gym stuff—I figured that was one place she wouldn't look." Lucille's face is haggard, dark circles prominent under her eyes. The crisis began last week; Lucille has already gone to a Parents, Families and friends of Lesbians and Gays (PFLAG) meeting for support and met Tony, who is regarding her as anxiously as a hen might a chick venturing from the nest for the first time.

"She took all the phones out of the house except one in her bedroom," Lucille says. "That way I can't call Sue. And she drove over to Sue's parents' house and sat outside in her car so I couldn't go over there." Lucille chuckles. "I already had. She missed me by about three minutes. I had a chance to tell Sue what was happening before my mom showed up."

We're all drawn in by the drama, perched on the edges of our seats. "Then what?" we ask.

"My mom stormed in to talk to Sue's parents. Sue had come out to her father when she was fourteen, but her dad told my mom that he'd forgotten all about it. He said he hadn't taken it very seriously. He said he'd talk to Sue, though he still didn't think it was serious. He was telling the truth, see. He *doesn't* think it's serious even if we're together." But it develops that Sue is three years older than Lucille, a dangerous gap for both girls—Sue could be charged with contributing, and Lucille, as a minor, could be made a ward of the court or institutionalized. "My mom photocopied all the letters," Lucille says.

Brad and I glance at each other. Lucille doesn't seem to realize the implications and no one has the heart to tell her. When I make a minimal attempt, Lucille shakes her head— her mom is just upset. She'll calm down. "She's making me go to therapy," Lucille says. "She thinks I've been brainwashed." Mom *did* let her come to the meeting, we remind ourselves, and surely that's encouraging.

To shake ourselves free of gloom, everyone begins talking about the circus-like atmosphere on Bourbon and St. Anne. "Can anybody get into a bar?" I ask the sixteen-year-olds. Tony sounds like a veteran. "Oh, sure, anybody can get in."

"Even straight people," Bob grouses.

"It's good to be able to see members of the gay community," Tony says. "Even though I guess it isn't the best side. People puking in the street isn't particularly a good side."

Tony says that it was in a bar that he first saw people of the same sex kissing. "It was great. We were in these four walls, it was protection."

Caroline is so agitated her fingers draw patterns in the air. "I'm so sick of straight people coming in the bars 'cause they think it's cool. If I ask a woman to dance, and she gets all uptight . . . well, 'Hey, honey, you're in a gay bar.' "

Someone pounds on the door. It's Lucille's mom. "Bye," Lucille calls, waving courageously.

"I hope she comes back," Brad says sadly.

"I saw her at the PFLAG meeting," Tony reports. "She can keep going there anyway." No parental consent is needed at PFLAG.

"I hate this," one of the facilitators says. "We're not allowed to do outreach in the schools; we can't post the fliers; we can't put together an after-school or summer sports team . . ."

"Why not?" I ask.

"Too provocative. We have to maintain a low profile. The center's applied for funding on the basis of our offering youth services. If the youth services get cut because of controversy, the whole center might have to close because we can't exist just on donations."

"So the youth group is supposed to drive the center," I say, "but that means the youth group has to be kept squeaky clean."

"Which means we can't reach the kids who need help the most."

"And it's less controversial to have sixteen-year-olds

hanging around in bars than playing on a softball team," I conclude. It makes a revolting kind of sense. Presumably anyone in a bar is already lost, a denizen of that dark and mysterious land across the barricades. Besides, boozing and partying is what gay people *do*—if the kids were playing softball, a few straight people might be enticed to join in (like Lauren's friend at William Woods in Missouri wanting to "pretend" so she could play on the lesbian volleyball team). Then where would we be? All mixed up and not neatly restricted to our own side of the street.

And indeed, that's how the meeting ends. When the oldsters tune back in, we discover that the younger people are still complaining about straight people at the bars (seems those straight people just can't stay away, no matter how unhealthy the venue). "I've got the perfect solution," Bob announces proudly. "See, where I'm from, the bar's hidden under a railroad trestle, and it doesn't have a sign or anything. You can only find it word-of-mouth, so that keeps the straight people away."

It's all I can do to not burst out laughing. Back to the '50s we go. Perhaps the cops could return the bricks we tossed at them at the Stonewall too.

"I think there's a downside to that solution," Joan Ladnier says mildly.

"i got this little nickname, outmonster."

The next day I'm still upset about the youth group's self-imposed low profile. Reaching fifteen kids in six months in a city as large as New Orleans is truly pathetic, especially when several of those kids came in "preseasoned"—that is, from groups in other cities. Then I realize that in the eyes of the authorities, a scared kid is someone who could still be "saved." Better these kids are isolated and tormented and struggling—maybe they'll repent and "change their minds." And the powers-that-be at the Lesbian and Gay Community Center are more concerned with the survival of the institution as a whole than with challenging the assumptions of heterosexism or standing up for the needs of young gays and lesbians. What they've got now is as good as it's going to get, at least for a while.

As I was leaving the meeting, it occurred to me that no one checks the signatures of the parents—the kids can just sign the forms themselves. But gay and lesbian kids—who are often over-responsible and over-good, as if exemplary behavior can make up for who they are—rarely take the easy way out. When I truck out to Xavier to talk to Caroline that morning, she tells me of hassles attendees have had getting the forms signed. "This guy Kevin says every time he asks for the note on Saturday morning, he has to go through hell, he has a *huge* fight with his parents. Thank God he has his own car that he paid for with his own money, because there's no way he'd ever get out of the house." Kevin was described by the facilitators as very out and comfortable, a kind of good-cheer party boy who tries to help other kids adjust. He wasn't at the group I attended.

"Does he ever mention anything about this to the facilitators?" I ask.

Caroline shrugs. We are sitting on a stone bench in a pleasant grassy square surrounded by imposing buildings. Signboards are staked into the turf, each trumpeting the merits of a Miss Xavier candidate: "A phenomenal woman, defying odds and expanding opportunities," "A rose with substance, strength, and inner beauty." Unfortunately, the campus is flanked by Interstate 10, so freeway noise drowns out the birdsong and offers a Braqueish backdrop of ramps and interchanges to the green-surfaced tennis courts.

Caroline Anchors offers her own angular counterpoint to her more conservative schoolmates. A nineteen-year-old freshman, Caroline wears a shapeless patterned dress, a head scarf, long earrings, leather sandals—perfect attire for the West Village, but outlandish for a black Catholic college in New Orleans, where everyone, boy and girl, is smartly coiffed and turned out in conventional good taste.

Caroline's separateness is not limited to her clothes. She grew up in a Jewish suburb of Philadelphia, the product of two upper-middle-class black professionals who set a lot of store by the accomplishments of their children. Bright, energetic, articulate, and attractive, Caroline's one of the beautiful people—a girl who had two big challenges in high school: adjusting to her parents' divorce in her freshman year and dealing with her lesbianism. Luckily, being gay turned out to be pretty terrific—she loved her youth group, loved Woody's, the bar she frequented, loved the constant parties in and around Philly and the group house everybody hung out at. "We called it Frank's house, though other people lived there too. I swear, everybody who is gay and under the age of twenty-five in Philadelphia has been to Frank's house. It's just . . . it's just great. I'm ready to go back home now."

It took her a while to get to Frank's, of course. "I always liked women, but I got a name when I was in the fifth grade. This guy asked me, 'Are you a lesbian?' I'm like, 'What's a lesbian?' And he tells me that I'm going to go to hell and all these wonderful things. So I ran around and told everybody that I liked this one friend of mine who was a guy, so that nobody would think I was gay. It was incredible, I used to chase him home from school. To this day he still thinks I'm insane. His buddies would throw rocks at us. It was like so insane, because I knew why I was doing this. I knew.

"Then, in the seventh grade, I just sort of blocked it out and I became like asexual. These friends I'd run around with . . . if we saw people kissing in the hall, we'd mess with them. We were really mean. Not mean—"

"Sarcastic," I supply.

Caroline nods. "One of them finally came out. And all this stuff came back to me about liking girls when I was younger, and I'm like, 'Oh, no!' So I ran around trying to date guys. The last guy I dated was really handsome and really intelligent and a really great guy. So I'm like, 'If I don't like this guy, I've got to be gay.' We went out for three months and never touched each other. Finally I told him."

Then she told one of her teachers, who introduced her to another gay student, who in turn brought her to under-twenty-one night at Woody's. "I was so terrified. I didn't know what to wear, what to do, where to sit. I was around all these people I didn't know, and it was already like so formed . . . Everybody who goes into that club gets this attitude: 'I am Diva. Don't talk to me.' I was like, 'How do you get into these cliques?' But then I went to the youth group and I met all these people . . ." She laughs. "We had so much fun. And we didn't go out and drink. We never did. We'd have these parties. Like during Gay Pride, they were saying, 'Yay, gay youth! We really want you guys to march.' But all the parties were for twenty-one and over. So Frank opens up his house and gay people from all over Philly come, like two hundred or four hundred people and every-body knew everybody else."

When she tells me these stories, her face becomes ani-mated, and she laughs with delight at the antics of her pals. Her sojourn at Xavier is told much more haltingly. In the same way that Brandon revealed the information that he'd been thrown out of the dorm in Portland, Caroline delivers her litany of horrors in an almost offhanded manner, as if this next part isn't really important.

It took Caroline a while to catch on to the fact that she is persona non grata at Xavier, or perhaps something even worse. This is a testament not only to her basic self-esteem, but to her certainty that the East is the moral and ethical center of the universe.

"I didn't realize the first semester," she says. "I try and think the best of people until they really give me a reason. You kinda have to like slap me."

What happened was that Caroline, fresh from her gay youth group in Philly, blew into New Orleans cocky and content just to be herself—witty, intense, and wanting *real* interaction, not superficial chitchat. Why had she picked Xavier? She wanted to enlarge her family of choice: "I was like, 'I've lived in a white community all my life, and this is where I want to go.' This was my first choice school. Be-cause of the pre-med program. Because this was a black school."

A few things put her off right away, like the way sorori-ties chose people based on the lightness of their skin, and how Creoles were considered socially superior. "A lot of bullshit," Caroline says. During her orientation session, a teacher said of the French Quarter, "You'll see a lot of sights, see a lot of fags and sissies."

"I could not believe this," Caroline says. "In any other college, you woulda got slapped down so fast for that shit. You couldn't do that stuff in my *high school*."

While Caroline was having trouble getting used to Xavier, the other students were having trouble getting used to her. "This one girl . . . she's really popular. I told another gay person on campus that she's gay, and she like freaked out. She said, 'I told you, I'm not that free with my business.' I said, 'She's *gay*. I don't understand what your problem is.' I said, 'Listen, why do you *care*?'

"It happens that I bring people out whether they want to or not. Like, I mean, not necessarily to other people, but just out to themselves. In high school, I got this little nickname, Outmonster. I'm like, 'Come on, I know you're gay. Let's go here, let's go there.' "

Outmonster comes to Xavier, Xavier trembles but closes ranks with a vengeance. Early on in the first semester, Caroline gave a speech about going to the 1993 March on Washington and ended it with "That's why I'm proud to be a queer American."

"There's this whole black lesbian thing," she says now. " 'We don't want visibility. We don't want to be known. We want our lives to be very simple.' I heard from this straight friend that people were angry at me. She said, 'Most of them live off campus and they want their lives safe, and they're not happy about you saying stuff about them.' "

During that first semester, already branded a renegade, Caroline made friends with a fellow student named Naomi. Naomi's other friends soon made their displeasure felt, and Naomi finally cut the connection.

"Then they go to this party, and this whole bunch of drunk frat boys freaked out on them. One of them got up in

Naomi's face and started screaming at her, calling them a bunch of dykes.

"They came and woke me up at two in the morning to tell me about this. I was really tired, and there were like eight girls in the room, and they're really, really angry. So I'm like, 'Okay, I'm sorry this happened to you, but I don't see where I come in.' They sat there and screamed at me, 'I don't appreciate being called a dyke.' Naomi didn't say anything the whole time. All she said was, 'I was really scared he was going to hit me.' I felt so bad for her because her friends kept talking about dykes this, dykes that, and I just knew she was really upset.

"I never talked to them again. They'll sit right next to me and not say anything to me at all. If Naomi's not around them, she'll talk to me. If she's with them, she acts like she doesn't know me."

By December, Caroline was effectively frozen out, and by March '94, when I met her, she was enduring the Xavier version of a West Point silencing: she eats by herself, studies by herself, talks to hardly anyone. Just the day before, after she'd gotten her tray, she realized there were no empty tables in the cafeteria. "All these people were looking at me because they knew I didn't have a seat. I said to the person who runs the cafeteria, 'Can I have a takeout? I don't have anywhere to sit.' And he's like, 'There's a whole bunch of seats.' I said, 'I can't sit there.' He said, 'Sorry.' So I had to sit with these girls who were none too happy to have me at their table. It's kind of bad."

This is the understatement of the year. Women clutch themselves when she passes in the hall. People talk about her loudly and then inform her when she confronts them that their conversation is private. Gay students won't speak to her even if they run into her in the Quarter, and straight students, protecting those "at risk," gather round their gay friends to proclaim them untouched by Caroline's peculiar contagion. The sickness analogy is apt, because more than anything else, Caroline is treated as a foreign body which must first be isolated and then cast out. After all, she's committed an unpardonable sin: saying she's queer, naming others, and acting like none of it matters. "I thought I was such a hard-ass when I came here that it wasn't going to bother me. And it does, you know," Caroline tells me sadly.

Her loneliness is excruciating. She hasn't dated anyone since she came South, hasn't touched anyone or had anyone touch her. "It's hard," she says simply. She pauses and looks off toward the tennis courts. "There's no place to meet people. The youth group, they're all men. And Charlene's [lesbian bar], they're really a lot older. I went to this birthday party, and there were all these black professional women. I was really impressed, but I mean, they were upward of like thirty. It's like, 'You've got a job and a car and you're gonna deal with somebody with no money and no car? C'mon, that's a drag.'"

Her sister, ten years her senior, tried to warn her. "She said, 'Are you sure you want to go there, because it's black, it's Catholic, and you grew up in this white, mostly Jewish environment.'" This wasn't the first time Caroline had worried her sister. When Caroline was in high school, her sister consulted her gay buddy: "'She's coming out that early. Is she okay?' In high school, everything was cool. She's like, 'All right, but you better not come out in college.' And I'm like, 'Oh, why not?'"

When she went home during Christmas, her friends in

Philly chanted, "Transfer, transfer!" One friend advised her to get out immediately. "He told me, 'It's gonna get worse. It's gonna get a lot worse.' He's from Florida. And he's telling me, 'You didn't grow up in a black community like I did. I know black people. They're not gonna take it. They're not gonna be able to handle it.' I don't know," she concludes. "It's just very, very different.

"Now I'm worried. I didn't make this decision [to transfer] until it might be too late to apply. Bryn Mawr has early admissions."

"Do you feel like you have to not go to a black school?"

"Yeah, and that sucks because I've always been very pro both my communities. It's not like they're separate from each other either. Some people have gotten the courage to come up and ask me stuff. And they're like, 'That's white people's business.' I start naming people to them, Langston Hughes and James Baldwin and Bessie Smith. And they're like, 'That's bullshit.' People don't want to see. And I'm like, 'Well, you can say it's white to be gay, but when you think about it, it's actually white to be homophobic. Gays weren't a big problem with cultures in West Africa, they were a part of our community.'

"So it just really makes me upset, that they can say stuff like dyke and faggot right in class. That they can use it in a speech and the teachers say absolutely nothing. This is how this stuff continues!" The last time someone said faggot in class, Caroline stood up and gave her own speech. And when some guys in her biology lab were knocking gays, she barreled in over their objections that she should mind her own business: "If you're in a room full of white people and you overhear somebody say something about 'nigger this

and nigger that,' wouldn't you jump up and say something?" She closes her eyes for a moment. "I wanted to get
organic chemistry out of the way before I transferred. But I
can't stay here for another year."

A nun comes by and says hi, the first person to speak to
us in several hours. A number of people have wandered by
to stare at us, and I worry that my presence is making it
worse for Caroline. Caroline brightens at the nun's greeting
and says hi back, then introduces me as a writer from California. A little later a student says hi. She's really only curious, and I suspect someone dared her to find out why Caroline's talking to a woman with a tape recorder. Caroline's as
cheery with the student as she was with the nun.

Seeing her bewilderment, watching her attempts at
good-heartedness and civility as people are being thoroughly odious to her, brings back painful memories. I was
given a choice in the spring semester of my junior year in
college: live off-campus and speak to no one once I'd walked
through the gates, or take a senior year away and graduate
with my class. I had no intention of being treated like a
pariah just because they'd discovered I was a lesbian, so I
chose the latter option. Now, twenty-five years later, Caroline isn't offered a choice—she is simply demonized. When
I see how young she is, how vulnerable, I begin to understand my own history, to forgive myself for morbidly dwell-
ing on that episode in my life. At the same time, I'm devastated that anybody is still enduring this kind of agony.

"I'm so sorry this is happening to you," I tell her when I
stand up to leave. She shrugs again and looks down at the
ground, blinking back tears. When she looks up again, her
eyes are determined. Caroline Anchors is no weakling. As
long as she can remember what it's like in the real world, in

Philly with her friends, she'll be all right. She just needs to get out of New Orleans . . .

I talk to Caroline again in May. She'd been thinking of calling me, she says. She sounds a little hysterical. When I first met her, getting her to admit anything was wrong was like pulling teeth. Now she's breathing too hard and I can feel her shaking through the phone. She went to talk to the admissions people at Bryn Mawr, she reports. They were very sympathetic. She hopes they'll accept her. In any case, she can leave Xavier soon. Very soon. A couple weeks, that's all.

Then the floodgates burst. She was attacked in her room. Just two days ago, early Friday morning. Two girls. They threatened her. They pushed her around, screamed at her. She had a chemistry final at 8 A.M. She didn't sleep after the girls left, stayed up crying and freaking out. She's sure she failed her test. Do I think she should call Bryn Mawr to tell them why she's going to get a bad grade in chemistry?

No, I say. Maybe you didn't do as badly as you fear. Has she reported any of this? Has anyone helped?

She reported some of it, she says. A week earlier two different women threatened her in the hall, telling her they were going to mess her up. She went to the dean about them. Then the two from Friday asked the dorm mother to "tell that bitch we're gonna get her." The dorm mother dutifully relayed this threat to Caroline, and that night they shoved into her room, yelling that they were going to kill her. Why?

" 'We're guilty by association,' " Caroline repeated, her voice full of wonder. "They kept saying that, over and over. I don't run with these girls. How could I make them guilty? Some fraternity guys called them dykes last fall and they've never gotten over it. They said, 'We already told you this is a black Catholic school. We're not ready for no marches or revolution. So just shut up your ass.' "

"They want you in the closet."

"Right," Caroline says. "And that is exactly what I cannot do."

Cannot do because the Caroline who has sustained her through all this misery is proud and out. Cannot do because she might as well live free or die. Cannot do because she'd be bowing to the worst and killing off the best.

"I can't believe how naïve she is," says the Texan who transcribed Caroline's tapes for me. "I'm surprised she hasn't gotten herself shot. She's in the *South*. She doesn't seem to know what that means. People get shot for being *Methodist*."

But how could she have known? Coming from where she did, from a protected and protective environment, how could she have imagined that she—brilliant, funny, incisive—could set off a virtual nuclear meltdown in the land of the conservative black elite?

Caroline is too much of an anomaly for anyone but the top administration to support. The dean of student housing was sympathetic, but even she said, "To have them [the perpetrators] kicked out of the dorm is a little harsh, don't you think? I'm sure you don't want this on their records."

"I don't think she realizes how serious this is," Caroline says. I can feel her shaking all the way to California.

Did anything precipitate the altercation in her room? Well, she'd given a talk about homophobia in her speech class the day before, but she doesn't think that had anything to do with it. Her teacher graded her down on it because she didn't include psychiatric opinions on homosexuality. "I told him my subject was homophobia, not homosexuality," she says. "He said I was going to get a lower grade anyway. Don't you *really* think I should call Bryn Mawr?"

"i just gotta date as many guys as possible."

In mid-May, just as Caroline is preparing to escape New Orleans, I'm heading back to Louisiana, to the west this time. As I cross the border from Texas, I heave a sigh of relief: I like the informality of Louisiana, the way people pull over on the highway and break out their fishing rods. It's a state full of renegades, where people truly do leave you alone. At least that's what I *think*. Neely Boudier sees it differently. "I thought havin' a fiancé would shut up all the rumors," she says, shaking her head. "Even if he *is* in college. But they say I just got rid of 'im so I could be with Star." She stares thoughtfully out at the river a few miles south of Lafayette, at the shimmers of heat dancing above the edgy blue water. We've set up shop halfway down the long grassy bank; cars whiz by on the road above us, trailing an occasional wail of a radio. "Seems like it almost made it worse."

I've been writing to Neely for months. She told me about the fiancé, about the gay guy who took her to the prom, that she was bisexual. Never once did she tell me about Star, and yet Star has been the subject of discussion since moment one of my arrival. Star, I learn, is very difficult. Star has moods. Star throws fits. Soon I will meet Star.

I asked Neely if I could interview her in December 1993. I heard about her from a girl in San Francisco who periodically sends Neely care packages of gay literature. When Neely was sixteen, she sought out a gay pen pal service and was given my friend's address. The two have been corresponding ever since. Most of Neely's other gay pen pals are closer to home—Texas and Arkansas and Missouri.

As a fish breaks the surface of the river and flops back down in a lazy spiral, I remember Neely's last lines to me: "Well, I still don't have a girl. I do, however, want one." I wonder if she's let on to her other correspondents about Star, with whom she's been involved for two tumultuous years.

In January, Neely sent me a letter in fancy script saying she had decided she didn't want to be interviewed. "I think it would be safer if I didn't at this moment," she wrote, and noted that both her best friend and "a second opinion" had corroborated her decision. The best friend lives in Texas, the second opinion is her fiancé whom she despises, and I can't get an answer from her about whether Star's angry that Neely eventually consented to the interview. "Star is always angry," Neely says.

In her March change-of-heart letter, Neely wrote: "There were reasons why I couldn't do it. One was, my best friends that know told me that if I was found out . . . you know. Well, secondly, I had no transportation to meet you. Third, I was just a little scared about all the legal formalities that may be floating around . . . I've finally come to the conclusion that if I follow my best friends' advice, then I won't be leading my own life . . . It would be what they want me to do and not what I want to do."

I too was conflicted as I set off again to Louisiana. Despite that line about wanting a girl, her letters had become increasingly full of news about her prom dates and her fiancé. It occurred to me that she might have been so lonely she was *pretending* to be gay so I would continue writing her, and now that we were finally about to meet, she'd realized the truth would come out and she wanted to prepare me. But the real story is far more complicated and sinister than simple loneliness, though deep inside, where she can hardly get at herself, Neely must be immeasurably, horribly lonely.

But now she's shifting her lean body, offering another angle to the sun. Even though it's only May, and even though she works practically every minute she's not in school, she's building a good tan. "It's my Indian heritage," she says. "French and Irish and Indian. By the way, you don't have to disguise my physical appearance. Everybody in Lafayette looks alike—it's 'cause we're all related." With her curly, auburn-highlighted hair, blue eyes, and upturned nose, she's adorable, and she knows it. Just eighteen, finishing up her junior year at Acadiana High School in Lafayette, she flounces around like a latter-day Scarlett O'Hara, but with an Annie Oakley twist—she's what I'd call a tomboy femme.

"When I was about fifteen, my mother said, 'Well, you need to quit playin' with the boys. They're gonna think you're chasing them.' So I went and made friends with the girls. Then after about six months, I got tired of it, and I went back and started playing pool and everything else again, like we used to. I still don't know half of them girls to this day.

"I never wanted to get married," she says. "I never wanted kids. I just wanted to grow up, be a doctor, get my dog and my truck and live happy." Living happy does not mean living alone, and it was imagining the future that tipped Neely off to her sexuality. "The thought of coming home from a hard day's work at the hospital and saying, 'Honey, I'm home!' and seeing a guy standing there . . ."

Her face is full of gloom. "It was just like, 'Now what?' Seeing a girl there was a lot better for me. So I finally decided, 'Okay, that's what it is.' But our school is real prejudiced about that. They don't mind black people, but it's just . . . they don't like *that* at all."

To say Neely is in the closet is so minimizing that it's misleading. She is in multiple closets, on multiple levels, and some of them have mirrors and others don't. Her day-to-day existence occurs in the interstices of "don't ask, don't tell," a charade gay people have played for generations, and its self-denying flip side, "don't tell *ME*." As she grows older, and adult responsibilities and desires intrude, it becomes harder and harder to confine herself to all the right little boxes.

She is a dutiful daughter: "My mother's given up a lot for me. I owe her everything." She is a good Catholic: "God knows everything, so why would God allow me to be born this way if it's wrong?" And she's a responsible worker, a loyal Louisiana girl ("I don't understand how you can live where you can't eat good"), and a warmhearted friend who really listens when you talk.

Getting from where she is now—in hiding even from herself—to shouting "Honey, I'm home!" to that imaginary girlfriend is the part that's confounding her. First there's her senior year to be negotiated. Then there's the college in nearby Lake Charles that offers a nursing degree. Once she gets her RN, she'll apply to medical schools out-of-state. It will only be then that she can let down her guard. "I can't come out here because of the doctors," she explains.

With their letters of recommendation, the doctors can make or break her medical career, and apparently each is more outrageously homophobic than the next. "You should hear them," she says, rolling her eyes. Neely works as an admitting clerk at the hospital, gathering valuable experience and the inside dope on hate. "You should hear what they say about AIDS. If they knew . . ." She shudders. "And lotsa their kids go to Acadiana. The kids might let on about me to their parents if they knew." So she tries to squelch the rumors at school, but her efforts sound as successful as fighting a forest fire with a broom.

Neely goes to Whisper's, the gay bar in Lafayette, almost every weekend. But she's always with her pal Henry, who is also totally in the closet, so everyone at the bar thinks they're a couple, especially after they arrived late one Saturday night decked out in their prom finery. Neely does nothing to correct that impression. "They don't talk to me 'cause they think I'm straight," she says. Does Star go to the bar? "Star's too young," Neely says.

Star sent Neely a huge bunch of roses just last week, Neely confides—right to the information desk yet! Neely had to snatch the card away and tell the nurses the roses were from a guy who's been pursuing her. All the nurses were abuzz, because everyone knows about John, the college-going fiancé who zooms back to see her every chance he gets and who *is* furious that Neely is talking to me. "As if this is gonna make me gay," she says scornfully. "Like if I go watch *Gone with the Wind*, I'm gonna become straight again."

Her schoolmates are more perceptive than the nurses. "We can hear 'em talking about us in the halls. The people they basically aim it at is this boy and me and Star. So we flirt with guys to keep 'em guessing." Fiancé John is supposed to contribute to the heterosexual assumption, but Neely is hard put to erase the contempt from her voice whenever she speaks of him. "Everybody's like, 'Well, why did you date him in the first place?' See, I had Star on my back. She's the type where she really gets into hugging and stuff, and with all these people around here, I'm constantly watching out for the doctors and everything. I wanted to hold back, so he was just there."

I'm trying to keep it all in my head while a part of me is distracted by this stuff about the doctors. Is she paranoid or what? And it sounds like all the gay people in town think she's straight and all the straight people in town think she's gay. Who's kidding whom? And how come she never told me about Star?

Neely flips over again like a pancake on a griddle and starts talking about how hard it is to find those elusive girls she wants. "With women, you can't tell which ones are gay and which ones are straight," she complains, stroking her flat stomach, "unless they're actually at Whisper's. It's like learning another language. You're kind of frustrated until you get the gist of it, you know?"

"So you haven't had a relationship?"

"No."

"Does Star want a relationship?"

"She considers us dating, but I don't. I mean, I get jealous when guys come up and try to have a relationship with her. But when she goes to do something, I can't. Not with her. There's other girls that I would, gladly, but with her I can't. I'm just not attracted to her."

"That's awkward," I say sympathetically, thinking the other girls are more desirable only because they're safely unattainable.

"But it's her I'm gonna be stuck with," Neely says with a smile. "I'm gonna be old and gray in my rocking chair and she's going to be wheeling herself across the porch, trying to beat me to death with her cane." Her smile is edging toward the beatific. "She's going to be arguing and complaining . . . You watch. It's gonna happen."

As she talks, she keeps glancing up at the road above us. It develops that she's worried that her mother might drive by, glance out the window, and recognize her daughter, who at this moment is supposed to be out shopping with Star. This particular shopping expedition is going on a little too long, Neely realizes, and she better get home. Meeting me tomorrow will be complicated, because her mother wants her around, but Neely has a plan that involves taking her mother on a long early morning walk to exhaust her, then inventing another shopping spree with Star, necessary since today's travails yielded nothing.

As I listen, I'm wondering why, at age eighteen, she's still accounting for every hour to her mother. Neely's got her own questions. Would I like to meet Star? Can Star come along tomorrow? Sure and yes, I say, as long as I can talk with Neely for a bit beforehand. That's fine, Neely says, and gives me inexplicable directions to Whisper's in case I want to go—it's unlikely I'll see her there since, in spite of the early walk with Mom, she won't hit the bar until midnight at the earliest. She has to find a ride 'cause "my mom will let me drive to anywhere on this godforsaken earth, but she won't let me drive to 'that fag bar.' People are like, 'Why don't you sneak?' But she's given up so much. She had to raise me, I'm not gonna lie to her."

The next day, over lunch at a Cajun restaurant, I ask her what would be different if she were straight. Her imagination doesn't extend beyond marrying the fiancé she loathes. Well, does she feel she's missed out on anything? "No, 'cause regular straight people, some of *them* don't even date people, because they're waiting for this or that. And I've always got Star there, dragging me around." She smiles and tells a long story about how she yanked off Star's bikini top and ran off with it so Star had to cross a public road barebreasted. "Oooo, she was so mad!"

Which leads Neely to admit she really *is* attracted to Star, but then why does she pull away every time Star tries to kiss her? And when Neely starts to kiss Star, "I just quit, for some reason. And I don't know what it is. I don't know if it's that I'm scared or what. Even if she just wants to kiss like, you know, regular, I can't. I don't understand it. I sit there and I think, 'Why?' "

We are both aware that the moment to meet Star is fast approaching. Neely has hardly touched her catfish étouffée, and the concerned waitress has come by several times to ask if anything's wrong with it. After she refills my iced tea, I ask Neely one of my stock questions, what she fears about being gay. Unlike some kids, who seem surprised that I'm asking, Neely can tick her fears off on her fingertips: "The biblical aspect. And my mother. I know she would love me anyway, but I would probably have to be celibate while she's alive, to make her happy. And then, the last thing, the doctors. In New Orleans, it would be fine. But while I'm here, I wouldn't be able to work anywhere. So I just gotta date as many guys as possible."

But I'm stuck on point two. "Would you really be celibate for your mother?"

"That's a good, really hard idea, because she's given up a lot for me." Neely's mom raised her alone in a small rented house near the downtown mall where she works as a hairdresser, and Neely worships the ground she walks on.

About five years ago, her mother's lifelong diabetes became more debilitating, and she's had several operations. Each time she missed work for a month or more, so Neely's contribution is necessary to keep the family intact. Her mom also suffers from high blood pressure, and Neely's afraid of what will happen if she finds out Neely is a lesbian.

"She must suspect," I say.

"She's asked me but I told her I wasn't." Neely stares at her hands. "There've been times I wanted to tell Momma about me, but it's just . . . I know it would be a shock to her system. I want to wait until the right time. But if I wait too long and she, you know, she dies, she'll never really have known me."

We're sitting in a restaurant with Neely staring at her uneaten food and me wishing I had something more to say than no matter how deeply you love someone, you can't buy a life by erasing your own. But that does not get at the heart of Neely's fear—that she will lose her mother. She hopes to strike a bargain with this quixotic God who makes people gay but doesn't want them to sleep with each other—I'll keep the girls at bay as long as you let Mom live. I'm thinking Star has as much chance with Neely as that snowball does in hell when Neely glances at her watch: "Oh, we've got to leave right now. We're supposed to be there in five minutes!"

As we speed out to another river, this time north of town, Neely tells me she decided last week that she had to break up with her fiancé. He is so truly awful that she can't take him anymore, she says, and anyway, he's not serving his purpose as a cover. Star writes him letters implying Neely is dating other boys "just to screw with his head," but even poor John realizes Star is Neely's main squeeze—as does everyone else. "They all gossip about us," Neely says. "It's gone on now for at least a year and a half, and it keeps getting worse. They ask if we're going to the prom together or if I'm jealous of some guy Star's dating . . . I just can't understand why they're saying all this stuff—I mean, even though it's true—but how do they *know*?"

As we pull into the dusty parking lot, Star is leaning on the fender of her car, arms crossed, a scowl on her face. But when Neely emerges from my rented Sundance, she has to suppress her grin. "We just got talking," Neely explains to Star's shrug. Star, who is even skinnier than Neely, has dark hair cut in a close-fitting cap, long-lashed brown eyes, and a single stud through her right earlobe. She's wearing jeans and a blue and red striped T-shirt. She sizes me up and dismisses me in a second. My potential as a rival seems the extent of her interest, though in later letters, Neely is always careful to add that Star has said hi.

No puzzle how anyone knows: the dynamics between the two of them are so obvious I'm surprised Neely's mom hasn't wised up, but then I guess denial can work for her as well as for Neely. Star is a year and a half younger, but clearly the ringleader with her temper and her moods. As we start walking toward a distant river, the two quickly forget about me and start doing what comes naturally to people who are dampening down their sexual energy but still can't keep their hands off each other—they begin punching and teasing and pushing, with Star's resentment on simmer, always ready to come to a boil. "Oh, we fight," Neely turns to tell me, just after she's caught Star a good one on her calf.

"Do we ever," Star agrees. She shoves her dark hair away from her forehead—apparently *she*'s not related to

Neely—and skewers me with big brown eyes. I suspect she'd be a very funny person if she weren't so frustrated by Neely.

Neely tells me that Star is pursued constantly by boys. "And it makes you jealous," Star says. Neely admits this is true, that certain boys drive her into a rage. The boys, I decide, must be heavy into self-immolation because Star would offer them nothing but scathing criticism and put-downs. Maybe it's a relief from girls on the marriage hunt, or perhaps they find her a challenge.

The two tell me a long fable about yard dogs and then, embarrassed, cast me sidelong glances and ask if we have alligators in California. We have sea lions, I tell them. They want to know what we eat out there on the coast. Nothing sounds appealing—they'll stay right here, thanks. Neely's mum about the future in Star's presence, and I suspect there are taboo topics aplenty: careers, education, travel, relationships, pretty much everything that doesn't relate to day-to-day interactions, or at most a couple weeks off. Neely's vision of their future together picks up again at age eighty, when sexuality between them is presumably a dead issue, when they can be together in the old age home without all that damn gossip. The sixty-some years between now and then is a vast and terrifying plain of im/possibility.

As we turn back up the nature trail we've been meandering along, Star allows that Neely will look nice in a shroud.

"What's that supposed to mean?" Neely asks.

"I drove past your mom on the way here," Star says, examining her fingernails. "She saw you weren't in the car. You better start thinking up an excuse or you're dead meat."

Neely stands stock-still—even the mosquitoes stop humming. "I'll say you dropped me off at Wal-Mart and went somewhere else," she says.

"Why would I dump you at Wal-Mart and then go outside the city limits?" Star asks reasonably.

"I'll say you drove me home first," Neely says.

"But your mom was probably going home. You're not there now, are you?"

"I'll think of something," Neely says desperately. It's only when she seems about to cry that Star relents.

"I *did* see her," Star confides, "but she didn't see me."

"Are you certain?"

"Certain. She drove right on by."

Neely practically faints in relief as a triumphant smile crosses Star's face. But tormenting Neely can't always substitute for being able to love her. And how long can Neely keep herself suspended in that deep freeze of a closet, never advancing beyond mid-adolescence when adult choices must be made? Because Star is so undeniably in her life, Neely must either acknowledge Star's real role or function in a strange netherworld of half-lies where one never grows up, dates never become relationships, and friendships are all built on artifice.

With these two, that old if-they-were-straight exercise takes on fresh teeth: mothers would not be in danger of keeling over, doctors would not be a threat right up there with Saddam Hussein, roasting in hell wouldn't be the next step after fun and games in the old age home, school wouldn't be an exercise in useless camouflage, and boys might be friends rather than foils. They would be dating someone they liked and kissing someone they loved rather than holding their noses through intimate acts with people they'd rather share a pizza with. But the memory I'm left with as I drive up to Houston to catch my plane home is Neely so perplexed, so terrified by something as simple and natural as love.

queer high and the house of bazaar

Mention Harvey Milk High School to anybody gay or lesbian and watch the rapture spread. "A gay high school? God, I would have given anything to go there!"

"Hasta be in New York, right? They've got everything!"

"You could talk in the halls, go to the prom, *be* someone."

Though the discomfort of feeling invisible in high school is not limited to gays and lesbians, it seems logical that a high school just for gay kids would begin to address the problem. And an all-gay school should also solve the difficulty of too *much* visibility. As ostracized Xavier University freshman Caroline Anchors says, "In a gay school, you'd be able to do all those normal things that everybody else does, like dating, without having it be a big political thing."

So everyone was shocked and disappointed when I revealed the terrible truth: that Harvey Milk High is head-quartered in a wing at Manhattan's Hetrick-Martin Institute, the nation's best-known social service agency for gay youth, and for reasons both physical and philosophic, it serves a maximum of thirty kids.

No leafy campus, no crowds of boisterous teens roiling down the hallways, no supportive counselors and teachers, no peals of laughter amid banging lockers, no same-sex proms. "Humans are ever hopeful," a friend of mine sighed, after describing this vision of a paradise that doesn't differ much from the standard variety, an experience most people, gay or straight, recall with dread. What I came to call "the Harvey Milk wet dream"—and I was equally guilty of indulging in these flights of fancy—is a good indication of just how alienated we are; when we can convince ourselves we would have loved high school if only it'd been queer, we're deep in Never-Never Land.

The people at Hetrick-Martin, however, are in the business of reality. When I described Queer High to Frances Kunreuther, HMI's executive director, she labeled it not only a fantasy, but most likely a dangerous and classist one at that. "We don't live in a gay society," she says. "Ninety percent of the population is straight. If we don't help students integrate into the straight community, I just don't know. They aren't going to have the option to have separate businesses. Sometimes I laugh at people who go to college with their gay organizations and their gay dorms and then they come to work here. It's not real to think everybody can work in that world."

I make the women's college argument, that four years of a sheltered, nurturing environment provides girls with such strength and self-esteem that they burst forth at graduation confident enough to take on the universe.

"But women's colleges are mostly for elite people," Frances argues. Then she shrugs. "There are different models. There's no one answer to the issue, which is discrimination and prejudice. And it ain't getting solved fast in this society, at any level, no matter what minority you are."

Frances is in her early forties; she keeps a busy schedule giving speeches to civic groups and squiring dignitaries around Hetrick-Martin's chaotic complex. She has to look good to straights and real to gays and be hard-nosed and charming all at once. Since I can reliably accomplish only one of these tasks, I'm impressed. "Most of the young people call up and say, 'I'm gay or I'm lesbian, can I come to your school?' And we say, 'What's the problem?' 'Well, it's not really a problem, but I'd like to go to a gay school.' We don't take those people."

"Why not?" I ask, thinking how hard it would be to make that call.

"Because we're really a school for hard-to-reach youth. We're not a regular high school. We're an alternative school. And we do believe that, both for the youth and also for the system, the gay and lesbian youth should stay where they are. We should be changing the system to accept them, not pulling them out of the system for their own school. That to me is really going backward—separate but equal.

"So we go into the school. We'll talk to the principals, talk to the teachers, talk to the youth. I'd rather try to change the school and make it acceptable for that younger person.

"Also, we can't go on the middle-class model about how

you leave your family to come out. We work with young teenagers of color who don't have a lot of resources. A lot of them won't go to college, they'll live at home. They don't want to give up their communities. So if Hetrick-Martin is not in the community, we're not doing our job."

Harvey Milk High is the darling of the media; in spite of Caroline's dream, its students are ultravisible. "It's like going to school in a fishbowl," says Andy Humm, Hetrick-Martin's policy coordinator. "We have to protect the kids from constant interview requests and people wanting to take tours." But the school is only part of Hetrick-Martin's mission. The agency, begun in 1979 by A. Damien Martin of New York University and his partner, psychiatrist Emery S. Hetrick, supports several other programs: an after-school drop-in center that shares space in the high school wing; counseling services on-site and by phone for crisis calls that come in nationwide; Project First Step, an outreach center for street kids that provides clothing, showers, hot meals, and referrals to shelters; an education and training arm that sends staff members and youth into schools and institutions throughout metropolitan New York; and an advocacy project that's developing an agenda for sexual minority youth, distributing literature to social welfare agencies about sexual minority youth, and supporting HIV/AIDS education for all youth. Such a huge public education and outreach effort did not exist before HMI came along to do it.

When I ask Frances what's changed for gay youth since '79, she says she can't speak to that, but then she relents: "It's remarkably different and remarkably the same. In '79 just to come out as a gay or lesbian youth was so daring. For a fifteen-year-old to be open about her sexual orientation, to talk about it, to meet people . . . it was almost inconceivable. That's really changed. It's easier for people to come out and to come out in a way that's less painful. But it's the same in that people still go through an enormous amount of isolation. There's also the reaction of the religious Right; the backlash is part of what's changed. And families still don't get it, even the most liberal families . . ."

She tells me about a speech she gave at a chapter of the ACLU. "Now these are very liberal liberal liberal . . ." She runs out of words. "The first guy says, 'I think bringing up the issue of gays and lesbians in high school is persuading them to go into a lifestyle, that you could have tipped them the other way. How could they really know their sexual orientation at that age?'

"These are not bad people," Frances assures me. "These are good people."

I don't tell her about the good people proselytizing outside the City in Portland every Friday and Saturday night; as much as we'd like to believe it, "good people" does not equal allies, because good people don't seem to empathize any more easily than bad people. Frances echoes that thought with a sigh. "Being gay is such a difficult concept for people to understand."

The main focus of HMI, Frances says, is to work within the family and the community. "These kids are not going to leave their families to come out, unless they're on the streets, and that's not the way we'd prefer their coming out." A great deal of counseling is done by phone, since parents typically refuse to come to HMI. Kids can receive counseling over the phone or at the facility. "There are a lot of young people who are closeted in our community, and we don't necessarily encourage them to come out if that's the way they need to survive. We do a danger assessment to see if it's safe for them to come out.

"It's tough to handle if someone is not in their gender-appropriate role. There's a certain toleration level. A little bit of a sissy boy in the gay community, that's fine. You can be a butch girl. But we have youth who are beyond those lines, and they have the hardest time. They just really cannot hide."

Unless, of course, they can pass. "We have some not-gender-conforming kids who pass at the school," Frances says. "One gave a presentation to our board of directors, and I'm sure they thought she was a girl." A fleeting smile crosses her face. "It's very tough on those youth. The families really don't know what to do. If they're conforming, that's something they can hang on to.

"I think the gay movement is both adult- and youth-oriented in a very bizarre way," she adds. "We either objectify youth or we ignore them. We have a hard time figuring out how to integrate them, how to be appropriate role models and set boundaries. I get so mad at people who say, 'Well, they can handle themselves. They have a lot of power as teenagers.' That's bullshit. You don't feel like you have power when you're nineteen."

Hetrick-Martin is at Astor Place, a few steps from a subway station, a welcome change from their dingy old location out on the West Side Highway. Enter the Astor Place building's elevator any afternoon and you'll vanish into that roiling mob of kids—though diminished in size—I fantasized for

Queer High. The girls are roughhousing, the boys are more aloof, casting a disdainful eye at the antics of the uncouth girls. Once upstairs, however, the boys enter into the spirit of HMI's after-school program, which includes a lot of sharing stories, pouring back and forth past the heavy door that guards the entrance to the Harvey Milk School wing, and darting in and out of the building (always via the ever busy elevator) to grab a hot dog or a soda or just run around.

Meanwhile, HMI is conducting all its other services, so phones are ringing off the hook, adults are being toured through the facilities, Harvey Milk students are engaged in their own after-school activities, and staff members who, taken together, are a wonderful example of the continuum of gender are themselves slamming in and out of the elevator and the doors to the inner offices or to the school. This is just what takes place to the right and center as you exit the elevator. Off to the left is the separate wing where a stream of street kids, counselors, and staff is buzzed into Project First Step. The lobby, then, is a scene of constant chaos, and for me, unused to large gay-operated and -staffed institutions, it has a fairy-tale quality about it as well, a "You mean we can do this too?" air.

The racial mix reflects the New York metropolitan area: HMI says it serves forty-five percent African-American, thirty-five percent Latino, five percent Asian and Native American, and fifteen percent white. This breakdown doesn't do justice to the reality of island lilts, accents, and racial and ethnic blending that make determining race not only difficult but spurious. One might say that about the gender breakdown too, given the number of boys in drag and makeup (which looks hastily applied to me but is apparently simply casual, as opposed to the real jobs at night). But since the girls are hanging around in big clumps and not mixing much with the guys, it soon becomes obvious that there are more boys (sixty-five percent to thirty-five percent), and that part of how the girls maintain territory in a largely male space is to stick together.

"We're much better than we used to be," Frances tells me. HMI has tried various methods of appealing to girls, like hiring female interns and making a game of reducing the amount of campy bitchiness boys can indulge in during groups—what is perceived as an amusing give-and-take by the boys seems a universal turnoff for girls, driving them away in the space of a couple meetings. "But it's also much harder for girls to get out after school," Frances explains. "Girls simply don't have the freedom that boys do."

Project First Step is almost clinically isolated. The street kids don't mingle with the after-school crowd, and there's a strict locked-door policy on the wing. The locks are to protect the kids from scrutiny ("This is their living room"), but the separation seems odd. In the vast majority of youth programs, such disparate services would never be offered on a single site, but a feature of trying to cover the gamut of gay youth concerns is that you can be dealing with nearly anyone, from a girl in a private school to a boy living in an alley. Perhaps the needs of the kids are so different that they truly do have nothing to say to each other; still, I'd rather that assumption weren't turned into a foregone conclusion. Of course, maybe the kids *don't* want to mix—as I discover when I talk to William, there seems to be plenty of animosity between the Harvey Milk students and those who come for the after-school program.

William, a senior who will graduate from Harvey Milk High two months after my April visit, asks that I use his first name but not his last. He's a big guy at age seventeen, racially indeterminate (he marks himself "other" on forms), mous-tached and burly, with deep brown eyes and a quick shy smile. According to David Nieves, a staff member who runs the peer education program, William used to be so with-drawn he'd hardly talk. When he came to Harvey Milk High, he was failing in school. "I wasn't having any harass-ment problems, but I was isolating myself from the rest of the students. I knew if I came out, there would be conse-quences, either verbal or physical, and I wasn't willing to do that."

William took a chance and came out to a counselor at his old school. "I figured if she was a counselor, she had a certain responsibility to help me, whether she agrees with homosexuality or not. And she did." With William's per-mission, she began the paperwork to transfer him to Harvey Milk and also confided in several of his teachers. "It was really an odd situation. My teachers knew I was gay and I was failing because I was having problems with it. But the students didn't know."

When he entered Harvey Milk at age fifteen, he'd had no contact with gay people. "The first year was really try-ing. I expected that gay people were going to be so great. You know, 'When I come out, gay people are going to be so nice and they're going to help me.' But then I met them and there are a lot of gay people who are pretty horrible."

"How were they horrible?"

"Because of people's own internalized hatred," he answers. "Taking that in, eventually they're going to let some of it out. Sometimes they let it out on the people closest to them, like the other kids."

"Like people are too negative or critical?"

He's nodding. "About themselves. And about other people. But it's a few, not everyone, and the teachers try to counter it." He pauses, remembering the unpleasantness of some of these first contacts. "Plus in our old place we had to walk down Christopher Street and see all the people. And that was weird in itself."

"See gay people?"

He sighs. "See gay people and see . . ." His voice trails away.

"Them falling out of bars?" I suggest.

"Yeah." He's nodding again, but it's not really what he means. I suspect that William, like the girls in the groups, doesn't care for behavior that seems to him to flirt at the knife-edge of ridicule and self-hate, but he's uncomfortable telling me that, possibly because he thinks it isn't right, and possibly because David Nieves is hovering over us, listening to every word. The agency deems it necessary to have staff members sit in on interviews, and I'm finding this practice oppressive, especially given the strict time limit David has set.

"What were your stereotypes?"

"I can look back and say it was really horrible. All the stuff I saw on TV was like effeminate white male middle class. Now I see the whole spectrum, everything from really poor to extremely rich. All different kinds. And now I see the problems in the gay community, and the separations within the high school, the different groups. Back then my view was very limited."

"How about older gay people?"

He shrugs. "I've met lots of great older gay people, lots of bad. Lots of the kids I know don't feel comfortable at the Gay and Lesbian Community Services Center because they feel pushed out and they're not listened to, so what's the point of going there? There's some support, but not enough."

William's mother, though "severely religious," is able to accept him. "She feels that human beings are inherently evil, and as much as you try to change them, they're always going to be evil people. That's why she's worried about me sometimes, 'cause she knows I'm fine, and that I'm a good person, but she's afraid other people don't see that. That they're going to judge me by the way I look or by the way I act."

Since William looks like a gentle, sweet man, I'm not sure what she's worried about, but then he lets on that he used to have green hair. "She went crazy," he reports. "She was like, 'You could get killed!'"

William volunteered for the peer education program shortly after he came to Harvey Milk High. "Does everybody at the school do these presentations?" I ask.

William sounds horrified. "Oh, no. It's part of the Institute."

"Why did you volunteer?"

He smiles. "It sounded like a thing that would look good on a résumé. And it would give me experience in speaking." William has done more than seventy-five presentations to schools and professional groups as one member of a pair of speakers. A staff member, usually David, also comes along for moral support.

"You've done seventy-five in two years?" I'm astonished.

"Yeah, to at least a thousand people."

The audience is told only that some people from Hetrick-Martin are going to speak to them about human sexuality. The speaker-pair begins by asking the students (or adults) to call out their stereotypes of homosexuals. "We don't disclose at the beginning of the training," David interjects from his stool in the corner. "Otherwise, they hold back—"

"Or they're too open," William says. "You can't finish the training 'cause they get into your sexuality before you want them to. You need a chance to speak to them first person to person, not as a gay person."

"So they're looking at you as someone they can identify with," I say.

"Not disclosing earlier also means not personalizing a workshop," David says. "If you personalize it, it can turn very hard when you're sitting in front of a classroom and you're hearing all these horrible words that come to mind when people hear 'homosexual.' Later on, when our sexual orientation is discussed, most of the time they're shocked. They never believe that you are. Because you don't fit the stereotype. So they start thinking, 'Wow, you really never know.' It could be your brother, your sister, your mother, your father."

"Mostly we do young people," William says. "And they're curious. They want to know. The hard time comes from adults. A whole lifetime of hearing something, they don't want to change it. They seem a lot more cold."

"Do you ever feel like a gay public relations man?"

He smiles. "Kind of. But I make it clear I'm just one voice in a really big spectrum."

When I ask what it's like at Harvey Milk, he sighs, probably sick to death of the subject. He's been through three directors and a move, but he likes the recent changes, he says. The school day has been lengthened, there are more group classes, and outside resource people are being invited in to teach. "Before I wasn't challenged as much," William says. "Now I am, maybe too much." He sighs, no doubt thinking of all the projects he has to finish in the few weeks before he graduates.

"It sounds like it'd be great in terms of teacher-student ratio," I say. "What is it, one to five?"

William frowns. I can tell he's afraid I'm going to paint too rosy a picture, and he's been trying to tell me, in pretty obvious code, that there's something not quite right in Denmark. "Then again," he cautions, "you have to think that the students are not coming from the greatest backgrounds. They may be troubled in their own ways, when it comes to relating to teachers and respecting other people. It's no utopia. And if you look at the school as a microcosm of a big high school, we have the same problems. Plus our homes. So it's problems on problems."

"Do the kids date each other?"

He shakes his head. "It's more like a family kind of thing. Maybe it's because all the kids don't like each other as people. You see the little idiosyncrasies. You have to spend all day with these people, you don't want to be in a relationship with them too."

"What about the kids who come to the after-school program?"

"There's conflict at times," he says, and starts ticking the reasons off on his fingers. "We have to share the same space. And maybe the kids in school feel the kids in drop-in can do whatever they want, don't have to follow the teachers. And maybe the kids in drop-in feel the kids in school are getting it easy because they have to go to regular schools and the kids at Harvey Milk don't. But I've seen both sides, and I don't think it's easy either way."

William mentions schisms and cliques so often that I begin to suspect that he's feeling excluded. That turns out to be somewhat of a misreading: William has support from David (and probably others) to not fit in where he doesn't want to. His criticism begins with a more general indictment of fracturing in the gay community: "The gay community is just so isolated in its own little place. I fear that may happen more and more. There will be like more extremist activists. More conservative gay people. More isolationist lesbians over here, and like, minorities over there. I see that right now. I don't see the community coming together.

"Gay people are just as judgmental as everybody else, if not more. The subcommunities within the gay community are very different in themselves, and when I'm hanging out with different cliques of gay people, I act differently with each group. There are some things that are allowed in some groups that are not in others."

"You mentioned earlier that you didn't fit into a group," I say.

"I don't have a need to fit into any groups. Right now I'm moving between groups." He doesn't look happy about it. I want to continue on this track, but David is pointedly looking at his watch, so I leap to a Big Question: "So what are the major issues facing your generation?"

"I would say that the one big issue is, we grew up with AIDS. Like from as young as we can remember, we saw it. And even though a lot of us know how to protect ourselves, that doesn't mean we're doing it."

"Why? Self-destructive? Couldn't happen to me?"

"My closest gay male friends have told me, 'I'm going to get AIDS anyway, so it doesn't matter.' And they've heard that since they were little. They grew up thinking that one day they might be HIV-positive."

David, who at twenty-eight does not fit William's narrow definition of his generation ("older than fifteen, younger than twenty"), chimes in anyway. "When I came out, me and my friends used to say, 'Well, we're gay, we have AIDS.' I wasn't even sexually active until I was twenty-one, but when I was sixteen, I knew I 'had' AIDS." He raises his dark eyebrows to see if I understand the irony. "A lot of my friends, since they already 'had' it, they didn't protect themselves. And a lot of them are gone. It was pretty ugly, seeing your friends doing all this stuff because they knew they were going to die anyway. But I decided to take another road. [A friend] told me, 'You don't have to fit in a group. Just be yourself.' I remember me and my friends talking about it. 'Oh my God, which one of these groups are you supposed to stick into?' You go through so many changes as a teenager, trying to figure out which one of those places you're going to fit in."

"If you go between groups, you feel left out too," William interjects, wanting to remind us that he's lonely and right smack in the middle of this, not safely out the other side and patting himself on the back for having made the right choices. "The club group, the community center group, the activists . . ." He sighs. "You know people from all different places, but you're kind of nowhere."

As I thank them, and William ambles off to complete a photography project, I see why he limits his peers to a five-year range: David is remembering his dislocation, while William is still living his. That William feels dislocated in the heart of the gay community may seem ironic, but that "irony" brings several things to light. As far as gay youth are concerned, Hetrick-Martin is a lone island; the ocean surrounding it, including the big mix of cliques and groups we term the gay community, remains chill waters. Furthermore, islands get submerged: Hetrick-Martin and Harvey Milk High can't isolate themselves from the splintering, even if every staff member tries to be supportive of every kid. Kids look to each other for cues, and in their need to belong, copy the prevailing community's values and missteps. Finally, no institutional setting can hope to replace "home," whatever that turns out to be.

William is right on track in his search for his own home, the primary occupation of all teenagers, gay and straight. Fortunately, he has David to tell him it's okay to take his time, even though he's had to swallow the bitter pill that simply finding the gay community did not save him. Or maybe it did. We humans are stern taskmasters—once we solve a problem, we deny its importance, only looking ahead to the next puzzle. In two years, William's gone from a withdrawn, isolated kid who was failing in school to an articulate, involved youth who moves between groups because he isn't satisfied with the answers he sees in them. He wants something else, and he has enough patience and tolerance for loneliness that he's willing to wait for it. His concern that I would get the "wrong idea" about Harvey Milk says more about how the school has succeeded than how it's failed—he's realistic about the foibles of himself and his schoolmates, and he's idealistic enough to believe it matters that he tells me the truth.

When I asked him what he was afraid of, he said he wished he had more straight friends and he was worried about going from a gay high school to a straight college.

"Do you regret coming here?"

"At times I do. You get tired of being in a room with the same people. Sometimes I don't want to be here."

"Of course, sometimes you wouldn't have wanted to be at your old high school either."

He chuckled. "Right. That was an everyday thing. Here it's like a once-a-year thing."

"i don't care if they come in a damn clown suit."

Fred Goldhaber, who has taught at Harvey Milk since the school opened in April 1985, is doing his best to maintain his composure. He's about to make another trip to the hospital; his lover is in intensive care. Small, round, and normally cheerful, Fred looks exhausted, but he doesn't want to talk about his troubles. He adjusts today's Mickey Mouse tie (he has upward of a hundred) and says, "Harvey Milk is a dream come true for me. When I finally figured out who I was at age twenty-one, I was really angry with the Board of Education for not teaching me about myself. I was like a detective story looking for clues. I was hoping I might be able to see that no other child has to live with a secret like that. Not that we teach gay topics here, because we don't.

But when something is absolutely relevant, we can say the truth."

"Is it really a goal of the school to return kids to their traditional high schools?"

"It has been listed as one of our goals in publications," Fred says diplomatically. Then he shrugs. "For a few kids, yes. For the majority, once they've been placed here, they get very comfortable and feel free and liberated because they can be themselves. Our goal is to see these kids get a good education one way or another." He pauses, considering. "The goal of Harvey Milk School is to create a world in which a Harvey Milk School is not necessary, but short of that—"

He's interrupted by his colleague, English teacher Donna Farnum. A soft-spoken African-American woman in her thirties, Donna seats herself at the same long counter Fred and I are using. Rooms at Harvey Milk are eclectic; the teachers share this narrow cell with its one countertop and several rolling chairs. Every other minute the phone rings or someone pounds for entry at the door to the school. When I arrived this morning, the students were divided between the two closed classrooms; all I could see through an interior window were backs and heads bent over desks.

"Anyway," Fred says after he puts down the phone and I greet Donna, "we've got our hands full just accommodating the students, making them feel safe, encouraging them to pull down the walls they build around themselves. They come usually angry, hostile, confused, troubled, scared. Either they've been exploited or molested, or outed by guidance counselors. The problems are not always other students, but insensitive teachers and administrators."

I ask the percentage of boys to girls. "About six to one,"

Fred answers. "In the past, we've had seasons where there'd be only one or two girls, and that's always frustrating for the girl. She wants to relate to other girls. One of the reasons we have less girls is that perhaps young lesbians are able to pass more easily. An effeminate boy hasn't got a chance in a regular high school, but a somewhat masculine young woman might."

"Quite a lot of girls come to the after-school program," I note.

Fred nods. "Harvey Milk is really a last-ditch effort for those kids who couldn't make it in the traditional schools, and I would imagine that a majority of the girls you see at drop-in are handling their regular school successfully."

"If everybody could come who wanted to come, do you have any idea how big the school would be?"

"I know that we turn away dozens of kids annually," Fred says. "Basically Hetrick-Martin sees us as a small program, and they envision us as staying small. We go to the agency and say, 'We'd like another teacher. We want a third room for classwork.' "

"We need that already," Donna puts in.

I ask them about the Queer High concept. Donna's worried that they'd lose the intimate setting that allows them to reach the kids. Fred can't picture it at all. "As long as parents think their children are their possessions, as long as parents oppose open discussion of AIDS and safe sex and homosexuality, I can't imagine a school where anybody could just show up and be taken in. Besides, we're just one group of people who put on masks in public schools. Kids who don't want to be identified as Hispanic or Jewish or whatever do it too.

"Wouldn't it be wonderful if in kindergarten you were

taught to be yourself?" he asks dreamily. " 'To thine own self be true.' You'd go around looking into who you are, and sharing with others, and finding out who you aren't. Instead they teach how to paint with a paintbrush, or sculpt with Play-Doh. They bring out the creativity, but they leave inside all the darkness and ignorance."

Fred comes back to reality fast when he spots a student wandering aimlessly in the hall. He sticks his head out the door to demand an explanation. The boy has a good answer —he's looking for a reference volume his teacher needs—so Fred lets him get on with it. He turns back to the conversation with a head shake. "I'm afraid that even if we were to open up these doors to a thousand kids, the ones who would need us the most would have the hardest time coming."

"I can't imagine a time," I say, "when gays and lesbians could take for granted the kinds of things heterosexual kids can."

"Just being themselves in the street," Donna agrees. "Walking down the block holding hands. The smallest gestures, the natural kinds of humanness. We're always having to process and negotiate. It's such a tiring thing."

"The kids who come here very often have to take these elusive routes home because they're afraid of getting beat up," Fred says. "On the streets, on the subway. Spooked, as they say. Someone who is in drag can get spooked on the subway."

Donna rolls her eyes. "If someone is in drag, forget it." Then she laughs. "But you know what? I really enjoy the kids. I don't care if they come in a damn clown suit. If they're in drag, jeans, a T-shirt, whatever, it's such a great celebration of life."

Fred describes a student so angry with the world that he

sat at the back of the room cursing under his breath for months. But when another student was killed, it was he who organized a program of poetry and dance, as well as a meal of chicken and rice, for a memorial service. "That's the most valuable thing we do," Fred says. "The kids just think, 'I want my credits,' but they come to us shut like a flower and we open them up. And it's a wonderful process."

"Do they get into identity stuff, like, 'Gay people do such and such, so I should do that too?' " I ask.

"Actually, they focus on their own community," Fred says. "On the balls."

Fred and Donna estimate that a third or more of the boys at Harvey Milk High are active in the New York house scene, the fancy-dress drag balls featured in Jennie Livingston's documentary *Paris Is Burning*. No wonder William complains about fragmentation, I think, if there's girls doing girl stuff and so many boys doing the balls. The houses that put on the balls are the equivalent of families, with mothers, fathers, sisters, and brothers, and like many families, they can be all-consuming.

Meanwhile, the phones are ringing off the hook, and Fred has things to do before he can leave for the hospital. As I get up to leave, Fred tells a quick story: "We once had a teacher who happened not to be gay. I felt she was pushing everything toward, 'Geez, we want kids, we want family, we want to be heterosexual.' That troubled me. At one point she asked, 'Who here would like to have children?' and one boy got up and said, 'I'd love to be a mother.' That's when I remembered that regardless of who is teaching the class, our kids are still our kids, and they will interpret things as they wish."

As I step on the elevator, I'm pondering the paradox of

wanting to reach more kids while simultaneously wishing not to be needed. I had asked Frances if it was HMI's ultimate goal not to exist. She shook her head. "We would exist just as a place for people to meet each other. That's an important function. I would like it that the ultimate goal is that people not come in such pain. But I don't see anything happening real quickly. If we go away sometime during the next twenty years, quite frankly it's going to be for other reasons, not because we're not needed."

When I returned from seeing Allyson Mount in Massachusetts, I stopped by Hetrick-Martin again, wanting to interview someone active in the house scene. But David Nieves told me that none of the twelve kids who were trained as peer educators—the only ones allowed to talk to the media —was in a house. Being in the ball scene seemed to preclude interest in public relations, unless, of course, what was being publicized were the balls themselves. After I whined and begged, David gave me ten minutes with a young man who had come to the agency that afternoon to participate in the after-school program. Those few minutes convinced me that I had to come back to New York to see these alternative families in action, and hopefully to attend a ball.

That I returned during the height of celebrating the twenty-fifth anniversary of Stonewall was not my choice, but I had to admit it seemed appropriate, to use HMI's favorite word. Seven months before that fateful day of June 28, 1969, I came out—which in the vernacular of the time meant I made love with someone of the same sex and didn't dillydally on the sidelines but plunged straight into a gay scene that was far more underground and circumspect than it is today. (As the milieu has changed, so has the definition:

coming out is now more likely to mean an acknowledgment of being gay to one's self, a milestone I cannot pinpoint, since it's something I've always known.)

Within a month of my coming out, I was asked to leave college when a "friend" reported my predilections to the administration. Because of the major social upheavals of the time—student strikes, the feminist movement, the incursion into Cambodia, the war, and Stonewall itself—I carry the distinction of being the last person booted out of Sarah Lawrence because I was queer. Only a little more than a year later, nine months after Stonewall, women were walking around on campus holding hands with their girlfriends; a year and a half later it would have been unthinkable to ask someone to leave because of her sexual orientation. During that time of turmoil, everything was held up to question, and changes of consciousness, when they occurred at all, tended to happen at the speed of light. The riot at Stonewall was thus both a parent and a child of its age and, along with all the human rights movements, proved an agent far more mind- and society-altering than a thousand hits of the finest acid. Having witnessed the sea change at Sarah Lawrence impressed upon me the power of not accepting *It's always been this way* as an answer to anything.

Visiting New York is still a mixed blessing for me, because the pain of my leave-taking has not dissipated. But Stonewall was so important to me in that early time of joining and defining community that I wanted to honor the drag queens and dykes, mostly people of color, who were fed up with rolling over for a society that despised them. I also wanted to congratulate my younger self that chose exile rather than humiliation or dishonesty. So when I heard that a phantom conglomerate called the House of Latex—a safe-sex education group composed of members of all the real houses in alliance with the Gay Men's Health Crisis—was putting on a ball the Sunday before Stonewall 25, at the start of the Gay Games, I made plane reservations.

"i go out there knowing i deserve respect."

It's steaming hot and still light when I line up with fifty other early birds outside the Marc Ballroom at Union Square in Manhattan. Almost all are men (or male-born), almost all are black or Latino, and the vast majority are twenty-five and under. I happen to be standing between two gay men my own age, one white, one black. The three of us form an alliance based on our mutual antiquity and our ignorance of what we're about to witness. The black guy has a friend who "does this stuff," but he himself has never been to a ball. The white guy, who works at *The Village Voice*, is here 'cause he thinks it'll be a kick. It doesn't take long before our trio is complaining. How come we can't just go in? How long can it take to let a crowd into a free event?

The fact that no one else seems to care derails our annoyance. We inch forward in the June heat, fanning ourselves with anything that comes to hand. A cop stands nearby, but nobody looks at him; he might as well be a three-dimensional recruiting poster. Finally I can't stand it anymore and roam up front to see what's taking so long. My report back to my section of the line that security people are scanning ballgoers with metal detectors causes a flurry of interest. "Are they white?" one young man asks me.

"I'm not sure," I say lamely, realizing I hadn't noticed because the answer, of importance to this black man, was irrelevant to me. He raises his eyebrows and turns away to talk to his friend.

As taxis whiz past and pedestrians step off the sidewalk to get around the line, which is growing longer by the minute, I recall the ten-minute interview with the youth at Hetrick-Martin that convinced me to come back to New York. Against his better judgment—and probably against policy—David collared a boy of seventeen who was wearing loose pants, a short-sleeved shirt, and casual daytime makeup of eyeliner and a lipstick so close to his own coloring it was almost unnoticeable. African-American, tall, and lithe, Evann Hayes was eager to tell me about the house community. "The people in the houses are from a lot of different ethnic backgrounds," he said. "You go around until you find the one that suits you. Kind of like fraternities," he added, trying to find an example that would make sense to me. "Maybe your friends are in a house or maybe you like someone or someone likes you."

Evann joined the House of Pendavis when he was thirteen years old. His house mother, Avis Pendavis, started the house when she was twenty-three, thirty years ago, and she's been the mother ever since. There is awe in Evann's voice when he speaks of her. "She's taught me so much," he said, then he touched his lip thoughtfully, glancing out at HMI's lobby, which was at that moment teeming with the after-school crowd. "You know, some people have a home life that's not very friendly. In the houses you have a mother and a father and brothers and sisters who take care of you, who accept who you are.

"Some people think the houses are bad things, that they teach us how to rob or lie. But it's exactly the opposite. We're taught self-respect, how to keep a job, how to function in straight society. We have competitions that keep us sharp, teach us grooming. The balls teach dancing and appearance and poise—" He was struggling for a word.

"Style?" I suggested.

"Yes, style! You have to develop your own individual style. And the members of your house help you do that."

"But if it's all this gay-exclusive drag stuff, I don't understand how it prepares you to deal with the heterosexual world," I objected.

He nodded to himself, as if he'd heard all this before. "Because it teaches you who you have the potential to be," he explained patiently.

"Self-esteem?" I asked.

He waved off my interruption. "Yes, but more respect. I go out there knowing I deserve respect for who I am. Before I joined the house, I didn't know what I wanted. Now I know I want to be happy. I didn't realize I had the *potential* to be happy.

"You know how the world sees us. They never show anything positive in the movies or on TV. The houses are such a positive force. We have rules—you have to have a job or be going to school, you can't use drugs, you have to be there when family members need you. *Paris Is Burning* showed only bits and pieces. It's so much bigger than that."

But then filmmaker Livingston had a different agenda: by zeroing in on the house culture and then widening her focus to crowds on New York City streets, she was demonstrating that the whole world is in drag. This fact is so obvious to the house participants—if to no one else—that it seems not only unnecessary to mention but irrelevant to an understanding of house society. The flip-flop vision that makes Livingston's film brilliant—extrapolating the behavior of everyone from those who are most excluded and marginalized, bursting the bubble of "other" in the process —is exactly what renders the film disappointing to those in the house scene itself.

"Do you associate with people who aren't in the houses?"

"Of course! I mean, teenagers are sometimes . . ." He wasn't sure how to put this. "Teenagers sometimes have the idea they can only associate with one group. So maybe when you're young . . . but when you get older you know more people."

"The balls must be fun," I said.

He was bubbling with enthusiasm. "Oh, they are! We help each other with makeup and our dresses and shoes. It's such a fantasy! Then I get up the next morning and go to work." He smiled at the juxtaposition of his two worlds.

"Do you feel like a different person when you're in drag?"

He paused, finger to his forehead. "No," he finally answered. "It's me, but more me."

Once past the metal detectors, we troop downstairs into a long, windowless, cement-walled room that reminds me of a chilly and uninviting church basement. But this room is hot as an oven and dominated by a three-foot-high, six-foot-wide runway extending a full two thirds of its length. The legions of folding chairs flanking the runway are soon occupied by an audience of several hundred noisy fans dressed in summer gear: loose cotton shirts coyly unbuttoned to reveal sculpted muscles and an unusual percentage of "outtie" navels, oversize pants, hair clipped close to the skull.

Everyone's hovering twenty-five feet off the ground, mostly from excitement, though drugs are no stranger here. Alcohol is—no beer is served, and I don't spot any flasks. Instead people are gulping down can after can of Jamaican iced cappuccino as they stand and model, pose and model, arch and preen like so many large cats. The teenagers are especially good at this; while keeping up a spirited conversation with friends, they know exactly how they look from every angle, who's looking at them from all those angles, who just left the bathroom with whom, and where the hell is my eye shadow/backpack/cigarettes/boyfriend?

What soon becomes obvious is that everybody has a mission, and the younger you are, the more vital that mission. Perhaps it's only ranging out to the hall to snag someone or insulting the girl on your left, but who knows? You might at any moment be tapped to apply lipstick to a bee-stung pout or race to the back room with the perfect accessory to complete the perfect costume or debate who might enter which category. What's mostly happening is showing off: bands of sixteen- and seventeen-year-olds with brave new muscles, brave new moustaches, and skin creamy, smooth, and soft as milk stride from the hall to the bathroom to the ballroom, stopping along the way to pose for the femme queens who are seated demurely in the folding chairs—that is, if they're not parading around the floor themselves or kneeling on the padded seats dishing dirt to those in the row behind them.

Keeping track of who's looking at me who's looking at you *who is she* means no one is willing to focus long enough to understand who I am, much less talk to me. All I accomplish during the several hours before the performance begins is to gather a few phone numbers from people too polite to tell me to fuck off. What I do instead is hang out with my two new pals, commenting on the action and reading the program.

The glossy white sheet we were handed at the door is a map of what's ahead, listing the order of the various contests. More important, it serves as a guide to entrants, who attempt to best fit whatever category they've chosen, which are all defined by perceived gender. Thus butch queens and femme queens walk the runway separately, in contests like BQ New Face (there's a contest for those who have never walked, and another for those who have never won, like a maiden race at the track), FQ Big Girl Runway Scandal (for heavyweights), BQ Pretty Boy Realness ("Do you still remain masculine having that flawless skin and being drop-dead gorgeous, while still having the girls and possibly the boys lust for you?"), BQ Executive Realness (for those corporate types), FQ Bangy Realness ("The ball has ended and you are taking the train home. Will you make it? Or will the train have a fierce delay because you got spooked?").

"She's a girl, right?" one of my companions asks, staring at a short-skirted woman in her late teens, a real heartthrob with her butterscotch skin, cap of dark hair, and spit curls tracing the outlines of high cheekbones. She's sitting a couple seats over from us in the same row. "I'm sure she's a girl," he says, his eyes narrowed as if this will help him decide. But then her boyfriend comes over and the two begin scoping out the competition for BQ New Face. "Amazing," my friend says.

As the witching hour approaches, eyes strike sparks,

mouths open and close without sound in the din, nostrils flare, teeth flash, fans flutter. Tingles of excitement chug up the spine and strong lean bodies stretch taut as a high wire. Finally Eric Bazaar, an African-American man in his late twenties, takes the microphone and announces that the ball has begun.

First we're treated to a video made by the House of Latex, the umbrella group that's banded together to educate the community about safer sex. People onscreen, all from the house community, talk about AIDS and other sexually transmitted diseases, but no one in the audience pays attention because they're yelling, "Go for it, honey!" at a femme queen twitching her behind or moaning, "Ronald!" or "Danielle!" when someone appears that they recognize. The sound track's full of information they know already, and whether they decide to put that knowledge to use is a matter of choice. The only part of the film that garners sincere applause is a statement that everyone needs to come together to help each other out—"we can't do it alone."

Another break in the action. By now it's after eleven, and nothing's happened yet. By counting up the number of contests in the program, assuming each is ten minutes in duration, the three of us project a conclusion at around four in the morning. Meanwhile, it's ninety-five degrees in the basement, and there are five hundred to six hundred people in a space meant for a couple hundred at most. "Serious cologne crimes here tonight," *The Village Voice* man says. "This is not a fragrance-free event."

It's not a baseball cap–free event either. There's plenty of 'em, worn backward and forward, along with garrison belts and those stretchy white undershirts that delineate muscles. And no one's having a bad hair day, except those entering FQ Hair Confusion, who've spent hours *trying* to have same. As we gulp at our chilled cans of cappuccino, we debate the average age. I go for twenty-six, but both my companions think twenty-one is more likely. To bolster his guess, *Village Voice* reads from the program, which explains that to win Face as a House, a house must enter four people: one BQ, one FQ, one "upcoming statement," and a "legendary face over thirty."

Both my companions roll their eyes. "Thirty? Oh, please!"

Then Eric's back onstage—or on the ramp actually, introducing the judges. Since each judge has to strut her stuff, this segment takes a good hour. But it's worth it, not only because, as Eric tells me later, each judge is a "living legend," but because his introductions are in the form of a rap-based patter that's complicated, quick, and very funny. When the judges are seated, the contest can begin. We check our watches. It's midnight, five hours after the doors opened. Even rock concerts in the '60s weren't this bad.

The judges are issued green flags (meaning "go") and white "detour" signs. Nobody wants to get one of those. Contestants for the first contest, FQ Realness, come slinking out of the audience. Among them is our personal favorite, Ms. Spit Curl. "She's gotta win," we breathe. But we're dead wrong. Once up on the ramp, she's far too diffident and awkward, moving like a gawky colt despite her '20s charm. The three who receive green flags, who advance to a second strut up and down the runway, not only can pass, but are twenty times gorgeous besides, with charisma and glamour and a walk that says *fuck me*, *fuck you*, and *don't you wish you could* all at once. None of this, I realize, can come easily; learning how to command—to possess—that runway must take enormous dedication and skill.

Nor do the butch queens get off easy. True, they don't have to sashay, but they *do* have to model their wares, and be manly about it too. And they've gotta vogue—that marvelous right-angled gymnastic dance of arms and legs that finishes frozen in the pose to top all poses practically in the judges' laps. Do they practice in front of a mirror holding their hands in weird Nefertiti-like junctures to their forearms? They must. Everybody's too good at it not to have spent months perfecting their moves.

The crowd allows the first few categories to go unopposed but then begins to razz the judges, living legends or not. Two hunky Latino butch queens in identical white undershirts and wide brown leather belts are rejected in favor of a tall, slender black guy, a decision that draws howls of outrage. No one qualifies for FQ Body, because no one is in the required bathing suit. School Girl Realness draws only three contestants, but School Boy Realness gathers fourteen competitors from the crowd, most wearing loose pants, hi-tops, backpacks, and carrying books. The clever guy that bounds up on the runway twirling a basketball on the tip of his index finger snares the Plexiglas trophy. Wholesome is apparently in this summer, because BQ Menace II Society draws only two very halfhearted gangstas. FQ Hair Confusion has great contestants, including one girl who walks topless, exposing a young man's hairless chest, but whose demeanor is so I'm-hot-'90s-woman, face so animated and compelling and aware, wild wild hair shooting out in a thick halo around her head, cascading over her narrow shoulders, that those flat pecs become just another form of female.

At 1:15 A.M., as we near the end of the short half of the program, another MC leaps up to the ramp to make an announcement. "We're going to have a fifteen-minute intermission," he says, which I translate to mean an hour or so. "And there's a big crowd of people outside who've been waiting to get in since ten. Could a bunch of you please leave?"

"For the cause," the three of us, now bleary-eyed, say to each other.

"it's as close to hollywood as a lot of us'll get."

"What's this realness business?" I ask Eric Bazaar a few days later. We're sitting in a restaurant on the corner of Christopher Street on Friday afternoon, thirty-six hours before the march kicks off. This is perhaps not the best choice. It's so crowded on the street above that it took five minutes to exit the subway station.

"It's just, you know, that you look real, that you blend in," Eric says. In spite of only seeing him on the end of the runway with a mike in his hand, I recognized him immediately. He has the requisite slender moustache of the butch queens and a mobile, fascinating face. Once you spot him, you don't want to stop looking.

"Blend in with what?"

"Straight people. If you're a butch queen nobody can spook you for being a gay boy and if you're a femme queen nobody can spook you as a man," Eric explains. What could be more obvious?

Eric is my last resort. Each appointment I made the night of the ball ("Two P.M. Tuesday by the fountain at Washington Square Park") has been broken, so I've spent a lot of time waiting on street corners and leaving unanswered messages on machines. My New York pals are amused— "Going downtown to meet another phantom kid?"—but I'm aware I have at least four strikes against me: I'm white, middle class, a woman, and in my forties. Eric has been the most helpful, though he wasn't able to cajole his seventeen-year-old friend into coming along. Now he says, "See, what it is, the upper class, the *white* upper-class gay community, they don't know *anything* about the ball scene. It's all minority, blacks and Hispanics . . ."

I had heard that the ball scene started in Harlem in the '20s, as part of the then-active nightlife of cafes and fancy dress fêtes. Eric shrugs. "Could be." Then he tells me as far back as he knows. "See, in the beginning, everybody wanted to look like Vegas showgirls, and then in the '70s it changed so that everyone wanted to look like models. When the '80s rolled around, they separated into butch queens—those are the boys—and femme queens, the transvestites."

"With this blending in," I ask, "do people pass as straight, or pass as women, in the rest of their lives?"

"Some people in the ballroom scene do. Some don't even care, they describe it the way it is. Me myself, I always try to blend in because when you come from Brooklyn or you come from the Bronx, from a rough neighborhood, you don't want people to know your business. When you get out in the Village, you can be more open."

"So you go back and forth?"

He's nodding. "You have two lives, the realness side in your neighborhood, and then when you get out here you can be free." Real is a role you play and free is a fantasy.

Where's the *real* real, I want to ask, but dumb questions like that are why these guys don't want to talk to me.

Besides, I've been having my own problems blending in in New York. When I wear a certain loose shirt that hides my breasts, people call me sir and act polite. When I'm wearing a tank top, people spin on their heels to do an exaggerated double take, and at least five or six times a day I get spit at, cursed, and have fists shoved in my face. Why this is happening on this particular trip is a puzzle. I'm spending more time than I usually do midtown, Stonewall 25 might be pissing people off (tiny pieces of masking tape reading KILL FAGS are stuck on subway steps all over Manhattan), and I'm almost always alone and thus a more tempting target than the Gay Games participants, who are usually traveling in big groups. Whatever the reason, it's not long before I'm wearing the shirt full-time.

"So the houses teach this blending."

"Well, not really—"

"But presumably the femme queens couldn't initially pass as women without some help."

"Right. They look up to legendary femme queens like Octavia or Tracy and say, 'I wanna be just like them,' and they'll start trying to look lovely like a real woman."

"It seems like all this would be expensive," I say. "Like in the ball you're hosting next month, you have a category where you have to be wearing '94 designer clothes."

He's nodding again. "Yeah. It's expensive. And some people steal—"

"Of course," I interject. Dumb again.

"—to get their outfit together, to compete against the

other person, to stand out from everybody else. Back when, they used to break windows on Fifth Avenue—"

"To grab something—"

He's pleased I'm finally catching on. "To grab something to wear to the ball the next day."

According to Raymond St. Pierre, a New York City public high school teacher and a volunteer at the Neutral Zone, an agency for street kids, the ball scene is beyond the reach of many. "My kids can't afford to go into the houses," he says. "They can't pay twenty-five-dollar entry fees for the balls. People who go into the houses are people who can go to discos." Raymond has other quarrels. "They perpetuate stereotypes with that whole realness thing, buying into some image of fitting into straight society." But what really gets his goat is the backbiting. "Kids get kicked out all the time," he says. "They're just left out in the cold."

Houses as elitist, assimilationist, exclusionary. In this layered society, there's always someone underneath the underneath, and it's tempting to shove around where you can. It's just as true that the ball society has given a boy like Evann Hayes a reason to care about himself. I tell Eric about Evann, how joining the House of Pendavis let him know happiness was possible in his life.

Eric sips at his water, listening gravely, then says, "Some kids' parents find out they're gay, the kids run away, and they become attached to the gay mother and father of the house." The house family serves as a literal substitute, Eric says, and often for kids as young as Evann's thirteen.

Eric joined the ball scene in 1983, at the age of sixteen, as a member of the House of Chanel. "The mother at that time—she's passed away—she was like a real mother, she looked out for everybody. There are houses that stick to-

gether like that, that are a real family. The House of Rich-
ards, the House of Xtravaganza, they're one big family."

"If people are broke, do the houses give them money?"

"Yeah. And they try to find jobs for people." Banks and
employment counselors, yes; marriage brokers, no. Sex,
Eric says, happens outside the house. "Otherwise there's all
kinds of trouble." And "house" usually can't be taken literally: "People don't live together. We have our own places."

"Do people get thrown out of houses if they become
problems?"

"Yeah. Maybe somebody steals or starts a fight and that
gives a bad reputation to the house, so you don't want that
person."

"What about this no drug rule?"

"Well . . . some houses do that. But anywhere you
have a club scene, there's people bound to be on drugs."
What concerns Eric is the fights, so much so that he mentions them several times. The balls have lately been plagued
by an outbreak of hostilities between houses, which have
erupted into physical battles. It's not only dangerous, Eric
points out, but also unfair to ballgoers who have invested
their hard-earned money only to have the evening busted
up by some hotheads. The possibility of fights was the reason, Eric says, for the thorough security check at the door.

He blames hair-trigger tempers and unfair judging for
the altercations. "People are *very* competitive. The balls
have gotten wilder. Lots of people don't work, and there's
drugs in the scene. But it really has to do with the people
who run the ball. A lot of people show favoritism and chop
somebody 'cause you want your house to win. See, when I
announce, I try to make everybody feel important. That's
why I get chosen a lot."

"How do kids find out about the balls?"

"Hanging around. The whole Village scene, they're always talking about a ball. And up on Forty-second Street."

"If a fourteen- or fifteen-year-old kid is hanging around—"

"Somebody'll say to him, 'You should be in the house to walk realness,' or 'You should be in the house for face.' Or just, 'You should come see a ball.' And that's how they get turned on to that.

"See, like I said, it's a fantasy. It's as close to Hollywood as a lot of us'll get. If you walk away with the trophy, you feel proud. Then everybody knows who you are. Once you walk down that runway, they start chanting your name, such as Avis Pendavis. Walking down the runway with people cheering you on—that's what people are trying to accomplish. They try to become legendary." He opens his fingers as if to encompass the world, so I'll see how this can happen, how a mere no one can become a someone. "The younger generation, they come into it, and the legendary people sit down and let the younger generation have their turn at fame. And there'll be a whole new group behind."

It happened after the judges were introduced and before FQ Realness began. As I sat on the edge of my seat, eager for the contest to start, Avis Pendavis, the mother of Evann's house, stepped up on the runway. Eric later told me it was the first time she'd walked in three or four years.

She was dressed in a tasteful gown, and she stood at the head of the runway for a long moment while the crowd went wild, screaming her name over and over: AVIS PENDAVIS AVIS PENDAVIS AVIS PENDAVIS. Her face was serene, almost otherworldly. She squared her shoulders, pushing back her hair, and began to walk the ramp slowly, no vamping, no camping. This was a woman gathering accolades from people who revere and adore her. Guys near the front of the ramp yelled, pointed, gestured, trying to attract her attention. As she noticed them, and she noticed each, she beamed at them for a long instant before she turned to someone else clamoring for her gaze. After she'd come halfway down the runway, a slow smile began to spread across her face, and the crowd let out a sigh, as if her eyes could set off a forest fire of good feeling, or her smile could bless the crowd. I could see why Evann had trouble finding a word. Style doesn't begin to describe Avis Pendavis—she has an incredible dignity and presence that is humanity at its best. And I understood exactly what Evann meant when he said, "She has taught me what I could be."

Watching her made me understand something else: the house society is above all a community based on hope. It's about not being felled by blows and slurs, about bearing witness not with fiery words or fervent testimony but through the body you carry into the world, the mundane made momentous. Avis Pendavis has risen above probably the two most powerful stigmas in our society—being black and transgendered—to emerge as a person of total calm. Or perhaps it is *because* she is black and transgendered that she has achieved this Zen-like state. There is nothing challenging about Avis Pendavis; she is not *reactive*. It seems almost impossible. No wonder they love her. No wonder they see in her something to strive for.

"She is a legend," Eric says simply. "She could make people fantasize. She could make it real."

Making the fantasy real, drawing the link between real and free, letting me be more me. Those in the house community learn realness to be safe, while at the same time creating a fantasy in which they can be someone in a society that devalues everything about them. They create alternate families that exist in an alternate world. In that world, the dominant language is refracted through a prism, broken into parts, and brought together again in new meanings that become personal to the community, not only separate from the disdainful society that surrounds them, but binding and defiant even in its supposed assimilation.

So why isn't Jesse Helms on the warpath about voguing and realness? Why aren't white fundamentalists worried that innocent, confused teens are being recruited by the House of Xtravaganza? Being too far out on the margin for people in power to notice can be a blessing as well as a curse.

How utterly logical that the gay members of communities already stigmatized by race and ethnicity would understand that kids need support in a world that doesn't want them. How apparent that groups which have had to rely on themselves for emotional and social sustenance would formulate a system which has survived for over seventy years and shows no signs of fading. And how beautifully instructive that the house culture realizes its future lies in its youth —kids who are not their own children, mind you, but too often someone else's castoffs. Showing a boy his own special beauty, giving him hope and confidence, are lifesavers.

The house community could teach the wider gay community a thing or two about mentoring teenagers. And if the world at large were to listen in, we might discover that children are not someone else's property, that each of us is responsible for everyone who comes along behind.

fear, fame, and fulfillment

from the talk shows to the pulpit

"if i can't even dream about it . . ."

When I met Brent Calderwood in March 1992, he was six-teen years old. He was tall and good-looking, but his shoulders were drawn forward as if he were warding off blows, and he'd only peek up at me shyly—quite a trick since he was eight inches taller. He later told me he'd been "fat and dorky" for years, and that his self-image hadn't caught up with what he now looked like.

I ran into Brent the very first time he attended the gay youth group at Berkeley's Pacific Center, a ramshackle Victorian on Telegraph Avenue three blocks past the perimeter of the Southside scene and its panhandlers, students, and street vendors. It might have been my first time at the group, too—or perhaps it was my second. Brent came a little late, so my presence had already been explained: I was writing an article on gay youth for the *Express*, the East Bay's alternative newspaper.

The guys—and of the seventeen or so at the meeting,

all but three of us were guys—were passing around a *People* magazine with Julia Roberts on the cover. While everyone else ogled the inside photo of bare-chested Marky Mark, Brent chattered on nervously about how much he loved Julia. He confided to an inattentive audience that he'd even plastered the walls of his room with her posters. Then, as if he suddenly realized where he was, he began to stammer. "That was when I was trying . . . I mean, when I thought I was straight . . ." He looked so bewildered and so lost at that moment that I fell in love with my subject, stopped being a journalist, and tumbled into the rabbit hole with him. When I spotted him after the meeting with tears running down his face, sobbing that he didn't want to be gay, that he wished it would stop, I wanted simultaneously to comfort him and to slay the heterosexist dragons who, above all, had made him fear himself.

Only one meeting later, Brent had come out to several people, including his hairstylist. "I just wanted to tell anyone I thought wouldn't give a shit," he explained. One girl said she'd always counted on Brent marrying her, and another wanted to take him shopping, warning him that if he wanted to be gay he had to start dressing better. His hairstylist wondered why he was telling her and theorized he must feel guilty. Brent was not dismayed by these minor debacles: "A month ago if I'd been asked if I wanted to become straight, I'd have said yes in a minute. Now no way."

The evening before the next meeting, he took the plunge and told Mom. "The words just wouldn't come out of my mouth. It was like they'd been in there so long there was a stranglehold on my tongue. She kept guessing things and finally she got it, and I said, 'That's it.' She gave me a hug and told me she loved me. I didn't expect it to be that good."

Less than forty-eight hours later, Brent and I convened at the Berkeley park colloquially known as Ho Chi Minh so I could interview him for my article. Things were moving fast, but he seemed a great deal less perplexed than he had during that first meeting. He acted like someone recovering from a long bout of amnesia, relieved to finally be settling into place, while at the same time anxious about being accepted as part of the family.

He told me he was the child of a divorce, the middle of three sons. His mother sounded overburdened, his father a remote workaholic. Brent was frightened of his father; he said that when he was a child, his father sometimes picked him up by his ears as a punishment. Brent surmised that his father's harshness stemmed from frustration, and since Brent's older brother had a serious heart ailment and the youngest was too little to be a target, Brent became the family punching bag.

"I didn't think anything was weird until I reached the fifth grade, when I started realizing maybe something was different," Brent told me as we lay on the grass surrounded by frolicking dogs and Frisbee-throwers. "When I was thirteen, I figured out the label. And that's around when I started being hassled in school, people calling me pussy and fag . . . By the ninth grade, I would be happy if I came home from a day in school and hadn't been called faggot or cocksucker once. That's a really sad standard for what makes you happy.

"One time I was in the locker room, and this guy who didn't like me starts going, 'Brent sucks dick, Brent sucks dick,' and soon the whole locker room was full of guys shouting this for like maybe three minutes. And I had to pretend I didn't give a shit about it, but really I wanted to kill myself. That's when I started cutting school. I had a 4.0 grade average, and within a few months I went to Ds and Fs."

The next year, Brent was expelled for cutting classes; no one tried to discover why his grades had taken a nosedive. His mother, believing he needed discipline, sent him to live with his father in Livermore, a conservative white suburb in Alameda County. The kids at Livermore High weren't as attuned to gay signals as they'd been at urban San Leandro High, barely over the Oakland line, or else the concerted campaign Brent had embarked on to erase clues to his gay identity was working: "I kept my hands in my pockets, said the right things, tried to sound not only straighter but less intelligent."

But now that he'd made the giant step of coming to the youth group, he was having a hard time treading contradictory paths: how could he learn to accept himself while he was hiding who he was? "I'm lying to myself and to the world every day that I'm in school," he said. "And there's no way I can be out in school without being totally ostracized, without violence."

Toward the end of the interview, he told me about his bouts of depression and anorexia, both of which seemed likely, given the necessity of "disappearing" the real Brent. Then he fished around in his backpack for his journal, wanting to show me the entries he'd written. Each began "Dear Brent."

"I must feel better about myself to write that, don't you think?" he asked. "Last week I just wanted to lash out at the straight world for doing this to me. For someone like me to be failing . . . I realize I've made choices, but when I first started cutting I felt I was making the only choice. It was for simple survival. I wasn't choosing to fuck up, I was choosing to not kill myself."

Brent was toying then with the idea of dropping out entirely; I tried to derail that notion, upset that someone so talented and bright would even consider leaving school. He ended up doing exactly the opposite—he came out the following October in his senior year, after meeting a girl who was bisexual but who wouldn't "tolerate me being fearful." They dropped the bomb together during a class discussion in which students were asked to reveal something no one else knew. "Most people said stuff like 'I like ketchup on my pancakes,' but three people said, 'I'm gay.' We fed off each other, 'cause we knew there were other people who would come out too."

Still, in Brent's eyes, self-affirmation was insufficient grounds for coming out—and self-affirmation (or a lover) is often all people have to cling to when the consequences of disclosure begin to mount. "I had spent so much time the year before in depression that I couldn't do it for myself. I didn't really like myself. I needed to do it for other people." Which meant Brent felt compelled to get active, ironically becoming far more visible than he would have if simple honesty had been enough.

He began by challenging what is probably the most common put-down in every school in the United States. "If you were to yell 'nigger,' teachers would come out of the classroom, people in the hallways would object. But 'faggot' is just public access, anybody can say it and it doesn't matter. That's the kind of attitude that keeps people invisible. I felt like I had to make myself more visible. I spoke at student council, I gave them a list of gay and lesbian hot line numbers, I hung up fliers about youth groups. Most of them were torn down, but at least I was doing something tangible."

When he walked into the locker room the day after he addressed the student council, a row of boys sat atop the locker unit above his bench. "They were staring down at me like vultures, whispering to each other. But there was this black guy, one of the only black people at Livermore, and we talked sometimes. He looked over at me and said, 'Hey, dude. Are you gay?' And I said, 'Yeah.' And he said, 'That's cool. Kind of like being black.' The rest of the time in that class, he dressed for PE next to me. I really admired that."

Were Brent not particularly talented, that might have been the end of his saga. He would have struggled through a difficult and contentious eight months, graduated, and gone on to more harmonious pastures. But Brent is an accomplished writer and artist, and perhaps even more important, he was a man on a mission. Soon after his student council speech, he met Rick Aguirre, publisher of *InsideOUT*, a magazine with a national scope and an international mailing list that's put out by Bay Area Sexual Minority Youth Network (sister organization to Brandon Clark's Portland-based OSMYN). Brent became a writer and editor at the magazine, and also began writing and doing illustrations for various gay and mainstream newspapers, including the Pacific News Services' youth supplement, *YO! (Youth Outlook!)*, which is carried in the *Oakland Tribune* and the *San Francisco Independent*. One of his pieces for *YO!* was a double-spread cartoon that told his coming out story. Because of his determination to spread the word, Brent ended up assuming a high profile in what was essentially a fallow field. There are very few gay youth activists, and even fewer who are willing to talk to the media. Half the Queer Nation members I interviewed in '91, though four or five years older than Brent and already safely ensconced in college, would not allow their names to be used in the *Express*.

Brent's father discovered his son was gay when a four-color photo of him standing at the portals of Livermore High appeared on the front page of not only the *Tribune*, but the other five papers in the consortium. "The article came out two days after Christmas. He'd picked me up at my mom's to take me back to Livermore, and I said, 'I guess you saw the article,' and he said, 'What article?' I said, 'I probably shouldn't tell you in a moving vehicle.' He stopped the car and went into a store. When he came out, he said, 'So, you're gay.' On the way home, he told me stuff like, 'The only thing you can do is be the best person you can be. You can't live anybody else's life. All I want for you is to be happy.'"

While Brent was happily surprised by his parents' reactions, he was realistic about what coming out would mean. "I knew my coming out wouldn't allow me to have the same everyday existence heterosexuals did. I knew I'd have more people treating me badly. But at least I wouldn't be treating myself badly. I'd rather be bashed by other people than by myself." Prepared for violence, he was unprepared for the fact that being willing to talk about it, particularly if he used clever turns of phrase like preferring to be bashed by others than by himself, would set talk show hosts salivating like Pavlov's dogs.

What he now calls "my little spiel" soon galvanized the next phase of his life: Brent as TV and radio personality. In short order, he was fielding calls from the sound media, and within the next few months filmed a segment for Fox as well as appeared on a couple TV and radio interview shows. He was also traipsing around the Bay Area making speeches on behalf of gay youth to various organizations. It seemed every other week he was giving a talk to one group or another or jetting down to LA.

But Mr. Personality was still persona non grata at school—especially after the *Tribune* article in late December. "There I was on the front page, in front of the 'Livermore High, Home of the Cowboys' sign, with my freedom rings and my little Castro outfit, talking about how harassment is really dumb. After that, when the teams would travel to a game, they were called 'the fag school.' Which was great, because they were the ones who were harassing me the most. Of course, they chose to see that as more of an excuse to be angry at me."

Brent is able to see the humor in it now, but he's been scarred by a coming out that, because he talks a good line and wields a clever pen, has taken an outlandish turn. What he does is to communicate very well, in the tender, meaty sound bites so essential to television, how he's felt growing up as a gay teenager. Because our society insists no such animal exists, Brent finds himself treated like a latter-day Ishi, the last of the Yahi Indians, with a combination of amazement and reverence. It could go to his head, but in large part, it hasn't; he's more interested in flexing his writing muscles than his ego.

Brent no longer hunches over like a turtle trying to crawl into its shell, though he continues to agonize over his body, and he's more often shy than not. At age eighteen, he's worried that he looks too mature to be sexually interesting. But does he want to attract men who only go after kids? He knows this debate is idiotic, yet his concern is real. While Brent's public image has taken off like a rocket—the professional kid—his private self is still writhing in the hot coals of adolescence, and the schism is most obvious in his tormented relationships. It's almost as if he's developed on two tracks: there's the charmer, with sparkling blue eyes, a jaunty smile, and short styled hair, and there's the self-abnegating cynic who can slide into insecurity and depression as quickly as Sisyphus's stone plunges downhill. His humor is never far under the surface, and can be so biting to himself or to others that sometimes it seems as if he's launching torpedoes from behind his long lashes. In spite of his celebrity, our talks tend to cover the same ground they have for over two years: me trying to convince multitalented Brent to go to a good college.

To me, it was a foregone conclusion that Brent would graduate from Livermore and then zoom off to school, there to be lauded and praised. After all, didn't he write terrific poetry? Draw wonderful cartoons? Wouldn't being gay even help him get in and be taken seriously once he was there? I was such a Brent advocate that I didn't care—let's use political correctness to our advantage for once, I thought. What I hadn't counted on was Brent himself and the different ways high school had affected us.

I endured high school in deep cover. College provided an escape from what had become tantamount to living behind the Iron Curtain, but it also gave both me and my audience (parents, friends, relatives) the illusion that Nothing Is Wrong, when, in fact, just about everything was. By coming out in his senior year, Brent had no such illusion to maintain, and he had become exhausted from the life he's led since telling the truth.

After the piece in the *Tribune* appeared, occasional harassment became a daily—even an hourly—event. "I couldn't go from one class to another, or around the quad, or even around town, without people yelling things at me. I was told that if I tried to go to the prom I'd be killed. But by the end of the year I'd racked up so many cuts I couldn't go anyway." Brent is dabbling his fork in his eggs as he remembers the events of eleven months earlier. For this interview in May 1994, we've graduated from Ho Chi Minh to Edy's, a cafe in downtown Berkeley that serves me a lunchtime hot fudge sundae and Brent a not much healthier Denver omelette, a far cry from the fast from hell he was on when we first met, Diet Cokes and Tic-Tacs.

"Why were you still cutting? To avoid being hassled?"

He's shaking his head. "No, the harassment made me feel powerful. They were reacting out of fear of me whereas before, when I was in the closet, I was reacting out of fear of them. No, I was still cutting because I was so busy nurturing myself and fighting other people that I couldn't focus on my schoolwork. I decided I didn't feel pride in graduating from a school that had treated me this way. If I graduated, I would only be doing it because I was trying to go about things in the conventional way. I'd already given up doing things conventionally. So I got my GED.

"College wasn't on my mind when I got out of high school. It just seemed like another institution that was important to heterosexuality. And I spent so much time concentrating on myself and accepting myself and fighting for other people that school seemed like the thing I had to get rid of in order to get on with my life."

Hmmm. Why do I suspect there's more to this story?

It's not long before he confesses that he's scared to go to college. "I'm just not ready to go back to school, to deal with meeting a whole new group of people. Everybody says college is so much better than high school, but I'm not ready to take the risk."

"It seems like a risk?" College to me was a refuge; I'm having a hard time reorienting myself.

"Oh, yeah." He clinches the matter by looking so haunted that I feel like I'm enticing him to return for another tour in Vietnam.

We are having this conversation only a couple months after I watched him receive an award from an educators' group for an essay he'd entered in a Bay Area–wide contest. Nervous as a colt before a race, he had paced around before the ceremony, asking me how he could relax. Should he smoke a joint? Did he look okay? Should he have a beer? Then he climbed on the stage, smiled shyly, and told a few jokes that were truly funny. As he read his essay, he glanced up a couple times, as if to make sure his audience hadn't drifted off past the reach of his imagination. All were still in place, listening raptly.

But would he let on to these educators or the talk show hosts that he's terrified to go to college, that he's suffering combat fatigue, that he can't bring himself to stiffen up his spine and unbutton his lip and sail back into battle? No, because that's his own private skirmish, cordoned off to the public until the wounded are removed from the field. He would rather lump college in with enforced heterosexuality and tell me how harassment builds character. He gets frustrated when I mutter that I'm not looking forward to a particular event. "Why bother to go with that attitude?" he snaps. Brent is the power of positive thinking made manifest; he's had to be.

During Brent's break from school—or what I hoped was a break since he wouldn't call it that—he occupied himself by working at the *Express* and at another paper his aunt edits. He also drew away from a number of his political commitments, including editing *InsideOUT*. He'd moved back into his mother's house in San Leandro after he received his GED in the summer of 1993; soon he trucked his books and artwork into the adjoining garage. Tossing and turning on a too-short sofa that serves as his bed, Brent would often come to work half asleep. He continued to make public appearances; sometimes I'd duck into his cubicle to chat and find him on the phone formulating a line on the Topic of the Month. But mostly he worked on his poetry and op-ed pieces and made friends outside the small world of the youth group.

All this was harder, of course, because of his age: "I can't get in ninety-nine percent of the really great bars," he tells me the first week of August 1994 as we scoot up to the Brick Hut, a lesbian-owned restaurant in Berkeley, for a quick lunch break. "There's no eighteen-or-up clubs for gay youth in San Francisco." What's there to do besides linger over lattes in the Castro or—horrors—go to the groups? Nevertheless, I imagine him on the gay equivalent to R&R; he was hanging around with gay employees from the *Express*, journeying to the Castro on weekends, and reading his poetry at gay clubs and bookstores, a very different reality from a year earlier in suburbia, when he would spend days responding to taunts and evenings cleaning up apples that were hurled at his father's house from passing cars. "Do you feel you've immersed yourself in a gay-friendly environment?" I ask him as he pours syrup on his Texas-style French toast; like most people, breakfast is his first meal, only Brent's breakfast happens around one in the afternoon.

"I don't think there is such a thing," he says, fork at half-mast. "I've found an environment that most straight people take for granted, which [consists of] people who are like me, some of whom I get along with and some of whom I don't. I don't feel like I've been swept into an underground world. I've just incorporated people like me into the life I've always had. And that's the place where I was able to make a decision about the rest of my life."

That decision, he tells me, is to go back to school. "I did what I needed to do in high school, but I missed out on my education. I want to learn more, explore more things. And college will be better than high school. In college I'm sure I won't be getting death threats." He ponders his French toast, then decides that sounds naïve, even Pollyanna-ish. "Even if I do," he amends, "I'm used to it, and I'll stand up for myself."

Then he sighs and says something I had thought all along. "If someone had taken the initiative and put me there, it would have been easy to go back to school. I wasn't willing to take the initiative because school had hurt me so much."

Brent has spent much of his year off trying to heal the schism between his public and private selves, a fracture that has the potential of a personal San Andreas fault. For this reason alone, I ended up believing that Brent's choice to take time for himself was the right one, no matter what his motivation. During that time he did a lot of thinking about how he functioned as a sexual being and what expectations he had of himself as a gay man within a gay and lesbian community.

"I know a lot of people whose way of coming out was having sex," Brent says. "For me that wasn't an option, because I was such a bad, geeky, ugly kid. I didn't feel like a sexual person, even though I started feeling sexually attracted to men around eight and masturbating at ten. So basically I came out on theory.

"The first time I ejaculated I didn't know what it meant. I ran to the bathroom holding myself, hoping I wasn't leaking out. I was, 'Make this stop, I promise I won't have these evil thoughts anymore.' "

"Evil because they were about men?"

He nods. "I think if I'd been having sexual thoughts about girls, I would have learned about masturbation the way most people do, by talking to their friends in the locker room. I would have been more chummy with boys."

Brent believes that apart from his parents' divorce, his father's sternness, and his own "geekiness," he would have felt insecure simply on the basis of his body "doing things I felt were wrong. Having to deny my body's natural impulses made me feel I couldn't trust my own physical being." He was locked in battle against himself.

"My parents got separated when I was in the fifth grade. I thought, 'Oh my God, this is my last chance. If they're divorced now, that means I won't have a male role model.' I didn't get along with my father, but I wanted him in my life simply because he would turn me into a man."

"You wanted to be cured."

"Oh, definitely. I wanted to get hypnotherapy, but then the hypnotherapist would have to know I was gay. And I was going to get married, up until around thirteen. When I was growing up I thought gays were all promiscuous and old men walking poodles on rhinestone leashes. But by the time I actually was going to come out, I felt, 'This will be so cool. I'll enter a community where there is no racism, no sexism, because how could people who are oppressed want to oppress others?' Later I realized that's often exactly why."

Right from that first day, when I saw him crying after the meeting at the Pacific Center, Brent's expectations have not lived up to reality. A starving man can hope for too much or too little, and Brent did a bit of both. "I thought the only reason I was shy was because I was gay in a straight world, and immediately upon going to the group I would meet somebody and everything would be perfect. When that didn't happen, I freaked out. I felt, 'What's wrong with me? Not even gay people like me.' "

He has not yet managed a good relationship. "A lot of my screwy relationships are because I'm a teenager, but there's more to it than that." He attributes the "more" to a potpourri of factors: how men are socialized to value sex over love, a lack of role models, and a childhood where men were not affectionate. "My first boyfriend knew I'd been anorexic, so he'd say things like, 'Can I see a picture of you from then? You might have looked better.' At the time I didn't see anything wrong. I thought that kind of meanness must be what it meant to be gay. I was repeating what I knew from my father. I have not allowed women in my life to be abusive, because I was brought up around women who weren't. I've had real relationships with women, but I'd never had a real male friend. How could I have a relationship with somebody if I couldn't be friends with him?"

Sexuality turns out to be at the center of this quagmire;

Brent is still battling himself. "Gay men grow up learning that we're never going to find love. That we can't. Two men can't love each other. It's wrong, it's evil."

"But once you fell in love you'd see the fallacy in that," I say.

Brent is shaking his head. "How can you get to the point where you can love somebody if you don't think it's legitimate to begin with?"

"So because a lot of gay people are struggling with internalized homophobia—"

"Including myself," Brent says. "I'm really out there politically and I can defend anyone's right to do what they want. But I have a lot of problems with sex. For instance, I've never had a complete sexual dream. I have dreams where I meet men but I never approach them. Or I approach them and then it turns out they've died. If I can't even dream about it . . ."

"I grew up learning that what I felt was wrong, and there was a lot of shame involved. Now that I've come out, I'm expected to suddenly forget all that. It took me a while to get to this point, and it'll take me a while to get out of it. Besides, it's hard to alleviate guilt on theory. All the sexual experiences I've had have been really gross. I haven't lost my ideals about love and soul mates, but until I experience something remotely healthy, it's all intangible and abstract."

He smiles at the waitress who comes to refresh his coffee, and we talk about Brent's friends, most of whom are women. Finally I ask what being gay will mean to him. "Sometimes I feel removed from the idea of being queer, of being deviant," he says. "Then all of a sudden it hits me: 'Oh my God. I'm gay. I'm gay in a straight world.' It used to make me want to cry; now my eyes get really big and there's this little twinge of shock. Then I smile, because I feel I've survived. Having to fight against a world that didn't like me, first for other people and then for myself, made me stronger, and made me love myself. It's made me more creative.

"And I don't think I would have been able to be part of this media blitzkrieg if I were straight. I wouldn't feel so empowered, or have a bond with my gay brothers and sisters, I wouldn't have created the bubble that made me intelligent enough or creative enough. On the flip side, I think there's just as much love out there for me, but it might be harder to find. Maybe my next real struggle will be finding an environment where love exists. Certainly not in the Castro," he says with a wink.

Which is where, in mid-September, after he's left the *Express* to pursue his college career, I next run into Brent. For a few minutes, we talk about the community college he's attending. "Disappointing," he says. "Rinky-dink." But that's not what's on his mind. "Oprah called. Well, not Oprah herself, but her people. Can you think of anything to say about the Helms amendment?"

"Voting for stupidity," I suggest.

A glint comes into his eye as he gives me a hug. "Good," he says. I know he'll think of something much better. "Call me with anything else."

As I hurry up Market Street to a meeting of my gay study group, I'm puzzling how to get him off the media trail and into UC Berkeley. Within a block, I decide I'm old-fashioned. Oprah needs Brent more than Brent needs Oprah, and with his brand of rough honesty, he makes an attractive spokesman. But I can't get over the fact that we need spokespeople at all. Brent has spent his adolescence first denying he exists, then proving it again and again. Even as he constructs his proofs for an eager audience, he's regarded as an anomaly, not as a representative, a perception troubling both for the community and for himself. Seldom is he allowed simply to be an individual, for that's the real luxury in life, one denied to those on the wrong side of a dozen different fences. When the gaze that's fixed upon you is cruel and myopic, your own vision, of necessity, turns to the long view. Maybe someday we'll be able to see what all of us have been missing.

"I'm getting a lot more festive."

When Greg Fowler came out to his parents, he stopped off first to tell a college friend who lives in a small town halfway between Atlanta and Albany, Georgia, where Greg's family lives. Greg had been intending to come out to his friend anyway, he says, but he was also hedging his bet: if his parents tossed him out on his ear, he wanted to make sure he wouldn't have to drive all the way back to Atlanta that night.

When he got to his parents' house, he left his suitcase in the trunk of his car. He tells me that's what hurt them the most, that he actually believed they might reject him. As he sips at his soft drink, he looks abashed. Still: "I'd seen so many friends' parents literally put them out on the street that it didn't seem like that foreign of an idea to me."

We are sitting in a restaurant a block from Metro Center in downtown Washington, D.C. When Greg appeared in the doorway of the Cafe Mozart, blinking in the glaring light of the streetfront deli, I saw a handsome, neatly tailored, self-assured African-American man. As he passed by the glass-encased cheeses and meats on his way toward the bar, he began to glance around shyly, and I realized this self-assured man was a youth a bit nervous to be looking for someone he didn't know, someone who would ask him to reveal himself in ways he never had before. He's so young, I thought. It was the last time I would focus on his age, not because he was guarded—in fact, he opened up more than he probably intended—but because once I stepped up to him, he immediately became the Southern gentleman, so set on putting me at ease that he did not again look as lost.

Greg had been referred to me by people he'd never met, other young gays who had read an essay about growing up that he'd submitted to *InsideOUT*, the magazine for sexual minority youth. "My memory of that day is as clear as crystal," Greg wrote in his essay. "It was the Sunday after my eighth birthday. I awakened from my nap in my parents' office suite at church. I looked over to the television set, and on the screen I saw my uncle preaching. 'God sent me to tell it like it is!' my uncle thundered as the crowd screamed with approval. 'Stop calling them homosexuals. Call them what they are—faggots!' "

For more than twenty years, Greg's family—his parents and his aunt and his uncle—have devoted their lives to building a large religious corporation from the ground up. Based in Albany, the Independent Holiness Religious Churches claims close to a thousand churches worldwide, several publishing arms, and a television station. Greg's parents function as top administrators and sometime preachers; the man Greg calls his "ex-uncle"—his uncle by a now dissolved marriage—is the Apostle Isaiah Revills, minister and founder of IHRC. "If there's such a thing as a modern-day religious prophet, he probably fits the bill," Greg says. "He's grown a long gray beard, he has these fiery eyes and a powerful, booming voice. But our relationship has never been that great."

Greg incurred the wrath of the prophet because he had the temerity to outshine Isaiah's sons. "There was this hierarchy, the sons of the people who ran the mission. The secretary's son, the leader's son, the chairman's son—there were six of us who sat on the top. My uncle's sons were technically on top, but they were never mentally as smart as I was. And a lot of people were looking to me to sort of . . ." He pauses, wondering how to put this without sounding immodest, and finally plunges in, choosing truth over propriety. "Groups in the church would say that they had these dreams that I was going to be something great. They said God had shown them."

"So you were being groomed?"

He nods. "There were times when I went along with it." This now strikes him as something to be ashamed of, but the prospect that he could use his abilities to perform good works must then have been compelling. "One night we were in Bible class, and the teacher never showed up. Me being the person that I was, I just decided to teach. The result was that I ended up teaching for the next couple months. I couldn't have been older than ten, and I was teaching the adult Bible class."

But whenever Greg shone, rain clouds would descend on everyone around him. "It's bad enough when one of the elder mothers of the church pulls you aside and says, 'I see great things in store . . .' But when that gets back to the parents, it causes bickering. It caused a lot more problems as I grew older, because I got asked to do more things. Once I did a speech for the church during a convention. There were at least five thousand people sitting out there. I get through this whole speech, and at the end, they stand up and start clapping. I'm just so happy to be through with the thing, I run out the door. I run around the church and come back in, and they're all still standing up clapping. But the politics of the church dictated that the next night the founder's son give a presentation. And everybody sort of modestly clapped, but nobody—"

"Went wild," I supply, picturing the scene.

"Finally some of the elders get up, telling everybody, 'Stand up and clap!' My parents were laughing . . ."

He smiles at the memory, this earnest young man who spurned the religious life that seemed to hold so much promise for the very secular world of public service in Washington, D.C. He's just wound up a winner in a reshuffling of jobs at the National Endowment for the Humanities, snaring the title of media relations specialist at age twenty-three. With his soft eyes that can be bashful and penetrating at once, I don't wonder that both the church ladies and the director of personnel at NEH believe this considerate and self-reflective man to be someone special.

"You must always have felt different," I say, "apart from being gay." I can't imagine growing up at the nerve center of a religious conglomerate, in a business that slathers a pretense of righteousness over the usual cutthroat machinations of any large corporation, much less one where factions have chosen you the wunderkind in a familial drama of succession worthy of the Greeks.

He nods. "It was very, very weird. And the politics of it were very, very difficult. We're not talking about a moderate church, we're talking very conservative. No movies, no sinful music. My junior year I was elected chairman of the prom, but I couldn't go, supposedly. And then I joined the marching band, which is another no-no, because they played secular music."

Greg felt different for other reasons as well. He skipped first and second grades, entering the third grade when he was five. All through school, he was two to three years younger than his peers. "For many years, I was the outcast. I was really smart, but my emotional development was a lot slower than everybody else's. I was still doing the buddy-buddy thing when everybody else was going on to the macho distance thing. Then somewhere between my junior and senior year in high school, before I turned fifteen, I went from Mr. Outcast to Mr. Popular, to the guy who actually beat out the quarterback for student body president."

"How'd you manage that?"

"Part of it was simply a desire to change. A big inspiration was my friend Charley. We used to think he bought his clothes straight out of *GQ*. I was wondering, 'How can I change my image?' and he said, 'Well, you need to dress better.' He literally mentored me to a different physical appearance, and that slowly gave me a different mental image. The result was the person who became student body president. I still have no idea how *that* happened."

The waiter comes to take our orders, so for a few moments we do a complicated dance of questions and decisions. "My best friend at the time was this guy named Jason," Greg says, after he determines what kind of schnitzel he wants. "He was kind of a carouser. As he and I became closer, he stopped hanging around those people. A lot of his buddies didn't like me. They felt I had somehow tainted the good times they were having. They retaliated by hinting to Jason that I had more interests in him than were natural. It spread like wildfire. Even teachers were talking. But I didn't know anything about it.

"A couple weeks before I found out what was happening, Jason began to change. People were saying [to Jason], 'Well, if he's interested in you as more than a friend, and you're hanging around him, then maybe you're interested in him too.' That's as close to being excommunicated as most teenagers ever want to be. He began to play this double game of trying to be my friend, but at the same time trying to keep them appeased. He'd talk about me behind my back and do things that were very subtle."

Jason also did something that was very unsubtle, but Greg isn't ready to tell me that part yet. He sips at his soda, and the waiter comes with Greg's salad but not mine. After we reiterate what we ordered, Greg returns to his story. "Remember I'm only fifteen. Very naïve. And I'm going through this phase where I need approval and acceptance. I'm thinking something's wrong, but Jason wasn't telling me anything. Finally I take this girl home, and she just comes right out and tells me what's going on.

"I was devastated by that entire experience. It practically destroyed our friendship. I never talked to people about Jason. It was too painful a memory. And I totally isolated myself from everyone." That summer Greg got a job at an amusement park and quickly picked up the nickname Spooky because he'd go for days without saying a word.

"Did part of you think that what they were saying was true?"

"My immediate feeling was not that this is true. Mentally I was still far from that point where I could admit it. I still have difficulty thinking about it. A lot of that period is just a blur for me." But as he spears a green bean, he suddenly laughs and says, "Once when we were in Sunday school, the guys were ganging up on me about my eyelashes, saying they were entirely too long and beautiful for me to really be normal. I was so appalled by this thought that I went home and cut my eyelashes off. So a part of me acknowledged how I felt. The other part of me slammed shut any doors whatsoever. And for the next couple years, I didn't consider going on a date with anybody."

In his last two years of college, he dated a girl named Rita, but his primary relationship was with his best friend Sonny. Greg considers it a stroke of fortune that he met Sonny when he did, during a brief period when he was more open with people, before he returned to his protective shell. Sonny and he immediately bonded, and over the next two years, there were only a couple evenings they spent apart, girlfriend or no. When Sonny came out to Greg, it forced Greg to look at himself.

"So you were never lovers, just joined at the hip?"

He's nodding. "In the process of coming out, and helping each other deal with it, we ended up being in a relationship that became totally engulfing. We literally could not stand to be apart."

"What happened with Rita?"

He pokes at his salad. "I always tell people this: Rita is like chocolate mousse. A small amount is fine. Too much will make you sick. We could never get along for more than an hour. She's just a volatile woman.

"When I first met her, I was going through this cycle

of, 'I need to do the normal thing.' I was thinking, 'She's cute. I'd like to go out with her.'"

"Was she a cover?"

He ponders this. "Like I said, Sonny and I were practically living together, and people were starting to whisper. Once Rita and I were out dancing, and I literally made out with her on the floor. I was doing it very consciously, knowing people were watching us. So there was that element there, but I don't know how much. As time went on, it just wasn't working, and so we went our separate ways.

"Then Sonny came out to me. I was still very much in the closet, even with myself. It took me another month or so before I could even say the word 'gay.' Homosexual was a little bit easier because it's so scientific. Even to this day, I must admit I have a hard time saying 'gay.'

"Anyway, Sonny's coming out was what triggered mine. Because in the process of trying to help him understand what he was feeling, I began to figure out what I was feeling. And to put a name to it."

"And this is when you were eighteen?" I kept having to remember he'd graduated from high school at fifteen.

"I'd just turned nineteen. It's funny, because you know what you're feeling, and you know that what you're feeling is by definition something, but you can't admit that what it is is what other people refer to it as." I chuckle at the awkward syntax, but it's a faithful description of that sort of dual identity coupled with denial that some people carry on long into adulthood.

Later on, after Greg and Sonny had dissected to the bone the subject of what it might mean to them to be gay, they decided they needed input beyond their circle of two.

After deliberating for more than a month ("Each week we'd say we were going, and then we wouldn't do it"), they finally worked up the courage to attend the gay youth group in Atlanta. "We drove down the street real slow. We had some very negative images, like they're gonna kill us. Sonny was terrified. He's like, 'Greg, I'm not getting out of the car. I can't move.' I ended up going, 'Sonny, either you get out of the car or I'm going to march up there and bring them all back down here to you.' "

"What were you so afraid of? People seeing you? Who you'd find inside that house?"

"I think it was more of an irrational fear of facing up to who we were. And realizing that once we'd taken that step, there was really no going back. And the funny thing was, it was almost an addictive poison to us. We kept going to that group long after we should have stopped. But it was the only outlet we had."

"Why should you have stopped?"

Just as he's about to explain, two things happen: the waiter brings our entrées, and Greg's beeper goes off. The caller is his quasi-boyfriend Holden. I say quasi because from Greg's description, the two seem marvelously in love but they're holding off doing anything about it. "His mom doesn't like me," Greg confides when he returns from the phone. "Correction. His mom likes me. His mom doesn't like him hanging around me.

"Anyway," he says, slicing into his schnitzel, "while I think that almost any gay youth grows up quicker than the average youth, at the same time, because of the festive nature of the gay community, you are allowed a lot more free fun. Certain considerations or morals that you would have to observe if you were straight aren't there for gay kids."

"So if you break one major rule, then all the rest are off," I say, though I've seen it work in just the reverse—after breaking Rule Number One, you enforce the others doubly hard.

"If the emphasis is on being free and not on being considerate," Greg continues, "they're not growing up in the sense that they don't understand how other people's feelings are affected by what they do. So people can be petty or envious or have a lot more drama. The youth group in Atlanta was like that, plus Sonny is extremely attractive. From the very first night we were there, people were hitting on him. This one guy comes up to us and says, 'Why are you two standing off by yourselves? We don't bite. Maybe we nibble a little.' Sonny was so put off by that statement that he never spoke to the guy again.

"But the group helped us a lot. Not only to introduce us to other people, but to acknowledge that we weren't weird. Sonny and I used to worry terribly about turning into drag queens, transsexuals. But last year Sonny dressed up in drag for Halloween. He laughed so hard when he told me about it. It's funny when you look back on it, but when we were going through it, it was hard."

We both address ourselves to our food for a spell. Finally Greg says, "I read somewhere that part of the fun about being around gay men is the sense of living life to the fullest. And that's funny because the thing in high school that was killing me was not dealing with my sexuality. The very thing that's helped me more than anything to deal with the somber, quiet, spooky person I'd become is my sexuality and the community and the ability to, every once in a while, let things go. Because I need that. I need it very much. I spent a lot of years where 'These are the rules, and you follow them.' My uncle and my parents used to tell me when I was little, 'Your life's the only Bible some people will ever read, and you have to set the example. If those souls are lost and go to hell, God's going to hold you responsible.'

"Now when I talk to people, they throw scripture back at me. But I generally know scripture better, and in the Aramaic and the Greek. Even my parents think if I'd done my research I'd see that I'm wrong. But the fact is, I have, and all that was the process of me saying finally to myself that I'm okay."

"Do you still go to church?" I ask.

"For a little while, I went to MCC," he says, referring to the gay-oriented Metropolitan Community Church begun by Reverend Troy Perry. "But the minute they asked me to do anything beyond share in the congregation, I stopped coming. They wanted me to do a solo, they wanted me to do a sermon." He pauses and then shakes his head. "It's still very uncomfortable for me to spend any large amount of time in church. It's had a great impact upon my life. A lot of it was good, but most of the good was not a direct good. Most of the good has more to do with how I reacted to it than what it was intended to do. There's a very difficult reconciliation within that has to happen that goes beyond working out what your self-identity is, but reconciling that identity with everything you feel you are, or that you have been taught you are. Still, I'd do it all over again, if I had to, because I think I would end up like I am."

"And you like who you are?"

"I'm beginning to like who I am," he says with a tinge of surprise, as if he'd never expected to hear himself say such a thing. "It's funny, because Holden is one of those people who, every single day, tells me how much he loves me. Sometimes I have a hard time believing I'm lovable. And he says that's hard to understand because he sees so much to love." Greg arches a skeptical eyebrow. "Don't ask me, but he does."

"You of anyone should have some insight into the motivations of the religious Right," I observe.

"I can see the unnamed fear that a lot of people have, because it's something I experienced. I very much remember that fear Sonny and I had about going to the group. What were we afraid of? We had no idea. All we knew was that inside we were filled with these fears. We couldn't name them, couldn't tell you the source, but they were there. So when I hear other people going off, it's like, 'I understand your fear.' But unfortunately, people who don't have to deal with it personally have no reason to ever confront that fear, to really ask what they're afraid of."

"And there's plenty of propaganda telling people they *should* be frightened," I say. "Antigay videos like *Gay Rights, Special Rights* and *The Gay Agenda.*"

Greg is nodding and gesturing with his fork. "There's this insidious thing in those videos that suggests that their very presence, whether they *do* anything or not, is going to be the undermining of society. It's the root of all evil."

"Have you noticed you sometimes use 'they' when you're referring to gay people?"

He puts down his fork and looks at me, and we both grin at each other. "Well," he says. He chuckles, and then gets back on track. "I don't think that the vast majority of people in this country really care, one way or the other."

"Don't care about gays?"

"Don't care about gays as much as they think they do. A couple of years ago, Barney Frank made the statement to me that in this country, people are a lot less homophobic than they think they are, and a lot more racist than they think they are. But what we're going through right now is probably the dying breaths of conservatism. I think what will happen first is we'll get pulled more to the right, and people will be so devastated by the consequences that it will snap a lot further to the left than they anticipated."

"Did you grow up with that root-of-all-evil assumption about gays or the gay community?"

He's shaking his head. "I honestly did not know there was such a thing. I really didn't. You read my essay." In it, he describes how, after his uncle's thunderous speech, he asked his mother what a homosexual was. His mother gave a definition, told eight-year-old Greg that homosexuality was wrong, and mentioned a cousin no one in her family had spoken to for eighteen years because "he refused to change his ways." After all this daunting information, she added a softener: "I know everybody goes through a phase where they like being around other people of the same sex. You are probably going through it now."

"In my mind, I pictured the Path to Liking Girls," Greg wrote. "For the present there was a Closed Until Further Notice sign there, but I figured it would change as I grew out of the Phase.

"For all my brilliance," he reminds me, "I was a very naïve child. I was just trying to fit in. For instance, we all made up stories about girls, and I made them up like everybody else did. One night, during my senior year, we got called to the [church] office. Unknown to me, these other people really had been sleeping around. We got called in, and they all confessed to these things they had done. And they got to me and I'm like, 'Haven't done a thing.' My uncle was livid. There were the six of us, all boys, and all the parents . . . and I remember my uncle saying, 'What makes you think you're so special that you don't have to fall?' And I was like, 'I have no idea. I didn't do anything.' "

Greg's naïveté must have made what happened to him later that year all the more unbearable—enough to drive him to his summer of silence at the amusement park and years of solitude afterward. Now that we've ordered dessert, he's finally ready to tell me what happened with his high school best friend, Jason. "He calls me one night at home and says, 'Greg, can you come over right now?' And me being the person that I was, I'm always going to be there. I had this image of the ideal friendship, you always come when the person calls . . . I was such a naïve child.

"So I went over, and all my enemies were there, and they were all drunk. Jason gets up to go to the bathroom. He comes back out with his pants still down. And he comes over and his crotch is literally right in front of my face, and he's rubbing his crotch, and saying the most horrible things. He was like, 'Greg, you know you want it.' And I started crying, I was just crying like a baby. And when he saw I was crying, he stopped. He stood there for a minute, looking at me, and then he started crying. And the other guys stop laughing and are like, 'What the hell is happening?' And he knelt down and started wiping my face. And one of them asked why he continued to hang around me. I remember him saying, very low, 'Greg loves me. Greg loves me. And no one else does.'

"There was so much pain there," he says, sighing. Then he adds, "Even today, when Jason calls, I can feel the shields going up. But it's nowhere as bad as it once was. That has less to do with me forgiving him than me coming to terms with myself."

Greg believes his relationship with Holden has changed him for the better. "I'm becoming much more vulnerable to people," he says. "I'm starting to care. I'm starting to let people know how I feel, for the very first time in my life."

"You felt like it wasn't safe before?"

"Very."

"That makes sense, especially after you opened up with Jason and then disaster struck."

"One of the most potent phrases I remember from my childhood was, 'Never wear your heart on your sleeve, because if people can see it, they'll stab it.' I still feel that way sometimes. I identified very, very seldomly with other kids. I still find myself in the position of being intellectually a lot older but emotionally younger than I am. So my friends are often younger. Holden's probably the youngest . . ." Holden is not yet eighteen, and his mother has forbidden him to see Greg. "It's become almost a game now. Holden likes taking a challenge."

"What's your biggest fear?" I ask.

"Losing Holden," Greg says promptly. But that isn't really it. "It's more . . . losing what he's done for my . . . my self-actualization process. Making me feel worth something."

"It sounds like he's helped you be more self-loving."

Greg's brilliant smile lights up his face. "Holden would say that was the perfect way of putting it."

"Even if Holden went away, that feeling wouldn't," I assure him. "It's part of you now."

"Yeah. But he's important to me. I've always been able to love the other person, to do, you know, the quote-unquote Christian thing . . . but all that time, I was trying to show other people what I wanted . . ."

"Do unto others except that people didn't do unto you."

"And the result was thinking maybe I'm not worth what I'm asking. Holden gives me a lot of that confidence. And one of the reasons I love him so is that it's in his nature to be exactly what I need him to be."

I think he's finished, but he's still considering my question about fear. "I've gotten over my fear of hell," he says. "That took a long, long time. Then I saw it had nothing to do with my sexuality, but instead with rethinking the scripture. The Seventh-Day Adventists don't believe there's a hell, and I agreed with them after reading what they said.

"My next fear was never finding anybody to care about me. At all, in any sense. That fear went once I met Sonny. And then of course, there's the fear that maybe I'm not really worth it. That's probably my most serious fear."

"Were you afraid you were going to have to change?"

Change is not something Greg takes lightly. "I knew that there was some ambiguous monster that could not be explained that I'd have to face and that I'd have to become. I didn't know what it was, but I was very afraid of what kind of changes would happen to me. And the funny thing is, people are so impressed with the kind of person I've become. They're like, 'We never thought your stuffy ass . . .' I'm so much more comfortable with myself. So much more self-assured. You and I would never have had this conversation if I hadn't changed a lot.

"Even people who come out at an early age are forced to change, though their change usually comes from the other direction." Greg draws a diagram on a napkin while the waiter takes away our plates, explaining that everyone is moving toward a middle ground.

I'm at a loss. "In terms of flamboyance?"

He nods. "This one friend of mine floats up the stairs, while I'm the kind of person who walks up the stairs one by one."

"So you're getting more festive," I say, using his word, "while he's becoming more conservative—"

"Oh, I'm getting a lot more festive," Greg assures me. "So I did feel I was going to change, but I had no idea at the time that the change would be so good for me. I've known a lot of young people in the churches we have throughout the country, and a lot of them depress me. It's like they're caught in this downward spiraling trap and they have no way out of it. I often want to tell this one friend of mine, 'What you need is a good man.' But he wouldn't see the humor in it."

On the train back to Manhattan, my thoughts keep straying to Greg. When he walked me to the Metro, he said, "I really couldn't have done this interview two months ago. I didn't like myself enough. I was so afraid no one would ever love me."

The youngest son of eight children, for whom greatness was foreseen, who was petted and praised, believed he was unworthy of love. But when he saw himself through the eyes of a man who loves him, he was able to find love for himself.

The simplicity of it gave me hope, because what all of us are about, more than anything, is love.

Greg believes he was "saved" by his homosexuality: from a dismal, predictable future, from his own somber, strict personality. But was he somber because he was burdened by the weight of all those souls looking to him for guidance or because he was afraid of the "monster" he would someday have to face? Was his childhood oppressive or did it give him the strength he needed to become the idealistic, intensely curious man he is today?

Sexual orientation, race, class, and gender may be small portions of what define us as human beings, but assumptions are made about who we are based on how we fit within those categories. And we cannot escape our own double consciousness—if we are black, we cannot escape seeing ourselves as black, or as gay, or as women, so the definitions have meaning for us apart from whatever onus society assigns to them. One of my closest friends has said that she would find it ethically more consistent to be a lesbian, but in real-life terms she couldn't bear to spend all that energy on being deviant. I understand exactly what she means: I cannot imagine myself straight because so much of my sense of self has been won in apposition and in synchronicity with what society declares to be my most defining feature.

As Greg feels he is moving toward a middle ground of freer expression, he can look back at his own anxiety about how he would be perceived, and how he would perceive himself: "What I was looking for was this more normal . . . not normal, but you know what I mean—people who didn't feel the need to dress a certain way. They were themselves. I wanted the straight life of a homosexual. When Sonny and I came out, we considered it a major insult to have anything effeminate about us. We wanted to blend in. Now blending in is not so much a necessity, but more to do with being the perfect actor."

"Being a chameleon," I suggested, "able to fit anywhere."

"That's part of the empowerment," Greg said. "To take the struggle to fit in and the burden that places on our community and make it into something the other side never thought of, something the heterosexuals never thought of. So that rather than simply falling or stumbling under that burden, we feel like we're rising to the challenge.

"Some of the people I so dreaded—the queens—have been the very healing ones I required. Because they were on the outside what I was feeling on the inside: the way people looked at them was how I felt people were feeling about me. We use the term 'coming out' specifically for the experience of gay people getting out of the closet. But in reality, life, for everybody, is a big coming out process, and learning to deal with the things that make us all alike, as opposed to different."

Greg is like a man unwrapping a string of packages and finding wonderful gifts inside instead of the cruel practical jokes he expected. Best of all, the gifts—like Holden—are by their very nature exactly what he needed.

postscript

the nature
of difference

On one of my plane trips east, I sat next to a geneticist on his way to a convention in Paris. First we bemoaned the death of rain forests, then the falling water table in the Midwest, then the necessity to provide as much food in the next twenty years as has been produced in all of recorded history. We'd gotten to genetically altering the sex of fish (males put on poundage faster and thus can reach peak size faster), when he asked what I did for a living. I explained. There was a long pause. "When we find the gene for homosexuality," he finally said, "the abortion debate will be altered beyond recognition."

A few years earlier, when *Newsweek* devoted the final third of its cover story on "born gay" to an unapologetic consideration of aborting all those yet-to-be-identified lavender fetuses, I found myself shocked and devastated but not surprised—in my heart I'd always known most people considered me better off dead. Whether I believed a gene existed was immaterial to my horror at being dispatched so cavalierly. "What galls me," I said to my seatmate, "is that the question of abortion would even be raised, and raised in such a casual, certain manner, without any acknowledgment that what we're talking about is genocide."

He looked at me in surprise, and then he tried to explain, in a very calm and gentle voice, what he believed I was incapable of understanding. "It's like if you were born blind," he said. "You wouldn't know what it was to be sighted, and you'd go through life never realizing what you'd missed. But we, as sighted people, know exactly how the quality of that person's life has been lessened. So . . ." He glanced at me with pity. "For almost any parent, it wouldn't *be* a dilemma."

How can we get to liberty and the pursuit of happiness when we can't even agree on the life part? That a woman would think she's harboring an alien in her womb because her baby might end up elsewhere on the sexual orientation scale is why the gay community has become both a refuge and a ghetto, and why identity politics is a necessity and a scourge.

Author Dorothy Allison, responding to queer theorists who slam home the point that desire does not an identity make, says we should deconstruct heterosexuality first. In comparison to sex, sexual orientation is a cinch to deconstruct, but we are all—queer teenagers, queer computer nerds, transsexuals, Castro Street clones, lesbian separatists, queer straight people, gay actors and tennis players, and even those theorists—challenging the pervasive inequities that rest on sexism and gender stereotyping. Homophobia is a straw man to prop up gender roles and sexism, using demonized gay people as object lessons in what will become of you if you step out of line. Painting gays as "other" disguises the fact that this is a system in which everyone loses.

As I followed the geneticist off the plane, I was struck by the irony that a man who understood the permeability of the sex barrier (at least insofar as fish are concerned), would sacrifice his unborn son or daughter to sexual orientation, that most stretchy concept. And I wondered what he meant by the "lessened" quality of life. My sex life couldn't be as good as his? I couldn't love or be loved as well? My family was not as good as his? Though the last comes closer to the point, ultimately he wasn't saying much about me at all. What he meant was that he had no conception of how little and how much it means to be gay. He believed it would be a kindness to abort a child who might turn out queer. To him, being gay is so manifestly different that it begs humanity— one cannot be gay and be whole.

My geneticist exhibited a very common human failing: we equate different with lesser than. Which is why liberals, challenging the argument that some are less than others, have tried to erase (as they seem to embrace) difference, insisting everyone is the same. Besides being untrue, their notion of sameness—as if all of us were subject to a white male default mode—ends up guaranteeing the visibility of some at the expense of everyone else. In a class exercise at Allyson Mount's Deerfield, students are asked to describe themselves in two hundred words or less. In the first sentence or two, women identify as women, blacks as blacks, Asians as Asians; gays and lesbians would do the same if they weren't hiding. The only people who don't list their race or gender are white men—we all know who's the marker and who's the other.

Conservatives criminalize difference—those who are strangers are not only lesser than, but dangerous besides. Multiculturalism has its hazards too: by being allowed to speak only from our assigned lecterns (gay, black, woman, handicapped, Asian), we are stifling what is unexpected about ourselves as individuals and muzzling what is common to us all. A more interesting inquiry is why some differences carry an enormous charge while others do not, and what it is about human nature that makes us so quick to categorize, to compare, and to judge.

How can we help gay and lesbian teenagers? Since the '80s, in some major metropolitan areas, there's been what we might call a "first-level" response. This has consisted of organizing gay and lesbian youth support groups outside school which may or may not be run by youth, and may or may not be advertised or open to anyone who wants to come. Also included in the first-level response in some cities is social service-generated aid to gay and lesbian street youth, which could include counseling, health care, day centers, or even temporary housing. Although there was resistance to labeling youth gay or lesbian, these services started because it became clear to social service workers that some kids were deemed unacceptable by in-place programs for runaways (particularly those with religious ties), and that trying to return children to parents who had thrown them out in the first place was worse than useless. (An excellent overview of this and other issues is contained in social worker Nancy Taylor's paper, "Gay and Lesbian Youth: Challenging the Policy of Denial," in Teresa DeCrescenzo's valuable *Helping Gay and Lesbian Youth*, from Haworth Press.)

What links these two first-level responses—support groups and programs for street youth—is that the kids have self-identified, which means that according to the soft-straight paradigm discussed in the Introduction, they've already been "recruited." Thus these programs have been initiated with greater or lesser degrees of fuss, but at least have been allowed to continue, even in this reactionary climate.

The second-level response, directed toward the invisible kids who have not stepped forward, kids who are often frightened, lonely, or self-hating, causes a far greater reaction. What we as a community must do is accept that we are accountable to kids we can't identify but know are there, while at the same time acknowledging that our efforts to help them will bring us into direct conflict with the assumption that everyone is born straight. The longer that fallacy is allowed to linger, whether it is rooted in ignorance or hate, the more children will be scarred by growing up gay—or won't survive their adolescence. Joining the tribe no longer refers only to young adults entering the gay community; it means all of us caring enough about each other to accept responsibility for the kids who need us.

Several programs have arisen in the past few years to try to address the isolation of queer youth. Among them are the American Friends Service Committee's Bridges Project, which disseminates information, provides referrals to youth groups, and helped organize the Youth Empowerment Speakout during 1993's March on Washington. Bay Area Sexual Minority Youth Network publishes *InsideOUT*, the youth-run journal that includes a pen-pal service. OutProud is active on the Internet, raising issues pertinent to teens. Networking efforts like these can be invaluable to those who know they exist, but helpful as they are, they still don't reach the majority.

What we must do is mount school-based programs like Virginia Uribe's Project 10, which offers support groups and promotes tolerance for gay and lesbian teens in Los Angeles County high schools, and California's Project 21, which argues at the state level for the inclusion of positive images of gays and lesbians in textbooks. We need to fight for legislation like that in Massachusetts that upholds the civil rights of gay and lesbian students in public schools, including protecting students against discrimination and violence, providing information and referrals, and encouraging the formation of gay-straight support alliances. We need to lobby for curriculums in junior high and high school that explore the effects of discrimination and prejudice of all kinds. And we need to reiterate the obvious point that programs like these will benefit all students.

We must educate the educators: teachers, counselors, and principals are left on the front lines to confront hysteria and ignorance, when they themselves know not much more (in a 1992 study by James T. Sears, a quarter of prospective teachers believed they would be unable to deal fairly with a homosexual student). Gay and lesbian teachers must be encouraged to come out themselves, providing positive role models for kids who are starved for real-life images. In some states and cities, teachers are protected from discrimination, but they're still afraid, for the usual reasons, to come out. Teachers must make hard decisions about what message they want to send to kids.

Part of the educational effort aimed at teachers and school administrators must be focused on averting violence and harassment; teachers have to be encouraged (or required) to stop harassment and gay-baiting of kids on school grounds. "Faggot" is such a common epithet that adults barely hear it—but you can bet closeted gay kids hear it every time, whether it's addressed to them or not. Coaches and athletic directors use words like "sissy" and "pussy" as motivators. They'd be the first to claim "fag" has nothing to do with putting down gays, but tell it to the kids.

Massachusetts has been an interesting test case: the Governor's Commission on Gay and Lesbian Youth held hearings in December 1994, a year after the law was en-acted, to take stock. The number of gay-straight high school alliances had jumped from just five to thirty-five, but administrators have apparently tried to squelch some groups. And there was a dismaying amount of testimony from students that physical abuse has not decreased. Train-ing teachers, administrators, and school security forces in tandem with the enactment of such legislation is necessary. Again Massachusetts leads the way: the Gay, Lesbian, and Straight Teachers Network (GLSTN), an organization be-gun in 1990 and instrumental in encouraging the passage of the antidiscrimination legislation (and in developing the gay-straight alliances), created in 1994 a statewide compo-nent to train school faculties and staff. GLSTN is currently setting up chapters across the country.

An equally necessary adjunct is AIDS education in the schools. There is no better example of how homophobia harms every kid in this country than in the foot-dragging over AIDS education—incredibly, teaching kids about HIV could by itself disqualify school districts from receiving fed-eral funds. Newt Gingrich planned to hold hearings in the summer of 1995 (at the behest of Lou Sheldon of the Tradi-tional Values Coalition) to address the advisability of such legislation. Meanwhile, study after study has shown that teenagers tend to downplay their risk for HIV, only starting to use safer sex techniques as young adults. HIV infection rates for teenage girls are rising dramatically, even among teens with few sexual partners, because the vaginal wall is much thinner in girls than it is in women over eighteen. The heightened window of opportunity for infection isn't open long; all the more reason to let girls know the window exists.

Gay and bisexual teenage boys are also at particular risk. In a survey of seventeen- to twenty-two-year-old Bay Area bisexual or gay men, 9.4 percent were HIV-positive, and nearly a third of those surveyed reported having unprotected anal sex in the past six months. That last statistic points out the need for more realistic sex education, in which degrees of risk are made clear. If kids knew anal sex was many times more risky than oral sex, their decisions would at least be better informed.

The major source of help now for gay and lesbian teens is youth groups—and despite what we like to imagine, the groups hit only the tip of the iceberg. A lot of kids live nowhere near a group, and the ones who do often don't know of the group's existence or are too frightened to go. Some groups demand parental consent, which eliminates the majority of potential attendees. Some kids dislike the therapeutic connotation—"I'm basically okay," several non-groupies said to me, as if one must be downing Prozac to qualify. But people who *do* go often don't return, girls in particular, alienated by what Brent Calderwood describes as the trajectory of many groups: the ascendance of a bunch of queens who've hung out for ages, dissing each other and everybody else. Says Lee Garrett about the group she attended just twice: "They were so negative. I just couldn't take listening to it."

There's another exclusionary tactic as well: often groups give points to those who are strongly gay- and lesbian-identified, and who have come out publicly in their schools and to their families. But many teens are confused and unclear about who they are, whom they might want to be with, and what it all could mean. Adults themselves, though they usually won't admit it, slide around somewhat on the gender/sexual orientation continuums throughout the course of their lives, but ambivalence about these identities can be particularly distressing to kids, since it conflicts with that adolescent tendency to want to occupy a niche come hell or high water. "Grading down" for confusion—or making it seem as if ambivalence is a cop-out or a ploy to avoid censure—is cruel, particularly when kids often come to a group as a last resort, believing it to be the only place left on earth where someone might understand.

Very few groups offer help in the realm of definition or support for *not* deciding. In some urban areas, bisexuality has social cachet, but its acceptability seems chiefly limited to the philosophic and not the physical. Renee George, who is bisexual, must defend herself from taunts on all sides—including snipes from the facilitator of a gay youth group that ostensibly includes bisexuals. Transsexuals represent a greater slide on the gender continuum, and while many of the observations in this book apply to transsexual youth, transsexuals have concerns that are different and have the potential to be even more isolating. One of my great regrets is that I was unable to include a chapter based on the transsexual youth group at the Lavender Youth Recreation and Information Center (LYRIC) in San Francisco.

For all these reasons, we need to diverge from the '70s model of support groups and move on to goal- and skill-oriented groups, as well as recreational activities like camping trips, picnics, and softball and volleyball teams. Theater and video troupes can mount productions or make films;

writing groups can publish their work; art and photography groups can put up shows. As much as possible, these should be offered on school grounds as well as off (and be open to anyone), and if possible should be youth-run. In any case, efforts must be made to advertise in schools—the assumption that gay kids search out the gay press to connect with recreational and social activities is unfortunately false. But even more, a kid who is too frightened at fifteen to join a gay photography club might be able to gather up his courage the following year if he reads enough fliers in the meantime.

But won't the fliers be torn down? Who will put them up in the first place? The answer to the second question is hopefully teachers and a few brave students—the answer to the first is that given time, a flier or two will remain to be seen by those who need to see them. That is, they'll remain unless all funding to schools that "encourage homosexuality" is cut off by the Congress.

Which means that we can't depend on schools or on groups for our second-level response. Community action often means individual action. While gay and lesbian adults should be at the forefront in advocating public policy issues that benefit gay and lesbian youth, we can also devote time to more personal solutions. Teaching a kid a skill or offering informal internships in an area of expertise can be of enormous help.

Let's not forget the value of good, plain fun. What if all-ages gay and lesbian clubs like the City in Portland were scattered across the country? With its thousand-plus clientele per week, the City has done more to alleviate the loneliness and isolation of gay teens in the Portland area than any social service agency could hope to achieve—and made money besides.

Meanwhile progressive agencies push the envelope into second-level solutions. In 1989, Gay and Lesbian Adolescent Social Services (GLASS) in Los Angeles, which provides group homes for sexual minority youth, began a licensed foster care program for adult gays and lesbians willing to offer foster homes to children and teenagers. And several facilities have started to serve as an interface between HIV-positive youth and AIDS agencies that are not set up to deal with those under eighteen.

After the military hearings in 1993, we codified "don't ask, don't tell," a hoax that requires some of our citizens to hide the most important aspects of their lives so that the prejudicial thinking of other citizens can flower unchallenged by the truth. Chiefly impacting those from eighteen to twenty-two,the military is a way out of unhealthy situations for many youngsters. If only because the current "compromise" condones discrimination—and is interpreted by many teenagers as a worsening of military regulations— we must continue to press for an equitable resolution to this "less than" legislation.

It's hard to talk about liberation when we cannot safely cross a playground, yet that is exactly what we must do. We have to question assumptions and speak the truth about our experience, even if that truth is unpalatable. Talking about ourselves is dangerous; arguing public policy issues is dangerous; confronting the Right is dangerous. Our amazing advantage—and the reason we are such a threat—is that we are like an ocean washing up on every beach; we who come from every crevice of humanity can find and forge common ground anywhere, and from that common ground will come liberation not just for us, but for everyone.

———

A great deal can change in a very short time—a fact of adolescence that isn't as easy to see when you're in the midst of it. Although I wanted to get updates on everyone I interviewed, after a period of months I was able only to contact about half of my interviewees. Some are exultant, some have been disappointed, and some are fending off blows, but no one has lost hope.

Caroline Anchors, who was trying to transfer from Xavier University in New Orleans, called Bryn Mawr in July, wondering what had happened to her application. "You're in," they told her. "But we need financial aid statements right away." Caroline called her mom with the good news, and got the bad news: her mother refused to fill out the forms that would qualify Caroline for a partial scholarship. Her mother wants Caroline to return to Xavier, believing Caroline brought her problems on herself. Caroline says that's impossible: during the final weeks, she received death threats and was warned by a friend she was targeted for a beating on the last day of school. Her friend advised her to leave school that instant, but Caroline attended her last day of classes under the watchful eyes of the Lesbian Avengers, who accompanied her to a final and then helped her move out of the dorm.

In November, Caroline discovered her Bryn Mawr acceptance letter in a drawer, where her mother had hidden it. She is attending a community college in Philadelphia, struggling to keep up her spirits, still hoping to convince her mother to sign the financial aid forms.

In spite of my gloomy prediction, **Neely Boudier** did indeed become lovers with her friend Star. But going together hasn't affected the necessity to play straight with boys or to satisfy parents who demand the girls secure dates to proms and homecoming dances. Star's parents in particular have begun to monitor their daughter's dating, so the two girls spend a lot of energy constructing a heterosexual appearance for Star—deciding whom she'll go out with, what events she'll attend, and how many "straight" points each date might amass with Star's parents. On these occasions, Neely is torn with jealousy, and the ambivalence shines through her letters as she tries to maintain a good front for both herself and for Star.

Brent Calderwood attended a community college in Hayward, at which he was receiving straight As. But within a couple months he became seriously depressed, and dropped out of school and left his part-time job. "I didn't feel I was learning anything," he says. He pauses, pondering what happened. "For so long I'd hidden being gay, and then when I came out I was so proud. I coasted on that for more than a year. It's like I've been feeding off the good things about coming out, but now that the energy's dropped, I'm left with the bad things, like being scared of people and thinking everybody's against me."

He's applying for jobs again, though being interviewed is difficult for him. "I can do anything as an advocate—write articles, go on television, schmooze at conferences—but I find it almost impossible to sell myself." He thinks what he needs most is to move out of his mother's house. "There's a crucial point at which you need to become an adult," he says. "That's where I am."

In early January 1995, **Brandon Clark** moved from Portland to San Diego, "mostly because I've lived in Oregon my whole life and just wanted to move *somewhere* else. Maybe you have to leave someplace to realize how wonderful it is. I plan on being here for only a few years, depending on school." Brandon left the University of Portland after his first year. "It just became too difficult. I was basically the only out person there. Financial aid kept losing my checks, and a few of my professors didn't like me. Then they raised tuition a thousand dollars, and I decided paying for this type of education is masochistic." Nevertheless, Brandon was chosen as outstanding student leader, a prestigious student-awarded title. "That was a real shocker," he says. "I was very honored."

After leaving school, Brandon became a familiar figure at city and county meetings, and was soon chosen to be on the committee that allocates federal funds for HIV/AIDS prevention. He joined the Oregon Commission on Children and Families, and testified to a countywide commission that in response to his plea organized a task force to "make life easier for sexual minority youth" within the county. "It was hard to leave all of this. The people I worked with in Portland said I could be mayor in five to ten years. That is my new goal . . . and then move on to governor!"

A few months before the move to Minneapolis with her lover Vanessa, **Vic Edminster** decided she didn't want to leave Columbia. "Too cold in Minnesota," Vic says. "And I didn't want to go to a huge coed university, even for a year or so." Vanessa said she was moving no matter what, and the two split up. Vic soon began a relationship with a graduate student named Kathy with whom she'd become friends, and Kathy and Vic found "a wonderful house" in downtown Columbia, big enough for Kathy's two cats and Vic's new dog. Though it was late in the term, Vic was able to apply for a loan and reregister at Stephens, where she plans to finish.

"The last year has been really good," **Greg Fowler** says. "I finished my graduate degree in English, and now I'm debating what to do. Maybe teach for a year." Greg says he never intended to stay at his position at the National Endowment for the Humanities, but viewed it as a stepping stone to something more satisfying. "I don't feel I'm growing as a person here," he explains. "The environment is stagnant, and I really need to meet new people and experience new things. I think teaching—either college or high school— would expand who I am." How about his relationship with Holden? I can hear Greg chuckling over the phone. "We got to the point where we decided we should see other people," he says. "Except now it seems we spend more time together than we ever did, and those 'other people' just don't seem to materialize. I want to stay in the area," he concludes. "That would be best all around."

When I reached **Lee Garrett** by phone, she was bubbling with enthusiasm. After our interview in mid-February, she had buckled down to work and then segued right into summer school. Meanwhile, she'd come out to her mother— again: " 'Mom, did you hear what I just said?' 'No, dear, I didn't.' " Lee launches into her arching laugh. "I mean, what can you do?

"Anyway, I really got big into the gay thing over the

summer, met tons of gay people my age in Orange County. When school started again, I sort of became a hermit and lost touch with my friends. I had a bad drug problem too, but now I'm taking tons of vitamins and this thing that's supposed to wash out your head. But see"—and this was the cause of her delirious excitement—"I'm leaving in four days to go to college!" She names a good Eastern school. "I got in on an early admissions 'cause I'd done the summer thing. When I went for the interview, I thought maybe every-body'd think I was too LA, ya know, clubs and the city, but then I saw this gangster girl there, and I realized I can be whoever I want."

Not long after my March interview with Oakland's **Renee George,** she began cutting school. "Just kickin' with my friends," she says, referring to two gay guy pals she'd met in the youth group. "I was kinda depressed," she admits. A friend offered a job and an apartment in San Francisco, but when Renee moved out of the chaos of her mother's house, she found both job and apartment had fallen through. She ended up at a combination group home/shelter in San Francisco "living with a bunch of straight girls." After a couple months of that ("one of those girls was really crazy, and there was never food in the house 'cause it was a shelter too"), Renee appealed to her social worker. "I said I was bisexual, and that I shouldn't be there. I was afraid I'd get beaten up." She was sent to a house for older minors who have caused no problems but cannot live with their parents; located in a quiet suburb, the residents are all lesbian or bisexual. "The moment I saw the neighborhood," Renee says, "I knew I'd do anything to get in." She started back to school, is doing very well, and will graduate after she amasses enough credits to make up for what she lost in her junior year. She is happy enough—as happy as she can be living in a group situation, away from her mother, who has been attending substance abuse workshops and is, according to Renee, "much much better."

"If I'd grown up in the [social service] system," she says, "I'd be delirious about this place. I like the people, I like the house, I like pretty much everything about it. But it's not home."

"I love Smith!" **Allyson Mount** exults. After hating her last year at Deerfield, it's a welcome change. She was initially disappointed; Smith seemed too easy compared to Deerfield. And after a summer of full employment, she didn't like not supporting herself. She solved that problem with a work/study program at a day care center, and the rest— "Well, a lot of it getting better is being with my girlfriend." The two met in the dorms. "The funny part is that she'd read my piece in *Speaking Out* and had thought of writing to me."

No problems in the dorms, Allyson reports—"well, a little." A couple women moved out of their sixty-person dorm because they didn't care for the nearly fifty-fifty mix of lesbians and straight women. ("It just turned out that way," Allyson explains. "I mean, that's a high percentage.") The four dorms called the Quad, she says, are known to be homophobic: "Lots of drunk guys from Harvard hassling people on weekends." Allyson hasn't joined the campus Lesbian/Bisexual Alliance, which she describes as "only social. If it was political at all, I'd be part of it." I remind her that she'd been concerned about being open on the street. "I don't even think about it," she laughs. "We hold hands, whatever. But we still can't go to bars. They really card here."

Allyson is taking a lot of history courses, though she tentatively plans on majoring in sociology. When her father read her course list for the spring semester, he said, "So you're studying the oppressed." "I hadn't thought of it that way," Allyson says, "but he's right."

Lonely **John Swensen** did not stay in Santa Fe, but went to a college in the Midwest, where he's found a small number of gay friends—five or six, of whom only four are out. "I would like to try it myself, but I am afraid," he writes to me, and then describes an incident in which two girls who were spotted kissing were pelted with garbage, resulting in a serious injury to one of the girls. It's disappointing for John, who expected his college years to be an oasis of enlightenment. Still, "I would say that there are definitely college campuses where gays are truly accepted, and that the unwillingness to be open that I've found here is simply a function of this school." At the start of the second semester of his freshman year, he has begun applying to other colleges for a transfer, in spite of the fact that he finds the academics "simply outstanding," and that he's done well in a situation that demands a lot of student-teacher interaction and independent study.

"Since I've been here," he writes, "I have definitely grown as a gay man; I have realized how wonderful it is to have an identity, but I have also realized how potent the discrimination can be, and many days go by when I just feel like I don't exist, and that my interests will always be secondary to those of others. That is very hard to accept."

about the author

Linnea Due is a writer and associate editor at the *Express,* an alternative newspaper in Berkeley, California, where she lives. She is the author of three novels, *High and Outside,* *Give Me Time,* and *Life Savings,* and she was one of three editors of the anthology *Dagger: On Butch Women* (Cleis, 1994). Her feature on gay and lesbian teenagers won an award as one of the top six underreported stories of 1992 from Media Alliance/Project Censored.